Albert Venn Dicey

England's Case Against Home Rule

Albert Venn Dicey

England's Case Against Home Rule

ISBN/EAN: 9783337158682

Printed in Europe, USA, Canada, Australia, Japan

Cover: Foto ©Suzi / pixelio.de

More available books at **www.hansebooks.com**

AGAINST

HOME RULE.

By A. V. DICEY, B.C.L.,

HON. LL.D. GLASGOW AND EDINBURGH;

VINERIAN PROFESSOR OF ENGLISH LAW IN THE UNIVERSITY OF OXFORD;
FELLOW OF ALL SOULS COLLEGE, AND FELLOW OF BALLIOL COLLEGE, OXFORD;

AUTHOR OF LECTURES INTRODUCTORY TO THE LAW OF THE
CONSTITUTION.

THIRD EDITION.

LONDON:

JOHN MURRAY, ALBEMARLE STREET.

1887.

LONDON :

PRINTED BY WILLIAM CLOWES AND SONS, LIMITED,

STAMFORD STREET AND CHARING CROSS.

PREFACE TO THE THIRD EDITION.

THREE months have elapsed since the first publication of this book. The period is short, but meanwhile events have occurred which strengthen two at least of the positions maintained in 'England's Case against Home Rule.'

The Gladstonian constitution, I contended, failed to fulfil the conditions which it was meant to satisfy.

That this is so is all but admitted even by Home Rulers. The defence of the Gladstonian constitution has been abandoned, if not by its author, at least by his followers. Few indeed are the eulogies which since the dissolution of Parliament have been pronounced by the advocates of Home Rule on the Government of Ireland Bill. Criticism has not missed its mark; the vital defects of the measure pressed last summer on the acceptance of Parliament have been made patent to all the world.

Throughout my statement of the case against Home Rule the opinion is maintained that the discontent of the Irish people is due far more to agrarian than to political causes.

This opinion is, we now know, shared by the leaders of the National League. Their Plan of Campaign rests on an

appeal not to the sentiment of nationality, but to hatred
of rent. The Nationalists no doubt know their own business. Their conduct proves that they hold " no payment
of rent " to be a far more telling cry than " Home Rule for
Ireland." On such a matter their judgment is decisive.
Nor is the Plan of Campaign the sole circumstance which
adds force to my contention. A well-informed author has
within the last two months published an account of the
battle for tenant-right in France.* The farmers of Picardy
have for generations fought for their *droit de marché* with
all the arms used by the farmers of Ireland in defence of
tenant-right. The contest in France, as in Ireland, has
been disgraced by the vilest outrages, by boycotting, by
rick-burning, by the mutilation of animals, by the murder
of *dépointeurs*, or land-grabbers. In France, as in Ireland,
crimes have been committed with impunity in open day
and under the very eyes of an indifferent or sympathetic
population. Yet the tenants who have fought for the *droit
de marché* have not been galled by foreign legislation, and
they have never been divided from their landlords by
differences of race, of religion, or of politics. They have
opposed the law, not because it came to them in a foreign
garb, but because it ran counter to popular sentiment,
traditions, or customs. In Picardy indeed—and here the
parallel with Ireland fails—the feud of centuries has come

---

* See the very noteworthy article, ' Tenant-Right and Agrarian
Outrage in France,' by R. E. Prothero, *Contemporary Review*, 1886,
p. 832.

almost to an end. The reason of its cessation is worth notice. The peasants have in effect made good their rights, and the spread of peasant-proprietorship is depriving the *droit de marché* of its importance. The moral of these facts hardly needs to be pressed home. This much may be safely asserted. The policy of the National League, taken in connection with the history of tenant-right in France, justifies the opinion that Irish opposition to law is mainly due to agricultural causes and that alterations in the tenure of land may deprive the demand for Home Rule of all effective force. Such reforms, however, must, according to all English notions of fairness, be carried out with due regard to the rights of individuals. A sacrifice of private rights to the interests of the nation gives the sufferer an admitted claim to compensation out of national resources.*

A. V. D.

ALL SOUL'S COLLEGE, OXFORD,
    February, 1887.

---

* My readers may notice frequent references throughout this work to my treatise on 'The Law of the Constitution.' I have ventured to refer to the book, although it is my own, for two reasons. The principles laid down in it form the basis of many of the arguments contained in the statement of the constitutional case against Home Rule; these principles seem to me most fairly stated in language used before the appearance of the Government of Ireland Bill, and employed without reference to any political controversy.

PREFACE.

An author who publishes a book having any reference
to Irish affairs may, not unnaturally, be supposed either
to possess some special knowledge of Ireland, or else to be
the advocate of some new specific for the cure of Irish
discontent. Of neither of these suppositions can I claim
the benefit. My knowledge of Ireland is merely the
knowledge—perhaps it were better to say the ignorance—of
an educated Englishman. It is derived from conversation
with better informed friends, from careful attention to the
discussions on Irish policy which for the last eighteen
years have engrossed public attention, and from books
accessible to ordinary readers. If I can claim no special
acquaintance with Ireland, still less have I the presumption
or the folly to come forward as the inventor of any political
nostrum. My justification for publishing my thoughts on
Home Rule is that the movement in favour of the Parliamentary independence of Ireland constitutes, whether its
advocates recognise the fact or not, a demand for fundamental alterations in the whole Constitution of the United
Kingdom; and while I may without presumption consider
myself moderately acquainted with the principles of

Constitutional law, I entertain the firmest conviction that any scheme for Home Rule in Ireland involves dangerous if not fatal innovations on the Constitution of Great Britain.

To set forth the reasons for this opinion is the object of this work. The opinion itself, whatever its worth, is not the growth of recent controversy; it has been entertained for years, and has been expressed by me in various publications. This book is much more than a reprint; its contents are, however, in part made up of articles which have already been published. My thanks are due to the owners of the *Contemporary Review* and of the New York *Nation* for their permission to make free use of my contributions to the pages of their periodicals; it is a pleasure to acknowledge the exceptional liberality with which my friend, Mr. E. L. Godkin, has allowed me to publish on my own responsibility in the columns of the *Nation*, opinions of which he is himself the strenuous and most able opponent.

Nor are my acknowledgments due only to the living. Gustave de Beaumont's '*l'Irlande sociale et politique*' was placed in my hands by a friend after the plan of my argument was complete, and the writing of this book was in fact begun. From De Beaumont I learnt more than from any other writer on the subject of Ireland with whose works I am acquainted, and I found to my great satisfaction that his speculations curiously confirmed the objections I was prepared to urge against the policy of

Home Rule. It is a duty to insist upon the debt I owe to De Beaumont, because at the present moment no greater service can be rendered to Englishmen and to Irishmen alike than to press upon them the study of an author whose writings are far better known on the Continent than in England, and whose thoughts, though they may seem a little out of date, are full not only of profound wisdom but of practical guidance.

A. V. Dicey.

October, 1886.

CONTENTS.

CHAPTER VII.

HOME RULE—ITS FORMS.

CHAPTER VIII.

ENGLAND'S CASE AGAINST HOME RULE.

CHAPTER I.

NATURE OF THE ARGUMENT.

MY aim is to criticise from a purely English point of view the policy of Home Rule, or the proposal to create a more or less independent Parliament in Ireland; and as a result of such criticism to establish the truth, and develop the consequences, of this proposition—namely, that any system of Home Rule, whatever be the form it takes, is less beneficial to Great Britain, or (to use popular language) to England, than is the maintenance of the Union, and is at least as much opposed to the vital interests of England as would be the national independence of Ireland.

Aim and line of argument.

The train of reasoning by which it is sought to establish this principle, and the consequences which the principle involves, consists of the following steps: first, an examination into the causes which give strength to the

B

Home Rule movement in England, and the nature of the
arguments in its support used by English Home Rulers;
secondly, a statement of the advantages and disadvantages,
from an English point of view, on the one hand, of maintaining the Union, and on the other, of separation from
Ireland; thirdly, a criticism of each of the principal
forms * under which Home Rule has been actually presented to the attention of the public, the aim of such
criticism being in each case to determine how far the
particular form of Home Rule can compete as regards the
interests of England with the alternative policies of
Unionism and of Irish independence; and, fourthly, a
summary of the conclusions arrived at by this survey of
the policy of Home Rule. My endeavour will be to make
this survey without any appeal to prejudice, passion, or
sentiment, and with the calmness and fairness which a
scientific constitutionalist should display in weighing the
merits of any other proposed alteration in our form of
government, such for example as the introduction of life
peers into the House of Lords, or in estimating the value
of some foreign constitutional invention, such, for example,
as the Swiss Referendum or the Dual system which links

---

* These are—
  i. Home Rule as Federalism.
  ii. Home Rule as Colonial Independence.
  iii. Home Rule as the Restoration of Grattan's Constitution.
  iv. Home Rule under the Government of Ireland Bill, or, to
      use a convenient name, under the Gladstonian constitu-
      tion. Chap. vii.

together Hungary and the Austrian Empire. No citizen of the United Kingdom indeed can pretend to be an impartial critic of a policy which divides the whole nation into opposing parties. But during a period of revolutionary excitement, it is well to remember, that any legislative innovation, however keen the feelings of partisanship which it may arouse, is always in itself capable of being looked at from a logical or abstract point of view, and ought to be so looked at by jurists. To one class indeed among the advocates of Home Rule, the fundamental principle contended for in these pages will appear irrelevant to the points at issue between such Home Rulers and their opponents. Nationalists, who still occupy the position held in 1848 by Sir Gavan Duffy and his friends, and who either openly contend for the right of Ireland to be an independent nation, or accept Home Rule (as they may with perfect fairness) simply as a step towards the independence of their country, are naturally and rightly unaffected by reasoning which shows, however conclusively, that Home Rule may be as injurious to England as a complete severance of the political connection between England and Ireland. A Nationalist may say with justice that he is no more bound to consider whether England will or will not be damaged by Ireland's becoming a nation, than an Italian patriot was bound, in 1859, to show that Austria would not suffer by being deprived of Lombardy or of Venetia; he accepts Home Rule on the maxim that half a loaf is better than no bread, but a starving man is not required to refuse the offer of food because the donor cannot make the gift without getting into debt; nor does the acceptance of half a loaf afford the least presumption that the recipient would not prefer a whole loaf if he could get it. Some indeed of the considerations which tell in the eyes of an Englishman against Home Rule may indirectly lead an Irish Nationalist to the belief that the boon of legislative independence, if granted to Ireland, would prove the present of a stone in reply to a prayer for bread. But should a Nationalist be convinced that no form of Home Rule would benefit Ireland, he would cling all the more firmly to the faith that her salvation depends upon her taking her place among independent states. To Nationalists, therefore, even though at present they may be fighting the cause of Irish nationality behind the visor of Home Rule, these pages are not addressed. The position thay occupy is one of which no man has any cause to feel ashamed. The opinion that, considering the misery which has marked the connection between England and Ireland, the happiest thing for the weaker country would be complete separation from the United Kingdom, is one which in common with most Englishmen, and, it may be added, in common with the wisest foreign observers, I do not share; but fairness requires the admission that it is an opinion which a man may hold and may act upon, without incurring the charge either of folly or of wickedness. To Nationalists, however, these pages, as I have said, are not addressed. The

persons for whom they are intended are either Home
Rulers, in Great Britain or in Ireland, who *bonâ fide*
advocate the policy of Home Rule for its own sake,
as a policy good and wise in itself; or else Unionists,
who firmly believe that the whole State will suffer by
any attempt to tear up the Treaty of Union, but yet
are unable to give for the faith that is in them as
strong grounds of reason as they would desire.   To such
persons the importance of the principle (if true) which is
contended for throughout these pages must appear undeniable; it strikes at the root of more than one half of
the arguments by which Home Rulers from the time of
Mr. Butt to the days of Mr. Parnell have attempted, fairly
enough, and latterly with great success, to win over English
opinion to their cause, and it undermines the whole position
occupied by Mr. Gladstone and his English followers.
They assume, with undeniable truth, that the English
people will not at the present moment, except under
compulsion, acquiesce in Irish independence ; they further
assume, and must from the nature of the case assume, that
Home Rule under one shape or another presents a fair
prospect at least of advantages not derivable from the
maintenance of the Union, and is at the very worst so
much less injurious to British interests than would be
separation from Ireland, as to offer to England a reasonable
compromise between the just claims of Englishmen to
secure the prosperity of Great Britain and the greatness
of the British Empire, and the legitimate desire of Irish-

men for national independence. If the proposition which it is my object to maintain turn out to be sound, all these assumptions fall to the ground, together with a host of fallacies for which these assumptions form the necessary basis. The principle, in short, which it is my object to enforce—that Home Rule in Ireland is more dangerous to England than Irish independence—lies at the bottom of all the rational opposition made by Unionists to the creation of an Irish Parliament, and, together with the arguments by which the principle is maintained, and the conclusions to which it leads, forms the true and just and reasonable case of England against Home Rule.

The whole spirit and method of my argument is open to at least three plausible objections, which deserve examination, both because if left unnoticed they are certain to occur to and perplex any intelligent reader, and because their removal brings into relief the strength of my line of reasoning.

Possible objections to method.

First objection.—To deal with a burning controversy in the abstract and logical manner suitable to the discussion of the problems of jurisprudence savours, it may be objected, of theoretic, academic, or pedantic disquisition more fit for a University class-room than for the living world of contemporary politics.

1. Too abstract.

The force of this criticism does not admit of denial. My method of treating the question of Home Rule is

necessarily lifeless when compared with the vehement
rhetoric or heated eloquence which characterises public or
parliamentary discussion; it is also true that the argumentative treatment of matters affecting actual life always
bears about it a certain air of unreality.

If, however, systematic argument lacks the animation
of political discussion or dispute, it possesses its own
counterbalancing merits, and the mode of treating Home
Rule purposely adopted in these pages has, it is conceived,
two not inconsiderable advantages. The first of these
advantages is that it diverts the mind from a crowd of
personal, temporary, and in themselves trivial considerations, which, though they possess not only an apparent
but also a real significance, are at bottom irrelevant to
the final decision of the true points at issue. Whether,
for example, Mr. Gladstone ought to have proclaimed
himself a Home Ruler before the elections of 1885;
whether Lord Salisbury's reference, or alleged reference, to
twenty years of coercion was or was not judicious, and
did or did not receive a fair interpretation from his
opponents; whether Lord Carnarvon misled Mr. Parnell,
or whether the Irish leader was a dupe to his own astute-
ness; whether Mr. Chamberlain ought to have joined the
late Ministry, or, having gone into the Cabinet, ought
never to have left it; what have been the motives con-
sciously or unconsciously affecting Mr. Gladstone's course
of action—these and a hundred other enquiries of the
like sort, which engage the attention and distract the

judgment of the public, possess, in the eyes of any serious
thinker occupied in estimating the strength of the arguments for and against Home Rule, no material importance
whatever.   His concern is the merit or demerit of a legislative enactment.   He is not concerned at all with the
conduct or the character of legislators.   Mr. Gladstone's
motives may be the highest which can be ascribed to the
Premier by the voice of admiring friendship, or the basest
which can be imputed to him by the unfairness of political
rancour.   In any case they are irrelevant to the matter in
hand.   An unwise measure will not become a beneficial
law because its author is a saint or a patriot; a statesmanlike law will not turn out a curse to the country
because its defender is an intriguer or a traitor.   We all
see that this is so if we carry our view back to the
controversies of the last generation ; the personalities of
fifty or sixty years ago are reduced before our eyes into
their real pettiness.   The first Reform Bill still retains
its importance as a measure which for good or for bad
revolutionised the constitution ; its beneficial or per-
nicious effects are still traceable in the England of to-day ;
but its evils are not lessened by the acknowledged virtues
of Lord Althorpe, nor are its good effects marred by the
ambition of Brougham or the violence of O'Connell.   It
is no slight recommendation of any mode of reasoning, if
it suggests to us the prudence of judging the policy of
1886, in the spirit and by the standards which every man
of sense applies to the policy of 1832.   Academic dis-

quisition has its faults, but ought to produce academic calmness; a class-room is, after all, a better place for quiet reflection than the House of Commons or the hustings.

The second of the advantages which marks the proposed mode of argument is that a line of thought which fixes a reader's attention all but exclusively upon the probable effects of Home Rule is a preservative against the errors which arise from introducing into a dispute, bitter enough in itself, all the poisonous venom of historical recrimination, and all the delusions which are the offspring of the misleading tendency to personify nations. The massacres of 1641, the sack of Drogheda, the violated treaty of Limerick, the follies strangely mingled with the patriotism of Grattan's Parliament, the outrages which discredited the rebellion of 1798, and the cruelties which disgraced its suppression, the corruption which carried the Union, and the broken pledges which turned political union into a source of fresh sectarian discord—the calamities, the mistakes and the crimes which mark each scene in the tragedy of Irish history—afford to Protestants and to Catholics alike, an exhaustless mine of recriminatory invective. But to evoke the spectres of past ages is not the way to assuage the animosities of the present day. The crimes of bygone generations are subjects for curious investigation, but the determination of historical problems, even when conducted in the spirit of the calmest enquiry, never removes the difficulties of practical statesmanship. Apologies, at any rate, or diatribes pro-

duced by the necessity for palliating or for denouncing
the misdeeds of other times, only add a new element of
confusion to the turmoil of political warfare. Whether
the insurgents of 1641 massacred every Protestant on
whom they could lay their hands, or bear only an indirect
responsibility for the death of eight or nine thousand men
and women ruthlessly expelled from the lands, of which,
in Irish eyes, they were wrongful occupiers, is a question
to be settled by Mr. Froude, Mr. Lecky, and Mr. Gardiner;
but the barbarities of insurgent Catholics, and the retalia-
tory severity of Protestant victors, which mark the fury
of an internecine conflict removed from us by the lapse
of more than two centuries, have little to do with the
practical question whether it be expedient, at the present
day, that the local affairs of Ulster should be dealt with
by a Parliament sitting at Dublin, or whether members
from Ireland should have seats at Westminster. Recrimination, while it adds nothing to knowledge, disturbs
the judgment of statesmen and of electors; but not even
the reckless resuscitation of bitter memories, which ought
to be forgotten, adds so much to the confusion of the day,
as does the habit fostered by the illusions of language,
and by the falsely applied historical method, of speaking
and thinking of England and Ireland as though they were
two human beings, who, on closing a life-long quarrel,
might be expected to entertain towards one another
those sentiments of regret, generosity, or gratitude which
are proper to men and women, but can only by the

boldest of fictions be supposed to enter into the relations between classes or nations.   To this delusion of personification is due the notion that Englishmen of to-day ought to make compensation and feel personal shame for the cruelties of Cromwell, or for Pitt's corruption of Irish patriots; that we are in some way liable and should feel compunction for crimes committed by (possibly) the ancestors of the very men to whom we are now supposed to owe reparation.   To the same cause is to be attributed the absurd demand that the Irish Catholics should put on sackcloth and ashes for the massacres of 1641.   To this cause is due the ridiculous claim that living Irishmen should be grateful for the well-meant though most unsuccessful efforts made by the Parliament of the United Kingdom to govern one-third of the United Kingdom on sound principles of justice.   A Sovereign's plainest duty is to rule his subjects for their good according to the best of his power and of his knowledge, and the mere discharge of duty does not entitle a ruler to gratitude from the persons who are benefited by his justice.   A Parliamentary Sovereign, being the representative and agent of its (so-called) subjects, is *à fortiori*—if there can be degrees in such matters —bound to govern for the benefit of the people whom the Sovereign represents and ought to serve; and there is something strictly preposterous in the idea that Irish electors, who in common with the rest of the United Kingdom send representatives to Westminster, should glow with gratitude when the Parliament of the United Kingdom so far performs its duty as to enact laws from which Ireland derives benefit. No one suggests that Englishmen or Scotchmen should feel grateful either to Parliament or to their Irish fellow-citizens for the maintenance of good government throughout England and Scotland. And it would puzzle the wit of man to show, why one-third of the United Kingdom should be expected to entertain feelings never demanded from the other two-thirds thereof.

Second objection.—The habitual reference made throughout these pages to national interest as the test or standard of national policy has (it may be suggested) a touch of sordidness and selfishness, and implies that statesmanship has nothing to do with morality.

2. Too much reference to interest.

This impression may, it is possible, be conveyed to a careless reader by the form in which the case against Home Rule is stated; but no suggestion can in reality be more ill-founded. It will be seen to be unfounded by any one who notes for a moment the meaning of the term "interest" as applied to matters of national policy. The interest or the welfare of a nation comprises many things which have nothing to do with trade or with wealth, and the value of which does not admit of being measured in money. The interest, welfare, or prosperity of England includes the maintenance of her honour, the performance of all her obligations, and, above all, the strict discharge of every engagement which she has undertaken towards countries or to individuals. The protection, for example, of law-abiding citizens in the enjoyment of rights secured to them by law, the maintenance of peace throughout the length and breadth of the Empire, the suppression of lawlessness, the strict performance of every promise which the State has made to every man or body of men (whether poor or rich, whether belonging to the class of labourers, of farmers, or even of landlords)—the rendering, in short, to every man of his due —are things, which, without any improper extension of the term interest, fall under the head of national interests. Utilitarianism, in truth, being a body of principles applicable primarily to legislation and only secondarily to ethics, its doctrines hold true far more obviously in the field of politics than in the field of morals. On any wide view of large public questions expediency will be found to be only another name for justice. It can be neither the interest nor the duty of any nation to legislate in a way which produces more of suffering than of happiness. A policy opposed to the interests or the welfare of the United Kingdom as a whole, even though it may appear for a moment to favour some particular portion of the State, is, we may be well assured, a policy opposed not only to wisdom, but to justice.

Third objection.—To look at Home Rule mainly from an English point of view, to criticise it because of its bearing on the interests or welfare of England, is, it may perhaps be thought, to treat the whole

3. Exclusively English point of view.

matter from the wrong side, and to betray an indifference to the welfare of Ireland.   Home Rule, the objector may say, is a scheme for the government of Ireland.   It therefore concerns the people of Ireland alone, it should be subjected to examination from an Irish, not from an English point of view, and to consider it in any other light is to exhibit in a new form that callous disregard by England of Ireland's claims which has prevented the two countries from blending into one community.

It is of primary importance that this objection should be stated with all the force which can be given to it, for were it valid it would assuredly be, in the judgment of all just persons, fatal to the line of reasoning which my readers are invited to pursue.   The objection is, however, so far from being valid as to present my whole method of reasoning in a false light.   A main reason why an Englishman does well to look at Home Rule from an English point of view is, that this mode of dealing with the adjustment of the possibly opposed interests of England and Ireland is (paradoxical though the assertion may sound) both the least irritating and in itself the fairest method of meeting the demands of Irish Home Rulers; though—and this is the one certainly good result which has arisen from the changed attitude towards Home Rule of Mr. Gladstone and his followers—these demands may now happily be dealt with as claims put forward not specially by Irishmen, but by a political party which includes large numbers of Scotchmen and Englishmen.   The assertion, however, that

to look at Home Rule from an English point of view is
the way to minimise irritation, and to deal fairly
with a topic specially requiring fair treatment, requires
some explanation.

Experience of the world tells every man that in complicated affairs of private life, involving questions, say,
both of money and of sentiment, nothing so surely
prevents quarrels as to separate in the clearest manner
possible matters of business from matters of feeling. In
determining a dispute between *A.* and *B.*, a great step
is gained when a friend induces each of the parties first
to state clearly his exact legal rights and his exact
pecuniary interest, and only when these facts are made
clear to consider what are the concessions fairly to be
demanded from him as a matter, not of right, but of
liberality. Nothing, again, is plainer in the conduct of
controversies between man and man, than that if *A.*
intends to exact his full legal rights from *B.*, the most
irritating defence of *A.'s* conduct is his pretence of acting
solely with a view to *B.'s* own good ; and that, on the other
hand, no manner of enforcing *A.'s* claims against *B.* causes
so little unnecessary vexation to *B.* as for *A.* to say
openly that he demands his rights because they are his
rights, and because to demand them is his interest. Here,
if nowhere else, the rules which apply to private disputes
apply also to political controversies. If millions of
Englishmen refuse a request made by millions of Irishmen, by far the least irritating form of refusal is open

avowal that the reason for denying a separate Parliament
to Ireland is the irreparable injury which Home Rule will
work both to Great Britain and to the British Empire.
This assertion has the merit, which even in politics is not
small, of truth. If the Parliamentary independence of
Ireland threatened as little damage to England as the
Parliamentary independence of Victoria, an Irish legislature would meet in Dublin before the end of the year.
Englishmen, it is true, do not believe that Ireland would
in the long run gain by the possession of legislative
independence. It is not, however, the doubt as to the
reality of the blessing to be conferred on Ireland, but the
certainty as to the injury to be done to England, which
causes their opposition to Home Rule. To base this
opposition upon the probable inconsistency between a
Home Rule policy and the true interests of Ireland, involves the assumption that Englishmen are better judges
of what makes for the true interest of Ireland than are the
majority of Irishmen. The soundness of this assumption
must seem to any man, who either recalls the most obvious
facts of Irish history, or notes the depth of ignorance as to
all things Irish which prevails even among our educated
classes, to be open to reasonable question. What is not
questionable is that the assertion, in whatever form it be
made, that three millions of Irishmen do not understand
what is good for themselves must arouse in their hearts
deep and natural anger. If indeed the claim of Great
Britain to look in this matter of Home Rule solely to the

effect of Home Rule on British interests, were equivalent
to the assertion that because England is strong she ought
wherever her own interests are at stake to reck nothing
of justice, such cynical scorn for all considerations except
the possession of superior power would kindle just resent-
ment in the soul of every man, whether in Ireland or in
England, who believes that national morality is more than
a mere phrase, though even in this case open cynicism
might excite less disgust than cynicism veiling itself
under the mask of benevolence.   Happily, however, there
is in the present instance no opposition between truth
and justice.   Home Rule is no doubt primarily a scheme
for the government of Ireland, but it is also much more
than this : it is a plan for revolutionising the constitution
of the whole United Kingdom.   There is no unfairness,
therefore, in insisting that the proposed change must not
take place if it be adverse to the interests of Great
Britain.   This is merely to assert that the welfare of
thirty millions of citizens must, if a conflict of interest
arise, be preferred to the interest of five millions of citizens.
Home Rulers, it must again and again be repeated,
demand not the national independence of Ireland, but the
maintenance of the connection between England and
Ireland on terms different from the conditions contained
in the Act of Union.   To keep one's mind clear on this
point is of importance, because the result follows that, as
already intimated, a whole series of arguments or claims
which may fairly be put forward by a Nationalist are not

available to a Home Ruler.   A Nationalist, for example, may urge that the will of the Irish people to be independent is decisive of their moral right to independence, and that the perils which a free Ireland may bring upon England need not in any way concern him or his country. Whether indeed the principle of "nationality," or the contention that any portion of a State which deems itself conscious of distinct national sentiment may, as a matter of absolute right, claim to become a separate nation, can be maintained, is an enquiry not so easily answered in the affirmative as is often assumed by modern democrats. What, however, is here insisted upon is not that the principle of nationality is unsound, but that this principle does not cover the demand for Home Rule.   A Home Ruler asks not for the political separation, but for the political partnership of England and Ireland.   He wishes not that the firm should be dissolved, but that the Articles of Association should be revised.   There is not then the least unfairness in the answer that no modification can be allowed which in the judgment of his associates is fatal to the prosperity of the concern.   To crowds excited by pictures of past greatness or of past struggles, by the hope of future prosperity to be brought about by miracles wrought by substituting the rule of love for the rule of law, there may appear to be something prosaic, not to say repulsive, in the comparison of the relation between Great Britain and Ireland to the relation between shareholders in a trading company.   But at a period when a fundamental change in the constitution is advocated on grounds of faith, benevolence, or generosity, a good deal is gained by bringing into relief the business aspect of constitutional reforms. It can never be amiss to be reminded that, in the words of one of the most thoughtful among the advocates of Home Rule, "Government is a very practical business, and that those succeed best in it who bring least of sentiment or enthusiasm to the conduct of their affairs." It is at moments of revolutionary fervour, when men measure proposed policies rather by their wishes than by their experience, that every citizen needs to have impressed upon his mind that government and legislation are matters of reason and judgment, and not of inclination. Nor let any one imagine that the expression of the belief constantly avowed or implied throughout these pages, that Home Rule would be as great an evil to England as Irish independence, shows a reckless and most unbusinesslike indifference to the perils and losses of separation. My conviction is unalterable that separation would be to England, as also to Ireland, a gigantic evil. This position is fully compatible with the belief that there are other evils as great, or greater. If a man says that he prefers the loss of his right hand to the loss of his life, he cannot reasonably be charged with making light of amputation. It is however perfectly true that the line of argument pursued in this work must, if it be sound, drive those to whom it is addressed to a choice between the maintenance of the Union and the concession to Ireland of national independence.

CHAPTER II.

MEANING OF HOME RULE.

" Home Rule " is a term which, like all current and popular phrases, is, though intelligible, wanting in precision.   Hence it is well, before we investigate the different forms which schemes of Home Rule may assume, to fix in our minds precisely what Home Rule does mean and what it does not mean.

" Home Rule "—or, to speak more accurately, the policy of Home Rule—means, if we may use language with which we are all familiar in relation to the Colonies, the endowment of Ireland with representative institutions and responsible government.

What Home Rule means.

It means, therefore, the creation of an Irish Parliament which shall have legislative authority in matters of Irish concern, and of an Irish executive responsible (in general) for its acts to the Irish Parliament or the Irish people. Hence every scheme of Home Rule which merits that name is marked by three features—*first*, the creation of an Irish Parliament; *secondly*, the right o the Irish

Parliament to legislate within its own sphere (however that sphere may be defined) with habitual freedom from the control of the Imperial or British Parliament; and *thirdly*, the habitual responsibility of the Irish executive for its acts to the Irish people or to their representatives.

These three characteristics, which I do not attempt to define with anything like logical precision, constitute the essence of Home Rule. Other things, however important in themselves, are matters of subordinate detail, and open to discussion or compromise. The limitations to the sphere within which the Irish Parliament is to exert independent authority, the definition of the term "Irish concerns," the constitution of the Irish Parliament, the nature and appointment of the Irish executive (which, though it is no doubt generally assumed to be a Cabinet chosen in effect like the Victorian Ministry, by the local Parliament, might well, and indeed far better, be a President or Council elected, like the Governor of New York, by popular vote), the occasions on which the British Parliament should retain the legal or moral right of legislation for Ireland—these and a score of other subjects which at once suggest themselves to a critic of constitutions are of supreme importance, but in whatever way they may be determined, they do not touch the principle of Home Rule. A scheme, on the other hand, however wise its provisions, which lacked the essential characteristics already enumerated, would not meet the demand for Home Rule; an Act which did not constitute a Parliament for

Ireland could not possibly satisfy the sentiment of Irish nationality; an Irish Parliament which did not habitually, at any rate, legislate with independence of the Parliament at Westminster could not divest the law in Ireland of its "foreign garb"; an executive not responsible directly or indirectly to the Irish people could not give full effect to the legislation of an Irish Parliament, and the existence of such an executive would (if the true ground why law is hated in Ireland be its alien character) only divert popular hostility from the law to the government.

What Home Rule does not mean.
Home Rule does not mean Local Self-Government; Home Rule does not mean National Independence.

Local Self-Government means the delegation by the Sovereign, and in England therefore by Parliament, to local bodies, say town councils, county boards, vestries, and the like, of strictly subordinate powers of legislation for definite localities. The authority possessed by such local bodies extends over definite and limited areas (which themselves are often created by legislation); exists for definite purposes; is directly conferred or tolerated by Parliament; has no capacity of indefinite extension; and neither comes into competition with nor restrains, either legally or morally, the legislative authority of Parliament. Logically, indeed, there may be difficulty in drawing the precise line of demarcation between a plan for conferring on Ireland the minimum of legislative independence

which could without absurdity be dignified with the name
of Home Rule, and a plan for giving to the boroughs and
counties of Ireland the maximum of law-making power
which could, without fraud upon the intelligence of the
English people, be comprehended within the elastic phrase
" extension of Local Self-Government." But this logical
puzzle need give us no trouble; it is based on the fact
that every non-sovereign law-making body, whether it be
the French National Assembly, the American Congress,
or the London, Chatham and Dover Railway Co., belongs
to one and the same genus.* The casuists of jurisprudence may quibble for ever over the confines between
Home Rule and Local Self-Government; men of sense
engaged in the consideration of affairs thrust aside such
inopportune logomachy, and content themselves with the
knowledge that were the Town Council, say, of Birmingham or of Belfast endowed with tenfold its present powers,
it would differ essentially from any Irish Parliament
which, even though denied the Parliamentary title, should
represent the people of Ireland, and should have received
the very smallest amount of authority which could by
any possibility satisfy Mr. Parnell. Nor are differences
which may not admit of easy definition difficult for a
candid enquirer to discern. A town council, whatever
its powers, does not represent a nation, and derives no
prestige from the principle of nationality; the feeblest
legislative assembly meeting at Dublin would rightly

* See Dicey, Law of the Constitution (2nd ed.), p. 80.

claim to speak for the Irish people. A town council, whether of Birmingham or of Belfast, springs from and is kept alive by the will of Parliament, and cannot pretend that its powers, however extensive, compete with the authority of its creator. Should a town council use even its strictly legal rights in a way not conducive to the public interest, Parliament would without scruple override the bye-laws of the council by the force of Parliamentary enactment. The authority of an Irish representative assembly would from the necessity of things be, if not a legal, at any rate a moral check, I will not say on Parliamentary sovereignty, but assuredly on Parliamentary legislation. Extended rights of self-government, though given to every local body in Ireland, would not affect the relation between the people of Ireland and the Parliament at Westminster. The very aim of Home Rule, even under its least pretentious form, is to introduce a new relation between the people of Ireland and the Parliament at Westminster. The matter may be summed up in one phrase: Local Self-Government however extended means the delegation, Home Rule however curtailed means the surrender, of Parliamentary authority.

The distinction here insisted upon is of practical importance, for it is connected with a question so pressing as to excuse an apparent, though not more than an apparent, digression.

Local Self-Government.

English Radicals, and many politicians who are not Radicals, hold, whether rightly or not, that the sphere of Local Self-Government may with benefit to the nation be greatly extended in England. The soundness of this view in no way concerns us, and it is a matter upon which there is no reason, for our present purpose, to form or express an opinion; they also hope that by a similar extension of Local Self-Government to Ireland they may satisfy the demand for Home Rule. They conceive, in short, that it is possible to confer a substantial benefit upon the Irish people, and to close a dangerous agitation, by giving to Belfast and to Cork the same municipal privileges which they wish to extend to Birmingham or to Liverpool. The reasons for this belief are threefold: that Local Self-Government is itself a benefit; that Ireland ought, as of right, to have the same institutions as England; that Local or Municipal Self-Government will meet the real if not the nominal wish of the Irish people. This hope I believe to be delusive. The reasons on which it is grounded are— one of them probably, and two of them certainly—unsound.

Local Self-Government is one of those arrangements which, like most political institutions, cannot be called absolutely good or bad. It is a good thing, I suppose, at Birmingham, and was some fifty years ago a good thing in Massachusetts, and it may prove (though this is specula-tion) a good thing in an English county. Local Self-Government is not admirable at New York; it works less well than it once did in New England; it does not produce very happy effects in London parishes; we may well doubt whether it be really suited for modern France. Local Self-Government where it flourishes is quite as much a result as a cause of a happy social condition; the eulogies bestowed upon it contain a curious mixture of truth and falsehood. What is true is, that where self-government flourishes, society is in a sound state; what is false is, that Local Self-Government produces a sound state of society. The primary condition necessary for the success of self-government is harmony between different classes. The rich must be the guides of the poor, the poor must put trust in the rich. Men who are placed above corruption must interest themselves in the laborious but important details of local administration; men who might be corrupted themselves, must desire to place power in the hands of leaders who are as a class incorruptible. High public spirit, a detestation of jobbery, trust and goodwill between rich and poor, are the feelings which make good local or municipal government possible. There are certain parts of England, there are larger parts of the United States, where these admirable and rare conditions exist. Do they exist in Ireland? I need not answer the question, for if they existed our difficulties in Ireland would be at an end. If, indeed, there were a genuine desire for Local Self-Government, expressed by Irishmen themselves, every sensible man would at once surrender *à priori* theories in favour of the conclusions drawn by practical experience. But no such wish has been expressed, and until it is expressed, a thoughtful observer may fairly believe that Local Self-Government will not flourish in a country where are presented none of the conditions on which its prosperity depends, and he may conjecture that in Ireland, as in France, an honest centralised administration of impartial officials, and not Local Self-Government, would best meet the real wants of the people.*

* De Beaumont's opinions on this point are perfectly clear : they represent the judgment of an extremely able thinker, who approaches the problems presented by Irish society with an impartiality which from the nature of things is unattainable by any Englishman or Irishman. His utterances will moreover command the more respect from the consideration that De Beaumont, belonging as he did to the school of his intimate friend De Tocqueville, was inclined rather to overrate than to underrate the virtues of self-government; whilst as a Frenchman he possessed a knowledge which cannot fall to any Englishman of the benefits conferred upon the people by a good administration of the French type. The following extracts from a chapter too long for complete citation, which is written to show that Ireland needs a centralised government, deserve the most careful attention. The whole chapter, and indeed the whole work to which it belongs, ought at the present moment to be familiar to every English Liberal :—

" *Pour détruire le pouvoir politique de l'aristocratie, il faudrait lui ôter l'application quotidienne des lois, comme on l'a privée précédemment du pouvoir de les faire. Il faudrait, par conséquent, modifier profondément le système administratif et judiciaire qui repose sur l'institution des juges de paix et sur l'organisation des grands jurys, tels qu'ils sont constitués aujourd'hui. Et d'abord, pour exécuter cette réforme, il faudrait centraliser le pouvoir.*

*　　　*　　　*　　　*　　　*

" *Plus on considère l'état de l'Irlande, et plus il semble qu'à tout prendre un gouvernement central fortement constitué serait, du moins pour quelque temps, le meilleur que puisse avoir ce pays. Une aristocratie existe, qu'on veut réformer. Mais à qui remettre le pouvoir qu'on va retirer de ses mains ? Aux classes moyennes ?—Elles ne font*

The notion that Ireland or any one part of the United Kingdom ought, or has a claim, to have the same institu-

---

que de naître en Irlande. L'avenir leur appartient; mais ne compromettront-elles pas cet avenir, si la charge de mener la société est confiée dès aujourd'hui à leurs mains inhabiles et à leurs ardentes passions ?

" *Telle est aujourd'hui en Irlande la situation des partis, que l'on ne peut obtenir quelque justice des pouvoirs politiques, si on les laisse à l'aristocratie protestante, et que l'on ne saurait guère en espérer davantage, si on les donne aussitôt à la classe moyenne catholique qui s'élève.*

" *Ce qu'il faudrait à l'Irlande, ce serait une administration supérieure aux partis, à l'ombre de laquelle les classes moyennes pussent grandir, se développer et s'instruire, pendant que l'aristocratie perdrait son pouvoir.*

*   *   *   *   *

" *Il n'entre, du reste, ni dans mon désir, ni dans mon plan, d'expliquer la forme et le mécanisme de la centralisation qui conviendrait à l'Irlande, et dont je me borne à reconnaitre en principe l'utilité passagère pour ce pays ; je ne hasarderai, sur ce sujet, qu'une seule idée pratique.*

" *C'est que, pour organiser en Irlande un gouvernement central puissant, il faudrait de plus en plus resserrer le lien d'union qui attache l'Irlande à l'Angleterre, rapprocher le plus possible Dublin de Londres, et faire de l'Irlande un comté anglais.*

*   *   *   *   *

" *On ne conteste point que l'Irlande ait besoin d'un gouvernement spécial ; et s'il y a nécessité de la soumettre à un régime législatif autre que celui de l'Angleterre, il faut bien aussi des agents particuliers pour appliquer des règles différentes d'administration. Mais, ceci étant admis, l'on ne voit pas ce qui aujourd'hui empêcherait de placer le siége du gouvernement irlandais dans la première ville de l'empire britannique.*

*   *   *   *   *

" *La réforme de la vice-royauté et l'abolition des administrations locales d'Irlande ne sont, sans doute, que des changements de forme. Mais ce sont des moyens pratiques indispensables pour exécuter les ré-*

tions as every other part rests on a confusion of ideas, and is a false deduction from democratic principles. It is founded on the feeling which has caused half the errors of democracy, that a fraction of a nation has a right to speak with the authority of the whole, and that the right of each portion of the people to make its wishes heard involves the right to have them granted. This delusion has once and again made Paris the ruler of France, and the Parisian mob the master of Paris. The sound principle of democratic government—and England must, under the present state of things, be ruled on democratic principles—is, that all parts of the country must be governed in the way which the whole of the State as represented by the majority thereof deems expedient for each part, and that while every part should be allowed a voice to make known its wants, the decision how these wants are to be met must be given by the whole State, that is (in the particular instance) by the majority of the electors of Great Britain and Ireland. From this principle it does not follow either that every part of the kingdom should have those institutions which that part prefers, (though in so far as this end can be attained its attainment is desirable,) or, still less, that every part of the

---

formes politiques dont ce pays a besoin. Il faut que, pendant la période de transition où se trouve l'Irlande, ceux qui la gouvernent soient placés absolument en dehors d'elle, de ses mœurs, de ses passions ; il faut que son gouvernement cesse complétement d'être irlandais ; il faut qu'il soit entièrement, non pas anglais, mais remis à des Anglais."—2 De Beaumont, *l'Irlande, Sociale, Politique et Religieuse,* pp. 124-129.

kingdom should have the same institutions as every
other part. That this is so everybody in a general way
admits. No one supposes that because the people of
Leicester abominate vaccination the Vaccination Acts are
not to be extended to that borough, or that the wish of
the people of Birmingham in favour of free schools is
decisive in favour of making education in Birmingham
gratuitous. The will of a locality is admitted not to be
the expression of the will of the nation. No one, again,
fancies that the legal institutions of England ought of
necessity to be extended to Scotland, or the law of
Scotland to England. In Ireland recent legislation has,
and with general approval, established institutions which
no one alleges must, because they exist in Ireland, be
applied of necessity or as a matter of justice to England.
English tenants might in many cases, it is likely enough,
think the provisions of the Irish Land Acts a boon, but
no one would listen to the argument that simply because
under the special circumstances of Ireland special privileges are given to Irish tenants, similar privileges ought
to be conferred upon every English tenant farmer. The
idea therefore that because English boroughs or counties
receive an increased measure of self-government the same
measure ought to be extended to Ireland, though it sounds
plausible, is neither conformable to democratic principle
nor to our habitual practice, grounded as that practice
is on considerations of common sense and expediency.
The true watchwords which should guide English demo-

crats in their dealings with Ireland, as in truth with every other part of the United Kingdom, are not " equality," " similarity," and " simultaneity," but " unity of government," "equality of political rights," "diversity of institutions." Unless English democrats see this they will commit a double fault : they will not in reality deal with Ireland as with England, for to deal with societies in essentially different conditions in the same manner is in truth to treat them differently ; they will not—and this is of even more importance—perform the true function of the democracy, which is to remove by special legislation, mainly in a democratic direction, the peculiar evils which are the result of Ireland's peculiar and calamitous history.

Once realise that Local Self-Government is essentially different from Home Rule, and it becomes patent that the idea of satisfying the wish for Home Rule by increasing the municipal franchises of every township in Ireland is a dangerous delusion. Local Self-Government may be an excellent thing in its way—it is possibly (though I do not say it is) the thing which the inhabitants of Ireland ought to wish for ; but it is not the thing which they do wish for, and it has not the qualities which, if Home Rule be really desired by the Irish people, make Home Rule desirable. It does not meet the feeling of nationality ; it does not give the popular leaders authority to settle the land question ; it does not free the law from its alien aspect. The very reasons which make English reformers favour the extension of Local Self-Government in Ireland

prove that Local Self-Government, whatever its merits, is
no substitute for Parliamentary independence. Englishmen
recommend Local Self-Government because it does
not check the authority of the Imperial Parliament;
Home Rulers desire Home Rule because it does check
Imperial legislation. Brandy is good, and water is good;
but when a neighbour asks for a glass of spirits, it is
mockery to tender a glass of water on the ground that both
spirits and water are drink. The benevolent person who
makes the offer must not wonder if he receives no thanks.

Home Rule does not mean National Independence.
This proposition needs no elaboration. Any
plan of Home Rule whatever implies that there
are spheres of national life in which Ireland is
not to act with the freedom of an independent State.
Mr. Parnell and his followers accept in principle Mr.
Gladstone's proposals, and therefore are willing to accept
for Ireland restrictions on her political liberty absolutely
inconsistent with the principle of nationality. Under the
Gladstonian constitution her foreign policy is to be
wholly regulated by a British Parliament in which sit no
Irish representatives; she is not to have the right either of
raising an army or of endowing a Church; she is in fact to
surrender any claim to the rights of a nation in consideration
of receiving a certain number of State-rights. In all
this there is nothing unreasonable and nothing blameworthy.
One part of the United Kingdom is prepared to

National Independence.

accept new terms of partnership. But this acceptance,
though reasonable and fair enough, is quite inconsistent
with any claim for national independence. A nation is
one thing, a state forming part of a federation is quite
another. To ask for the position of a dependent colony
like Victoria, or of a province such as Ontario, is to
renounce the demand to be a nation. A *bonâ fide* Home
Ruler cannot be a *bonâ fide* Nationalist. This point
deserves attention, not for the sake of the miserable and
ruinous advantage which is obtained by taunting an
adversary in controversy with inconsistency till you drive
him to improve his logical position by increasing the
exactingness of his demands, but because the advocates
of Home Rule (honestly enough, no doubt) confuse the
matter under discussion by a strange kind of intellectual
shuffle. When they wish to minimise the sacrifice to
England of establishing a Parliament in Ireland, they
bring Home Rule down nearly to the proportions of Local
Self-Government ; when they wish to maximise—if the
word may be allowed—the blessings to Ireland of a separate
legislature, they all but identify Home Rule with National
Independence. Yet you have no more right to expect
from any form of State-rights the new life which sometimes is roused among a people by the spirit and the
responsibilities of becoming a nation, than you have to
suppose that municipal councils will satisfy the feelings
which demand an Irish Parliament.

D

CHAPTER III.

STRENGTH OF THE HOME RULE MOVEMENT IN ENGLAND.

A DISPASSIONATE observer will easily convince himself
that in Great Britain the movement in favour
of Home Rule is stronger than is believed by
its opponents.   Patent facts show that this is so.
In 1880 no single English statesman had avowed himself
its supporter; not fifty English or Scotch members of
Parliament could have been found to vote for an enquiry
into the admissibility of Mr. Parnell's policy.   It may
well be doubted whether at that date ten British
constituencies would have returned to Parliament representatives pledged to grant Ireland a separate legislature.
Contrast this state of things with the present condition
of affairs.   England has indeed pronounced decisively
against any tampering with the Act of Union, but the
leading statesman of the day has avowed himself a Home
Ruler; he is supported by eminent colleagues, and by
nearly two hundred representatives of British constituencies.   Scotland and Wales on the whole favour the
policy of separation; and if, as has been roughly computed,

Strength of move-ment.

of the electors of the United Kingdom, 1,316,327 have voted in support of the Union, the same computation shows that 1,238,342 are, to say the least, indifferent to its maintenance. These are facts which tell their own tale. The Home Rule movement has waxed strong. What is in England the source of its strength, and what are the arguments in its support relied upon by its English advocates?

Nine persons out of ten will reply that the Home Rule movement in England owes its origin and force to the patronage of Mr. Gladstone. No one who has watched the ebb and flow of popular feeling will underrate that statesman's influence, and few persons, whatever their political bias, will deny that but for Mr. Gladstone's conversion Mr. Parnell's teaching would not at this moment have gained for him as many as fifty disciples among English politicians. It may even be conceded that but for Mr. Gladstone's action no English party would, during his lifetime, have adopted the Parliamentary independence of Ireland as a watchword. But here, as in other instances, there is grave danger of mistaking the occasion for the cause of events, and if Mr. Gladstone's conversion has determined the form and increased the momentum of the Home Rule movement, it would be an error to hold that the prevalence of doctrines unfavourable to the maintenance of the Union between England and Ireland were wholly or even in the main due to his conduct. His conversion itself remains

Sources of its strength.

to be accounted for. This would (except to those critics who ascribe the most important acts of public statesman-ship to the pettiest forms of private selfishness) remain almost unaccountable unless it were regarded in the light, in which it ought no doubt to be looked upon, of an example of the facility with which a leader guided by keen sympathy with the real or supposed opinions or emotions of the moment follows, while apparently he guides, the phases of public opinion. Candour moreover compels the admission that, if Mr. Gladstone's action has led some politicians to " find salvation "—according to the miserable cant of the day—in the adoption of opinions which cannot be dignified with the name of convictions, many honest men both within and without the sphere of public life have under the countenance of a great name been encouraged to avow publicly sympathies with the demand for Home Rule which have been slowly matured, and have hitherto scarcely been acknowledged even in the convert's own mind. To any one who perceives that the force of a movement opposed to the traditions of English statesmanship must be attributed to some cause beyond the personal influence of a leader, the idea naturally suggests itself that the prevalence of conversions to the policy of Home Rule is due to the power of argument, and that the English people have been brought to see the expediency of conceding a legislature to Ireland by the same methods which induced them to abolish the policy of Protection. This notion does not correspond with known facts. Till a recent date hardly an argument was addressed to the English public in favour of Home Rule; no great writer or speaker even aimed at proving to the nation that a reform or innovation which has been rejected again and again as repeal had more to recommend it under a new name. Great changes in our institutions or policy have hitherto been preceded by lengthy, in general by too lengthy, discussion. The doctrines of Free Trade were established by Adam Smith seventy years before the abolition of the Corn Laws, and Protection was not vanquished till Cobden and Bright had, by laborious controversy, exposed its fallacies in every corner of Great Britain. The reasons in favour of Catholic Emancipation were stated in their full force by Burke more than forty years before a Roman Catholic was admitted to Parliament, and the whole case in favour of the Catholics had been argued out in the presence of the nation long before the passing of the Catholic Relief Bill. No movement ever appealed to keener popular sympathies than the movement for the abolition of slavery. Yet the Abolitionists made their case out—proved it, as lawyers say, "up to the very hilt," before a single slave was released from bondage. The Irish Church (it may be suggested) was abolished off-hand. This apparent exception to the regular course of long argumentative controversy which in England marks all great innovations has misled Home Rulers, yet the exception is only apparent. Long before 1869 the intelligence of England

—one might say of the civilised world—had been
convinced by the power of reason that the maintenance
in a Roman Catholic country, and at the expense of a
Roman Catholic population, of a Protestant ecclesiastical
establishment was an indefensible anomaly. The walls
fell at the first blast which sounded attack, because the
foundations had been argumentatively sapped and undermined for more than a generation. With the cause of
Home Rule it is far otherwise. Its sudden progress has
been characterised by a singular absence of systematic
discussion. No one supposes that its English advocates
are deficient in talent or in zeal. Mr. Gladstone, Mr.
John Morley, Mr. Bryce—to name no others—are as
competent apologists for any opinion they entertain as
can well be found. They have been put upon their
mettle; they have addressed the nation in Parliament
and out of Parliament; they have produced a certain
number of reasons, which deserve respectful consideration,
in support of their favourite innovation. But no candid
critic can feel that these eminent men, and other less
distinguished labourers in the same cause, have put
forward arguments of strength enough to account for the
undoubted conviction of the reasoners. Appeals to trust
in the people, to confidence in human nature, to the
strength of love as contrasted with the weakness of law,
to shame for our past misgovernment of the Irish, to
sanguine expectations of terminating a secular feud
which has caused wretchedness to Ireland and has

lessened the power of England, would appear in the judgment of orators addressing English electors likely to have much more weight with their audience than any attempt to prove that the establishment of a Parliament at Dublin will be conducive to the benefit of the Empire. Nor is this wonderful. The plain truth is that the strength of the Home Rule movement depends, as far as England is concerned, on a peculiar, though not of necessity a transitory, state of opinion. The arguments of Home Rulers, whatever their worth (and I have not the remotest intention of denying that they have weight), derive at least half their power from their correspondence with dominant sentiments. That this is so is admitted by the now celebrated appeal from the classes to the masses. It is in its nature an appeal from a verdict likely to be pronounced by the understanding or the prejudice of educated men, to the emotions of the uneducated crowd. The appeal may or may not be justifiable. This is not the point for discussion; but the making of such an appeal necessarily implies that the existence of certain widespread feelings is a condition requisite for full appreciation of the reasoning in support of Home Rule. The reasons may be good, but it is faith which gives them convincing power. They derive their cogency from a favouring atmosphere of opinion or feeling. Two features of recent controversy suffice of themselves (if proof were needed) to establish the truth of this assertion. The rhetorical emphasis laid by Home Rulers on the baseness of the arts which carried

the Act of Union is, as an argument in favour of repealing
the Act, little else than irrational.   The assumed infamy
of Pitt does not prove the alleged wisdom of Gladstone :
and to urge the repeal of an Act which has stood for
nearly a century, because it was carried by corruption, is
in the eye of reason as absurd as to question the title of
modern French landowners because of the horrors of the
Reign of Terror.   Even a Legitimist would not now base
a moral claim to an estate on the ground that his grand-
father was deprived of it through confiscation and murder.
But rhetoric is not governed by the laws of logic, and
insistence on the corruption or the criminality by which
the Act of Union was carried is an effective. method of
conciliating popular sentiment to the cause of repeal.   No
notion again has been more widely circulated or put
forward on higher authority than that past reforms have
been due in the main to the enthusiasm of the masses.
But no notion is more directly at variance with the lessons
of history.   In the eighteenth century the enlightenment of
the Whig aristocracy was England's safeguard against the
Jacobitism and the bigotry of the crowd.   Every effort
in favour of religious liberty was till recently the work of
an educated minority who opposed popular prejudice.   In
the last century popular sentiment would have denied all
rights to Jews ; in 1780 Lord George Gordon was the
hero of the people of England, and even more emphatically
of the people of Scotland.   And Burke was forced to
present an elaborate defence to his constituents at Bristol

for taking part in an attempt to mitigate the penal laws against the Roman Catholics. There is every reason to suppose that even in 1829 a *plébiscite*, had one been possible, would have negatived the Catholic Relief Bill. The mitigation again of the Criminal Law was the work of thinkers like Romilly and Bentham. These eminent reformers would have been much surprised to have been told that the uneducated masses were their staunch supporters. One of the greatest improvements ever effected by legislation was the reform in the administration of parochial relief. The new poor law was essentially unpopular; its principles were established by economists; its enactment was due to the Whigs, supported, as it should always be remembered to his credit, by the Duke of Wellington. It may be conjectured from recent legislation that at this very moment an indiscriminate renewal of outdoor relief would command the approval of the agricultural voters. Protection in the form of the corn laws was unpopular in England; this, however, cannot with fairness be put down to the moral or intellectual credit of the multitude. The corn laws were disliked because they enhanced the price of bread. Even as it was, the Chartists used to interrupt the meetings of the Anti-Corn Law League, and it is an idle fancy that the dangers of a protective tariff are in themselves more patent to the electors of England than to the democracy of France or of America. Trades Unionism is in many of its features a form of protectionism. If again we turn to foreign policy,

we must read history with a strangely perverted eye if we
hold that the people have in general condemned wars,
whether just or unjust. There is hardly to be named a
great war in which England has been engaged which has
not engaged popular support. In the struggle with the
American Colonies the warlike sentiment of the people
was undoubtedly opposed to the prudence and justice of
a small body of enlightened men, who found their representative in Burke. In England, it is true, no great
change of law or of policy can in general be effected until
it has in some sort been sanctioned by popular approval.
But to attribute every advance, or even most advances,
along the path of progress to the masses by whom a step
forward is finally sanctioned, is hardly a more patent
fallacy than the notion that because every statute is
passed with the assent of the Crown, to the Queen may
be ascribed the glory of every beneficial Act passed in
her name. To maintain, as every man versed in history
must maintain, that ignorance must from the necessity
of the case be the ally of prejudice, is not to deny to
the people their merits or virtues. If ignorance were
wisdom as well as bliss, every effort in favour of popular
education were folly. No doubt the rich or educated
classes are slaves to delusions from which the crowd are
free. This concession falls far short of the doctrine that
legislative progress is mainly due to the soundness of
popular feeling. That this doctrine should in one shape or
another have been promulgated, and have formed the basis

of an argument for a complicated change in the constitution, is a sign that the advocates of the innovation or reform feel instinctively that the strength of their case lies in its coincidence with dominant sentiment. Nor is it hard to see what is the condition of sentiment or opinion which favours the doctrine of Home Rule. The matter, however, is of such importance as well to repay careful examination.

For the first time in the course of English history, national policy has passed under the sway, not so much of democratic convictions, but of a far stronger power— democratic sentiment. Every idea which can rightly or wrongly be called popular, commands, even among persons who deem themselves Conservatives, ready assent or superstitious deference. Hence flow (be it at once conceded) some of the best characteristics of the age, such as the detestation of inhumanity ; the distrust in violent methods of government; the dislike to anything which savours of indifference to the wishes, or callousness to the wants, of the people. Hence the growth of the conviction that property has at least as many duties as rights, and of the faith inspired, rather by compassion than by reason, that the toiling multitudes can and must be made to share in the prosperity and the luxuries created in great part by their ceaseless labour. From the same source—from the prevalence of the democratic spirit—arise a crowd of dubious not to say ignoble ideas, as that the voice of the majority is the voice of God ; that it is a folly, if not a crime, to resist any widespread phase of belief or of passion ; that any body of persons claiming to be united by a sense of nationality possesses an inherent and divine right to be treated as an independent community. Many of these notions are radically inconsistent with one another. The dogma, for example, of the supremacy of the majority, or the conviction that legislation ought to aim at the greatest happiness of the greatest number, each belongs to a different order of ideas from the principle of nationality, and may easily come into conflict with it. This inconsistency does not lessen the influence exerted by the mass of democratic feeling. We may, however, well note that democratic ideas at the present day produce their effect far less by exciting enthusiasm (for they now kindle nothing like the fiery fervour which the doctrines of popular sovereignty or of human equality excited a century ago throughout the length and breadth of Europe), than by their singular capacity for dissolving the convictions which oppose the claims of revolutionists. Of this solvent power recent events have given us more than enough examples. One may suffice. The argument that because Irish householders have received votes therefore the majority of the electors of the United Kingdom must concede to the majority of Irish householders anything whatever having reference to Ireland which Irish householders desire, is logically absurd. But (combined, no doubt, with other causes) it convinced the Conservative Government of 1885 that the executive in Ireland was bound to bow to the will of the Irish people, and was relieved. from the obligation of enforcing at all costs the law of the land. Popular sympathies, moreover, blend in the minds of modern Englishmen with feelings of a much less generous and much less respectable order. Dislike of trouble, hatred to the performance of arduous public duties, a growing indifference to ordinary commonplace ideas of law and justice, contempt for the legal rights of individuals whenever these rights clash for a moment with the ease or interest of the public, exert an incalculable influence on the conduct, and in truth upon the convictions, both of Members of Parliament and of electors. It is not too much to say that the favour or acquiescence with which so-called practical politicians are prepared to accept Home Rule is grounded to a far greater extent than any one who respects the character of England likes to confess upon the *naïve* but intense conviction that it is too much to expect from five hundred and more English gentlemen that they should take the trouble of withstanding the continuous pressure exerted by eighty-six Parnellites. Cowardice masks itself under the show of compromise, and men of eminent respectability yield to the terror of being bored concessions which their forefathers would have refused to the threat of armed rebellion. It is unnecessary to explain how this condition of opinion, under which the best and the lowest feelings of human nature are blended in a current of democratic sentiment, predisposes large bodies of Englishmen towards acquiescence in the Home Rule movement. My aim is not so much to analyse with precision the mode in which the cause of Home Rule is fostered by the moral atmosphere of the day, as to insist upon the all-important consideration that the progress of the Home Rule movement is due rather to the encouragement it derives from prevailing sentiment than to any intellectual conviction on the part of Englishmen that it is dictated by considerations of sound policy.

CHAPTER IV.

ENGLISH ARGUMENTS IN FAVOUR OF HOME RULE.

To lay stress upon the consideration that the Home Rule movement in England derives its force from the condition of public feeling is not, be it remarked, equivalent to showing that the policy of Home Rule is unwise, still less that the policy of Home Rule is unlikely to be adopted by the nation. Masses of human beings must generally, as individuals must often, trust to the guidance of feeling. The difference between the sentiment which ought and the sentiment which ought not to determine national conduct is, that the one admits and the other does not admit of justification on grounds of reason or experience. Reasoning is the test, not the source of wise action. Slavery was abolished, the abuses of the *ancien régime* were destroyed, Italian unity was created under the stress of emotions which carried away thousands who could not have logically defended the impulse which governed their acts. But in these, as in other cases in which humanity has been carried forward along the path of progress by the force of emotion, the enthusiasm of the time could, in so far as it

Arguments by which Home Rule policy defended.

worked for good, be justified on grounds of reason. Man is (difficult though it often be to believe the fact) a rational being, in so far at least that he is constrained to defend on argumentative grounds courses of action dictated by feeling. From this law of human nature Home Rulers have neither the power nor, in fairness be it added, the wish to escape. Their influence is due to the condition of public sentiment, but they justify their policy by arguments which are the intellectual equivalents for the moral feelings which go to constitute the opinion of the day. Of these arguments, those which require statement and examination can be conveniently summed up under six heads—the argument from foreign experience—the argument from the will of the Irish people—the argument from the lessons of Irish history — the argument from the virtues of self-government—the argument from the necessity for Coercion Acts—the argument from the inconvenience to England of refusing Home Rule to Ireland.

Argument 1. Foreign experience.

The argument from foreign experience.—Home Rule under one shape or another has been tried in a large number of foreign countries, and has (it is alleged) been found everywhere to solve the problem of combining into one State communities which, like England and Ireland, were not ready to coalesce into one united nation. Each State throughout the American Union, each Canton of Switzerland, has something like sovereign independence. Yet the United States are strong and prosperous, and the Swiss Confederacy, which was a land at one time torn by religious animosities, and divided by differences of race, is now a country so completely at harmony with itself that without a regular army it maintains its independence in the face of the armed powers of Europe. Canada or Victoria have more complete liberty of action than any one dreams of claiming for Ireland. Yet Canada and Victoria are loyal, and under the guidance of men who, it may be, were yesterday rebels in Ireland, support the supremacy of the British Parliament and contribute to the splendour of the English Crown. The German Empire contains not only separate States, but separate kingdoms, such as Bavaria, ruled by kings or princes who certainly value highly the independence of their countries and the dignity of their thrones. The despotism of Turkey has not forbidden the local independence of Crete, and self-government has, it is hinted, produced acquiescence in Turkish rule. The autocracy of the Czar is found compatible with Home Rule in Finland, and Finland is the most contented portion of Russia. Norway and Sweden are united in feeling because they are not by law a "united kingdom," and act in harmony just because each country has a different constitution, and each is governed by its own Parliament. Denmark has, with benefit to herself, given local independence to Iceland, and Iceland is content. Austria and Hungary, after centuries of misunderstanding and twenty years of bitter conflict, have

E

finally composed the feud of ages by a compromise, which gives to the two parts of the Empire the practical blessings of Parliamentary independence, and concedes to Hungary at least the sentimental blessing of acknowledged nationality. The argument, in fact, from foreign experience, professes to be an induction based upon a foundation of instances as large as can support any conclusion of social science. In one land after another the existence of Home Rule, or, to use the curiously inaccurate phraseology of the day, of "autonomy," in one part of the State has been found consistent with the unity of the whole. An experiment which has succeeded in one set of cases ought to succeed in another, and England has no reason to dread a scheme of government which has been tried with success in other portions of the civilized world. Nor does the zealous advocate of Home Rule pause at the conclusion that the measure he recommends may, on the strength of foreign experience, be regarded as a tolerable evil or as a probable cure for a chronic disease. He suggests that it is a good in itself, and laments that ignorance led our ancestors to fuse Scotland and England into an United Kingdom, when they might, had they understood the principles of federalism, have left to each country the blessings of State sovereignty.

There is some difficulty in treating with perfect seriousness a line of reasoning which, proceeding from
Criticism on argument. the quarter whence it comes, holds up for our
admiration the wisdom or lenity of Turkish rule

in Crete, and extols the supreme justice of the system upon which rests the Austro-Hungarian monarchy, which implies that the arts of government may be learnt from the Russian administration of Finland, and omits all reference to the disastrous results of the attempt to endow Poland with some sort of independence, which bases weighty inferences as to the proper relation between England and Ireland on the concession by Denmark to the scanty inhabitants of a desolate island lying 1100 miles from her coast of as much autonomy (if that be the right term) as under the Crown of England has been enjoyed for generations by Jersey or Man, and which suggests lamentations over the splendid triumph of constructive statesmanship embodied in the treaty of Union with Scotland. *De minimis non curat lex* is a maxim of judicial procedure which in spirit applies to proposals for legislation. Arguments from Iceland and the like may be set aside as the ornaments or curiosities of debate, and may be allowed as much weight and no more as would be given to an argument in favour of petty states from the flourishing condition of Monaco, or to reasonings in support of Republicanism from the condition of Andorre. There is something slightly ridiculous in the zeal with which the advocates of Home Rule, using at least as much industry as discrimination, have scraped together every instance they can lay their hands upon of constitutions under which something which can be called Home Rule exists without producing palpable injury to the State ; it would however be unfair to deny some real weight to a kind of induction, which, if not convincing as argument, yet possesses undoubtedly a good deal of rhetorical effectiveness. Nor ought the concession to be refused that if there be any man dull or ill-informed enough to suppose that countries cannot be politically united unless they are subject to a common legislative power, the slightest knowledge of lands outside England is sufficient to make manifest his ignorance. When, however, the instances on which the induction is supposed to be founded are carefully scrutinised, it will be discovered that those examples which deserve attention are far less numerous than might be supposed from a glance over the lists (now well known to the public) of what may be termed successful experiments in Home Rule, and, further, that this limited number of instances does not go far to make out the conclusion in favour of which they are adduced.

At the present stage of my argument I purposely omit all minute examination of the applicability to the relations between England and Ireland, either of the English Colonial system or of federalism as it exists in the United States or in Switzerland. Any scheme of Home Rule must follow in some degree one or other of these models. It will, therefore, be necessary to consider in subsequent chapters how far either of them may admit with advantage of imitation. Two observations, however, may even at this point not be out of place. An English colony, such as Victoria, is a virtually independent

country, attached to England mainly by ties of loyalty or
of well-understood interest, but placed at such a distance
from the mother country that England could without
inconvenience, and would without hesitation, concede to
it full national independence when once it was clear that
Victoria desired to be a nation. Victoria, in short, is a
land which might at any moment be independent, but
which desires to retain or strengthen the connection with
England. Ireland, on the other hand, is a country lying
so near to the English coast that, according to the views
of most statesmen, England could not with safety tolerate
her independence, and also a country, which, to put the
matter in the least exaggerated language, feels the connection with England so burdensome that the greater part
of her population desire at least the amount of independence conceded to a self-governing colony. The case of
Victoria and the case of Ireland each constitute, so to
speak, the antithesis to the other. There is, therefore, at
any rate no *à priori* ground for the assumption that the
system which successfully regulates the relation of
England to Victoria is equally adapted for regulating the
relation between England and Ireland. The federalism
again, of America or of Switzerland is the consequence of
the existence of the States which make up the Federation.
The United Kingdom does not consist of States. The
world has heard of the difficulty of forming a republic
without republicans : this feat would appear to be easy of
performance in comparison with the achievement of

erecting federation without the States which form its natural members. In America or in Switzerland federalism has developed because existing States wished to be combined into some kind of national unity. Federalism in England would necessarily mean the breaking up of a nation in order to form a body of States. To the question constantly raised in one form or another, " Why should not the federalism which suits the United States suit England ? " the true answer is suggested by the counter-inquiry, " Why should not the constitutionalism of England suit the United States ? " The obvious and conclusive reply to both these inquiries is, that the circumstances of the two countries are totally different. There is, in short, no ground in the nature of things to presume that constitutional arrangements, which are well adapted for the condition of America, are well adapted for the totally different condition of the United Kingdom. To say this, be it noted, is not to pre-judge the question reserved for subsequent consideration, whether some kind of federalism may not supply the solution of the problem how to adjust the political connection between England and Ireland. It is no more than noting the often-overlooked fact that the admitted success of federal government in the United States gives no presumption in favour of its suitability for Great Britain and Ireland.

The experience of foreign countries to which Home Rulers confidently appeal resolves itself, if the matter be

carefully sifted, and if the colonial system of England and
the federalism of America be left for the moment out of
account, into the fact that two powerful continental
Empires maintain Imperial unity, and yet (as it is alleged
without lessening their strength) contain within their
limits States each of which enjoys a large amount of
independence. That neither the German Empire nor
the Austro-Hungarian monarchy suffers inconvenience
from the looseness of the connection between the States
which they each contain is one of those assertions
more easily made than proved to be true; but supposing
its truth to be, for the moment and purely for the
sake of argument, admitted, there will still be found
considerable difficulty in showing that either German
Imperialism or the Dual system of Austria-Hungary
contains lessons of practical value for the guidance of
English statesmen.

. What indeed is the precise inference which one is to
draw from the fact that the constitution of the German
Empire leaves, for example, to Bavaria a large amount of
independence it is not very easy to understand. The
whole circumstances of the German Empire are as
different from the circumstances of Great Britain as the
position of one civilised European country can well be
from the situation of another. The salient characteristic
of German history is that Germany consists of States
which until quite recently have never been politically
consolidated into a nation. The United Kingdom has for

nearly a century formed a political unit, and has now for
something nearly approaching two centuries been subject in reality if not in name to one sovereign Parliament. The whole scheme of the Empire, with its independent or semi-independent sovereigns, with its kings,
princes, and free towns, is something to which there is
absolutely nothing to correspond in the present condition
or in the historical development of England. The German Empire is the natural though strange growth of a
special and strange history. The sober English statesmen
who advocate Home Rule assuredly never dreamt any
dream so wild as that the Imperial Federalism of Germany could in any way be reproduced in the United
Kingdom. But if this be so, it is a little difficult to
understand references to the lessons to be drawn from the
position of such countries as Bavaria. For the difficulty
of applying German precedents to proposed innovations
in the English constitution lies far deeper than the un-
suitability to England of the forms of German Imperialism. The condition which has given birth to the
present German Empire is that in Germany the sentiment
of nationality has overridden the political divisions which
broke up Germany into almost disconnected and often
hostile States. In Germany the popular passion for unity
has compelled the formation of a United Empire. This
sentiment, and not the cumbersome device of an ill-
arranged constitution, prevents Bavaria from using her
independence in a manner inconsistent with the unity of

the Empire. The force which tends towards unity is constantly on the increase. The Empire holds in its hands the legal means of diminishing or indeed of destroying the independence of the States, and should the independence of a State ever come into conflict with the unity of the nation State rights will not, we may be sure, win the day. Nor, further, is it any accident that Bismarck whilst tolerating the existence of Parliaments will not tolerate the introduction of Parliamentary government. The acquiescence of Liberals in the evils of personal rule is due to the consciousness that the real authority of the Emperor is necessary for the unity of the Empire. Contrast all this with the condition of things under which Englishmen are adjured to concede a Parliament to Ireland. The leading features of the case, according at any rate to Home Rulers, are that Parliament is too weak to withstand the pressure exercised by eighty-six obstructives, and that Ireland, no less, as we are now at last frankly told, than Scotland and Wales, desires to relax the bonds of national unity. We are advised to dissolve the United Kingdom into a confederacy because Germany, through a clumsy form of confederacy, is growing into a united empire. This counsel confuses the stages of imperfect development with the stage of incipient decay; it ascribes to the childishness of approaching senility the hopes which are proper to the childishness of early youth. The point is worth pressing. The considerations which govern a confederacy as it is developing into a nation are very different from the considerations applicable to a full grown nation when threatened with dismemberment into a confederacy.

Deák's statesmanship undoubtedly found at any rate a temporary solution of the questions which kept Austria and Hungary at variance in a compromise which bears some analogy to the arrangement by which Home Rulers propose at once to loosen and to maintain the connection between England and Ireland. In the case of Austria-Hungary, the union which exists is not, on the face of it at least, a step towards unity, but rather the surrender of the endeavour to mould the two parts of the monarchy into a united empire. The Dual system is therefore the instance of the blessings attending Home Rule which is most sedulously thrust upon English attention. Let us see, then, what in outline this system is, and what are the causes which favour its existence.*

German jurisprudence has taxed hard its boundless stores of ingenuity and obscurity in the endeavour to find a proper scientific definition of the nature of the anomalous union which binds together the monarchy of Austria-Hungary. With the inquiry, however, what may be the precise class of constitutions under which we ought to bring a political arrangement which is "singular" in the strictest sense of that word, English inquirers need not

---

* For the constitution of Austria-Hungary see Ulbrich's *Oesterreich-Ungarn* in Marquardsen's *Handbuch des Oeffentlichen Rechts*; Francis Deák, with preface by M. E. Grant Duff; Home Rule in Austria-Hungary, by David King, in the *Nineteenth Century*, January 1886, p. 35.

concern themselves. The broad outlines of the Dual system, invented by the ingenuity of Deák, and accepted under the stress of necessity by the sagacity of the Emperor, may, for our present purpose, be roughly sketched in short, and, it is hoped, in not unintelligible terms.

The Dual system is a permanent alliance rather than a union between the kingdom of Hungary and the countries now represented in the Austrian Imperial Parliament, or (to use convenient though not quite accurate terms) between Austria and Hungary.

The essential features of this alliance or compromise, which is in its nature a treaty far more than an act of legislation, may be thus summed up.

At the head of the whole monarchy stands the Emperor-King. The rules for the succession to the throne indeed secure that the Imperial and the Hungarian Crown shall always devolve upon the same person. The Crowns, however, are distinct, the monarch on whose head they rest governs two distinctly different peoples, bound to him by different ties of allegiance. He has Hungarian subjects and Austrian subjects, but he can claim authority over no man as a subject or citizen of Austria-Hungary. The monarch (and this is a matter of supreme importance) is not only the nominal, but the real link connecting the two halves of his dominions. He is moreover a true ruler. Englishmen hear of a Parliament at Vienna and of a Diet in Hungary, of Austrian ministers and of Hungarian ministers, and they fancy that Francis Joseph is a constitutional king after the type of Queen Victoria of England, or King Humbert of Italy. No idea is more erroneous. He is the actual head of the State ; he is the real commander of the army.   In the Austrian Empire he exercises a predominant influence on the Government, and observers who look at the past exertions of Imperial prerogative, and who weigh well the immense power of temporary legislation reserved under the Imperial constitution to the Emperor, suspect that in his Austrian dominions, Francis Joseph might if he chose as easily suspend constitutional government, as he did in fact suspend it (though for a most legitimate object) in 1866.   In Hungary the parliamentary constitution is a reality, but the King of Hungary's authority is a good deal more than nominal.   The transactions between Deák and the Emperor become incomprehensible unless you allow for the influence conferred by Hungarian loyalty upon the King of Hungary.

This real monarch rules the monarchy with the co-operation of what might roughly be called three Parliaments.

The first Parliament is the Hungarian Diet sitting at Pesth, which constitutes the real and true legislature for Hungary, and which, in spite of the powers retained by or conferred upon the local legislature of Croatia, makes laws for the whole domain of the Hungarian Crown.   The King of Hungary appoints the Hungarian ministers, who are responsible to the Hungarian Diet, and are kept in office by the Diet's support.

The second Parliament is the Imperial Parliament, or *Reichsrath*, sitting at Vienna, legislating for the territories of the Austrian Empire which do not belong to the Hungarian Crown. The Emperor appoints the Austrian or Imperial Ministry, who are responsible to the Imperial Parliament, and need the support of the *Reichsrath;* it may well however be doubted whether an Austrian Premier does not depend for his authority far more on the will of the Emperor than on the votes of *Reichsrath;* the authority of the *Reichsrath* is, moreover, considerably restricted by the powers conferred upon the subordinate assemblies of the different countries, e.g. Bohemia or the Tyrol, which make up the Empire.*

Englishmen should note that the Hungarian Diet has as such no legislative authority in Austria, and the *Reichsrath* has no legislative authority in Hungary.

The third Parliament consists of the so-called Delegations.

These Delegations are two committees of sixty members each, elected by and from the members of the Hungarian Diet and the Imperial Parliament respectively, but though I have termed them " committees " they are committees which within their sphere have an authority independent of the bodies by whom they are appointed.

The function of the Delegations is to determine the " common affairs " of the monarchy, that is to say a strictly limited number of matters, namely, common finance, common military matters, and foreign affairs. On these

* Ulbrich, pp. 15, 76, 77.

three topics, and on these alone, the Hungarian and the Austrian Delegations are (acting of course with the Emperor) supreme. They determine the common Budget of the whole Austro-Hungarian Empire; they determine as far as legislation is required all questions affecting the Imperial army as a whole; they also determine, as far as their intervention is required, questions of foreign policy. The function in short of the Delegations is to deal with matters, and with those matters only, which affect the Austro-Hungarian State as a united body, and in its relation to foreigners. Hence three Ministers, the Minister of War, the Minister of Finance, and the Minister of Foreign Affairs, who act for the whole monarchy, constitute what is called the Common Ministry, and are appointed by the Emperor-King, and are responsible neither to the Hungarian Parliament nor to the Imperial Parliament, but simply to the Delegations. It is natural for Englishmen to conclude that the Delegations regulate matters, such for example as questions regarding customs, &c., which must affect every portion of the State, and must, if the two divisions of it are to be united at all, be regulated on common principles. But this is not so. The economical relations of the two parts of the Empire are determined by laws identical in substance, passed by the Hungarian and Imperial Parliaments respectively. These laws are enacted from ten years to ten years. It is therefore possible under the present arrangement that in '88 the existing customs union between Austria and Hungary may come to an end.* The position further of the Delegations is in reality that of two separate committees each representing a separate Parliament. Infinite pains have been taken to place the Hungarian and the Austrian Delegations on exactly equal footing. The Delegations meet alternately at Vienna and at Pesth, they debate in general separately, and come to an agreement through written negotiations ; they may have a common meeting. In this case the number of deputies present on each side must be equal, and by a vote of the majority at such common meeting, any question in dispute is finally determined.

The Austro-Hungarian system is therefore briefly this : two separate States, each having a separate administration, a separate Parliament, and separate bodies of subjects or citizens, are each ruled by one and the same monarch; the two portions of the monarchy are linked together, mainly as regards their relation to foreign powers, by an assembly of delegates from each Parliament and by a Ministry which is responsible to the Delegations alone, and which acts in regard to a limited number of matters which are of absolute necessity the common concern of the monarchy. This is the Dual system held up for our imitation. Picture it for a moment as actually existing in what is still the United Kingdom. We should have an English Ministry and an English Parliament at Westminster which had not the least authority in Ireland ; we should have an Irish Ministry and an Irish Parliament at

* See Marquardsen, 28-30.

Dublin which had not the least authority in England. Each Parliament would in point say of foreign policy be hampered by the superior authority of a third Parliament consisting of sixty English and sixty Irish members who sat alternately at Westminster and at Dublin to transact or perplex or obstruct the affairs common to the whole Empire. To imagine such an arrangement, to sketch out in one's fancy, for example, how the common budget decreed by the Delegations would be provided for by taxation imposed by the Irish Parliament, is enough to show that the Dual system is absolutely inapplicable to our circumstances. It could not last for a year, and if by any miracle it did last for that time, the whole British Empire would be reduced to confusion or ruin. The advocates of innovation exhibit the most singular mixture of despair and hopefulness. The presence in Parliament of eighty-six Parnellites makes them despair of the British constitution, which has existed for centuries. They hope or expect that three Parliaments, in two of which these very Parnellites, or men like them, would reappear, would harmoniously legislate for England, Ireland, and the British Empire, and this hope is based on the alleged success of that Dual system which has not without difficulty been kept going for not quite twenty years. The alliance of scepticism and credulity, of which we have often heard in the sphere of theology, is a startling phenomenon in the province of politics. The Dual system, however, it will be urged by its admirers, has worked well.

Admit the fact, the success is clearly due to circumstances negative and positive totally absent in the case of England and Ireland. The bodies united by means of the compromise do not, like the United Kingdom, constitute the centre of a world-wide Empire. Hungary has taken up arms against the Austrian Emperor, yet there has never been in strictness a feud between the Hungarians and the other subjects of the Emperor. The compromise or alliance manifestly met the interest of both portions of the monarchy: it restored to Hungary a constitution which for eighteen years or more had been suppressed, but which had never been given up; it secured, or went far to secure, the new constitutional liberties of the Austrian Empire. Hungary could not stand alone, and she knew it. The compromise was in reality a politic alliance between the two leading races among the many races governed by Francis Joseph. The Germans and the Magyars came to terms; the alliance strengthened them each against other foes. But with every political advantage the Dual system, of which the permanence is not as yet at all secure, might have proved as undurable as Grattan's Constitution of 1782 but for one circumstance, to which I have already directed attention. At the head of Austria-Hungary stands not an absolute, but a powerful monarch. The authority of the Emperor is the spring which makes the cumbersome machinery of a complicated constitution keep going. The matter is worth attention. The power of the Emperor William holds together the States of the German Empire; the power of Francis Joseph

F

keeps alive the Dual system ; where the Crown has a real authority trial may be made of experiments in the way of local independence, which are impossible in a State where, as in England, the true sovereign is an elective assembly.

Foreign experience then affords but a very tottering foundation on which to raise pleas for Home Rule in Ireland. It may no doubt be read by those who are already convinced that Home Rule is desirable in favour of their views. It may confirm a faith based on other grounds, more it cannot do. Fairly looked at, foreign experience tells rather against than for the doctrines of Home Rule. If appealed to at all, it must be taken as a whole. It then shows that Federalism is when flourishing a stage towards, not a stage away from, national unity ; it shows that a strong central power above Parliamentary control is almost a condition to the successful combination in one body of semi-independent States.* It shows that the whole tendency of modern civilization flows towards the creation of great States ; national unity is, so to speak, the watchword of the age ; this is scarcely a reason for breaking up the United Kingdom. The sagacity of Italian statesmanship rejected the plausible scheme of an Italian Federation. If Englishmen are to take lessons from foreigners they need not be ashamed of being instructed by Cavour.†

---

* This is, in my judgment, true even of such federations as the United States or the Swiss confederacy.

† John Stuart Mill, in his very remarkable pamphlet 'England and Ireland,' gives it as his distinct opinion that neither the Canadian

The argument from the will of the Irish people.—Eighty-six representatives of the Irish people represent the wish of Ireland for Home Rule. We cannot under a Parliamentary system of government go behind the result of an election. It must be taken therefore that Ireland wishes for Home Rule; and since popular government as it exists in England means nothing else than government in accordance with the wishes of the people, the wish of the Irish people for the Parliamentary independence of their country proves their right to an Irish Parliament, and terminates, or ought to terminate, all opposition to Home Rule.

Argument 2. Will of Irish people.

This simple argument, that because three millions of Irishmen, or for that matter three millions of Englishmen, wish for a thing, they are therefore absolutely entitled to have it, is not often put forward in its naked simplicity, but is constantly presented under various rhetorical disguises, such for example as the assertion that Irishmen have a right to manage their own affairs, that Ireland only wants to be left to herself, and the like; and impresses both the imagination and the conscience of the masses. There is a good deal to be said about the truth of the alleged fact on which the argument is based, namely the wish of the Irish people.

Criticism on argument.

Confederation nor the Dual system of the Austro-Hungarian monarchy afford models which could be followed in regulating the connection between Great Britain and Ireland. See 'England and Ireland,' pp. 32–37.

It might be worth while to note that the " people " in this
case meant only a majority of the electors, whose wish is
notoriously opposed to the ardent desire of a respectable
minority ; and it might be well to suggest that the constitutional pedantry which refuses to "go behind an
electoral return," *i.e.*, to see things as they are, is not the
same thing as either good sense or statesmanship.   But for
the present purpose it is better to admit that the majority
of the inhabitants of Ireland would, if a fair vote were
taken, express their wish for Home Rule, as they might,
probably, under similar conditions express their wish for
separation.   The argument in hand, however, even when
its basis is conceded, allows, according to the different
meanings which it may bear, of different answers.   If
taken in its most obvious sense, as asserting the absolute
right of a majority among Irish electors to any concession
with regard to Ireland which they are pleased to claim,
it may be met by another formula of equal cogency or of
equal weakness.   " The vast majority of the United
Kingdom, including by the way a million or more of the
inhabitants of Ireland, have expressed their will to maintain the Union.   Popular government means government
in accordance with the will of the majority, and therefore
according to all the principles of popular government the
majority of the United Kingdom have a right to maintain
the Union.   Their wish is decisive, and ought to terminate
the whole agitation in favour of Home Rule."   To any
sensible person who has passed beyond the age of early
manhood (for youths may without blame treat politics

as a form of logic) neither of these formulas can present a sound ground from which to defend or impugn legislation which involves the welfare of millions. The contradiction however between two formulas each of which if propounded alone would command the assent of a democratic audience is noteworthy. This contradiction brings into prominence the consideration that the principle that the will of the majority should be sovereign cannot, whether true or false in itself, be invoked to determine a dispute turning upon the enquiry which of two bodies is the body the majority of which has a right to sovereignty. The majority of the citizens of the United States were opposed to Secession, the majority of the citizens of the Southern States were in favour of Secession ; the attempt to determine which side had right on its side by an appeal to the "sovereignty of the majority" involved in this case, as it must in every case, a *petitio principii,* for the very question at issue was which of two majorities ought, as regarded the matter in hand, to be considered the majority.

It would however be doing injustice to the argument from the will of the people to dispose of it by dwelling upon the logical inconsistencies inevitably involved in every attempt to determine a question of practical politics by the application to it of *à priori* dogmatism. Formulas such as "the sovereignty of the people" often contain much solid truth hidden under an inaccurate and a too absolute form of expression. The assertion that the wish of the Irish people is decisive as to the form of constitution to be maintained in Ireland covers two genuine and in them-

selves rational convictions. The first is, that a body of
human beings who feel themselves, in consequence of their
inhabiting a common country, of their sharing a common
history and the like, inspired with a feeling of common
nationality, have, if not a right, at lowest a strong claim to
be governed as a separate nation. This is the doctrine of
nationality which, be it noted, though often confused with,
is at bottom different from, the dogma of the supremacy of
the majority. That the doctrine of nationality is, when
reasonably put, conformable with obvious principles of
utility may be readily admitted; but it is a doctrine which
can only be accepted with considerable qualifications. Its
validity was denied both theoretically and practically, and,
in the judgment of most English democrats, not to say of
most European Liberals, denied justly and righteously by
the Northern States of America, when the Southern States
claimed the benefit of its application. The argument
moreover from the principle of nationality in reference
to the present controversy proves too much. If the
Irish people are a nation, this may give them a right to
independence, but it can never in itself give them a moral
claim to dictate the particular terms of union with
England. The second conviction which underlies the
argument from the will of the people is of far more serious
import than any reasoning drawn from even so respectable
a formula as the doctrine of nationality. The dogma that
the will of the people must be obeyed often expresses
the rational belief that under all politics, and especially
under the system of popular government, institutions derive

their life, and laws their constraining power, not from the
will of the law-giver, or from the strength of the army,
but from their correspondence with the permanent wishes
and habits of the people. Home Rule, to put this matter
in its strongest form, means, it may be said, the application
to Ireland of the very principle on which the English
constitution rests—that a people must be ruled in accordance with their own permanent ideas of right and of justice,
and that unless this be done, law, because it commands no
loyalty, ensures no obedience. The whole history of the
connection between the two islands which make up the
United Kingdom is a warning of the wretchedness, the
calamities, the wickedness and the ruin which follow upon
the attempt to violate this fundamental principle not only
of popular, but of all good and just government. Home
Rule may appear to be an innovation. It is in this point of
view simply a return to the essential ideas of English constitutionalism, it is an attempt to escape from the false path
which has been pursued for centuries, and to return to the
broad highway of government in accordance with popular
sympathy. At this point, however, the argument from the
will of the people merges in the much stronger and more
serious train of reasoning derived from the teaching of
history.

The argument from Irish history.—Appeals to the lessons
of the past are at times in the mouths of Home Rulers,
as also of their opponents, a noxious revival of ancient

passions, or (it may be) nothing better than the use of an
unreal form of rhetoric; yet a supporter of Home
Rule may use the argument from Irish history
in a way which is at once legitimate and telling.

3. Argument from Irish history.

On one point alone (it may be urged) all men of
whatever party, or of whatever nation, who have seriously
studied the annals of Ireland are agreed—the history of
the country is a record of incessant failure on the part of
the Government, and of incessant misery on the part of
the people. On this matter, if on no other, De Beaumont,
Froude and Lecky are at one. As to the guilt of the
failure or the cause of the misery, men may and do differ;
that England, whether from her own fault or from the
fault of the Irish people, or from the perversity of circumstances, has failed in Ireland of achieving the elementary
results of good government, is as certain as any fact of
history or of experience. Every scheme has been tried in
turn, and no scheme has succeeded, or has even (it may be
suggested) produced its natural effects. Oppression of
the Catholics has increased the adherents and strengthened
the hold of Catholicism. Protestant supremacy while it
lasted did not lead even to Protestant contentment, and
the one successful act of resistance to English dominion
was effected by a Protestant Parliament supported by an
army of volunteers led by a body of Protestant officers.
The independence gained by a Protestant Parliament led,
after sixteen years, to a rebellion so reckless and savage,
that it caused if it did not justify the destruction of

the Parliament, and the carrying of the Union. The
Act of Union did not lead to national unity, and a measure
which appeared on the face of it (though the appearance
it must be admitted was delusive) to be a copy of the law
which turned England and Scotland into a common
country inspired by common patriotism, produced conspiracy and agitation, and has at last placed England and
Ireland further apart morally than they stood at the
beginning of the century. The Treaty of Union, it was
supposed, missed its mark because it was not combined
with Catholic Emancipation. The Catholics were emancipated, but emancipation instead of producing loyalty
brought forth the cry for Repeal. The Repeal movement
ended in failure, but its death gave birth to the attempted
rebellion of 1848. Suppressed rebellion begot Fenianism,
to be followed in its turn by the agitation for Home Rule.
The movement relies, it is said, and there is truth in the
assertion, on constitutional methods for obtaining redress.
But constitutional methods are supplemented by boycotting, by obstruction, by the use of dynamite. A century
of reform has given us Mr. Parnell instead of Grattan, and
it is more than possible that Mr. Parnell may be succeeded
by leaders in whose eyes Mr. Davitt's policy may appear
to be tainted with moderation. No doubt in each case the
failure of good measures admits, like every calamity either
in private or in public life, of explanation, and after the
event it is easy to see why, for example, the Poor Law
when extended to Ireland did not produce even the good

effects, such as they are, which in England are to be set
against its numerous evils; or why an emigration of un-
paralleled proportions has diminished population without
much diminishing poverty ; why the disestablishment of
the Anglican Church has increased rather than diminished
the hostility to England of the Catholic priesthood; or why
two Land Acts have not contented Irish farmers. It is
easy enough, in short, and this without having recourse to
any theory of race, and without attributing to Irishmen
either more or less of original sin than falls to the lot of
humanity, to see how it is that imperfect statesmanship
—and all statesmanship it should be remembered is
imperfect—has failed of obtaining good results at all
commensurate with its generally good intentions. Failure,
however, is none the less failure because its causes admit
of analysis. It is no defence to bankruptcy that an insolvent
can, when brought before the Court, lucidly explain the
errors which resulted in disastrous speculations. The
failure of English statesmanship, explain it as you will,
has produced the one last and greatest evil which misgovernment can cause. It has created hostility to the law
in the minds of the people. The law cannot work in
Ireland, because the classes whose opinion in other
countries supports the action of the Courts are in Ireland,
even when not law-breakers, in full sympathy with law-
breakers. This fact, a Home Ruler may add, is for his
purpose all the more instructive, if it be granted that the
errors of British policy do not arise from injustice or ill-

will to Irishmen. The inference, he insists, to be drawn from the lesson of history is, that it is impossible for the Parliament of the United Kingdom to understand or to provide for Irish needs. The law is hated and cannot be executed in Ireland because, as we are told on high authority, it comes before the Irish people in a foreign garb. The law is detested, in short, not because it is unjust, but because it is English. The reason why judges, soldiers or policemen strive in vain to cope with lawlessness is, that they are in fact trying to enforce not so much the rule of justice as the supremacy of England. The Austrian administration in Lombardy was never deemed to be bad—it was very possibly better than any which the Italian kingdom can supply; the Austrian rule was hated not because the Austrians were bad rulers, but because they were foreigners. In Ireland, as in Lombardy, permanent discontent is caused by the outraged sentiment of nationality. Meet this sentiment, argues the friend of Home Rule, by the concession to Ireland of an independent Parliament. The law which comes from Ireland's own legislature will be obeyed because it is her own law, and will be enforced throughout Ireland by Irish officials supported by the sympathy of the Irish population. Let Ireland manage her own affairs, and England will be freed from a task which she ought never to have taken up because she cannot perform it, and you will lay upon Ireland duties which she can perform but which she has never yet been either allowed or compelled to take up,

Irishmen for the first time will feel the full responsibility, because for the first time they have received the full power, of self-government. The argument, in short, on the Home Rule view stands thus: the miseries of Ireland flow historically from political causes, and are to be met by political changes. At the bottom of Irish disorder lies the sentiment of Irish nationality. The change, therefore, that is needed is such a concession to that sentiment as is involved in giving Ireland an Irish legislature. This is the reform by which the result of curing Irish discontent can be achieved, and it is a reform not incompatible with the interests of Great Britain.

This is (in my judgment) a fair statement of the historical argument relied upon by the advocates of Home Rule, though, of course, it allows of infinite variety as to its form of expression. It is a line of reasoning which rests on premisses many of which (as any candid critic must admit) contain a large amount of truth. It is logically by far the strongest of the Home Rule arguments. It is one, moreover, in which authorities who on other points differ from each other are in agreement. Mr. Parnell asserts with emphasis that Ireland is a "nation," and apparently holds that the passing of a good law by the Parliament of the United Kingdom is less desirable than the existence of an Irish Parliament, even should that Parliament delay good legislation. Mr. Gladstone attributes the inefficacy of laws passed by the

Imperial Parliament to their coming before Irishmen in a "foreign garb," and an author who is not in any way a supporter of the Liberal leader does not apparently on this point disagree with Mr. Gladstone. " If there was a hope that anything which we could give would make the Irish contented and loyal subjects of the British Empire, no sacrifice would be too great for such an object. But there is no such hope. The land tenure is not the real grievance : it is merely the pretext. The real grievance is our presence in Ireland at all. If there was a hope that by buying up the soil and distributing it among the tenantry we could make them, if not loyal, yet orderly and prosperous, even so the experiment would be worth trying; but, again, there is no such hope. The Land Bill of 1870 gave the tenants a proprietary right in their holdings. They have borrowed money on the security of that right at ruinous interest, and the poorest of them are already sinking under their debts to the local banker or tradesman. If we make them proprietors to-morrow, their farms in a few years will be sold or mortgaged. We shall have destroyed one set of landlords to create another who will not be more merciful." *

The only way of meeting the historical argument, containing as it does admitted truth, and sup- Criticism. ported as it is by high authorities, is to survey the broad phenomena of Irish history, and see

* Froude's 'English in Ireland,' vol. 3, pp. 581, 582.

what are the inferences which they warrant.* Whoever wishes to derive instruction from the melancholy history of the kingdom of Ireland must, as has already been intimated, rid himself from the delusions caused in the domain of history by personification. He must dismiss the notion that England and Ireland are persons to be charged with individual and continuous responsibility for the crimes or follies of past ages. He must check the natural but misguiding tendency of the human mind to imagine that in national affairs when anything goes wrong you can always, or indeed generally, lay your finger upon some definite assignable wrong-doer, that is, upon some man or some men who can be held responsible for political calamities or errors, as a murderer may be held guilty of murder, or a robber of theft. A calm critic should also reflect on the profound truth of the dictum (attributed by the way to an Irishman) that "history is at best but an old almanack," and, while not entertaining any great hope that antiquarian research can afford much direct guidance as to the proper mode of arranging the future relations between England and Ireland, remember that the most salutary function of the study of the past is to tone down those historical animosities which derive their bitterness from the ignorant habit of trying the actors in bygone scenes by moral laws to which they are not justly amenable. The moral function of an historian

* See especially on this subject 1 De Beaumont, 'L'Irlande,' Partie Historique, pp. 15-207.

is to diminish the hatreds which divide nation from nation and class from class, such as, at the present moment, do more to prevent real unity between the inhabitants of the two islands making up the United Kingdom than do unjust laws or vicious institutions. To a student who regards with philosophic calmness a topic which has mainly been dealt with by politicians or agitators, it easily becomes apparent that the crimes or failures of England, no less than the vices or miseries of Ireland, have to a great extent flowed from causes too general to be identified with the intentional wrong-doing either of rulers or of subjects.

One fact thrusts itself upon the attention of any serious student. England and Ireland have from the commencement of their ill-starred connection been countries standing on different levels or at different stages of civilization; they have moreover been countries impelled by the force of circumstances towards a different development. Englishmen forget, or (more strictly speaking) have never understood, how exceptional has been the path pursued by English civilization; they do not realise to themselves that the gradual transformation of an aristocratic and feudal society into a modern industrial State which still retains the forms, and in many points of view the spirit of feudalism is a process which, although owing to the most special circumstances it has been accomplished with success in England, has hardly a parallel in any other European country. Ireland on the other hand has,

despite the deviations from her natural course caused by
her connection with a powerful nation, tended to follow
the lines of progress pursued by continental countries, and
notably by France. A foreign critic like De Beaumont
finds it far easier than could any Englishman to enter
into the condition of Ireland, and this not only because he
is as a foreigner delivered from the animosities or
partialities which must in one way or another warp every
English judgment, but mainly because the phenomena
which puzzle an Englishman, as for example the passion
of Irish peasants for the possession of land, are from his
own experience familiar and appear natural to a Frenchman. What to the mind of a foreign observer needs
explanation is the social condition of England rather than
of Ireland. He at any rate can see at a glance that the
relation between the two countries has planted and
maintained in Ireland an aristocracy, aristocratic institutions, and above all an aristocratic land law, foreign to the
traditions and opposed to the interests of the mass of the
people. Let an observer for a moment take up the point
of view natural to a continental critic, and admit, in the
language of De Beaumont, that the primary radical and
permanent cause of Irish misery has been the maintenance
in Ireland by England of a "bad aristocracy," * or, to put

* "On ne saurait considérer attentivement l'Irlande, étudier son
histoire et ses révolutions, observer ses mœurs et analyser ses lois, sans
reconnaître que ses malheurs, auxquels ont concouru tant d'accidents
funestes, ont eu et ont encore de nos jours, pour cause principale, une

the same thing more generally, and it may be more fairly that the vice of the connection between the two countries has consisted in its being a relation of peoples standing at different stages of civilization and tending towards different courses of development. Here you find the original source of a thousand ills, and hence especially have originated four potent causes of the condition of things which now tries the patience and overtaxes the resources of English statesmanship.

First,—The English constitution has both from its form and from its spirit caused in past times, and even at the present day causes as much evil to Ireland as it has conferred, or does confer, benefit upon England.[*]

The assailants of popular government point to the misrule of Ireland as a proof that the Parliamentary system is radically vicious. They do not prove their

---

cause *première*, radicale, permanente; et qui domine toutes les autres; cette cause, c'est une mauvaise *aristocratie.*" 1 De Beaumont, 'L'Irlande,' deuxième partie, p. 228. The only objection which may be fairly taken to De Beaumont's language, though not to his essential meaning, is, that the words he uses occasionally suggest the idea that he attributes some special vice of nature, so to speak, to the landed classes in Ireland; whilst there is, of course, no reason to suppose that the original Norman invaders of Ireland were a whit worse than the Normans they left behind them in England, or that the Cromwellian settlers did not possess the virtues which distinguished Puritan soldiers. What De Beaumont really means is that the aristocracy, or landed gentry, have been from first to last placed in a false position, which has led to their exhibiting the vices, with few of the virtues, of aristocratic government.

[*] Compare 1 De Beaumont, ' L'Irlande Sociale,' &c., pp. 253–256.

G

point, because the calamities of Ireland afford no evidence
whatever that England, which has been more prosperous
for a greater length of time than any other nation in
Europe, has essentially suffered from the power of the
English Parliament. What these critics do prove is that
a representative assembly is a bad form of government for
any nation or class whom it does not represent, and
they establish to demonstration that a parliamentary
despotism may well be a worse government for a dependency than a royal despotism. This is so for two
reasons. The rule of Parliament has meant in England
government by parties; and whatever be the merits of
party spirit in a free, self-governed country, its calamitous defects, when applied to the administration of a
dependency, are patent. Down to 1782 Ireland was
avowedly subject to the despotism or sovereignty of the
British Parliament, and at every turn the interest of the
country was sacrificed to the exigencies of English
politics. Between 1782 to 1800 the nominal independence of Ireland placed a check on the power of the
English Parliament, yet in substance the English executive, controlled as it was by the Parliament at
Westminster, remained the ultimate sovereign of the
kingdom of Ireland. If Pitt could have carried the King
and the English Parliament with him, he would, in spite
of any opposition at Dublin by the adherents of
Ascendancy, have emancipated the Catholics, just as,
when backed by the King and the English Parliament, he

did, in the face of strenuous opposition in Ireland, pass the Act of Union. And even at the present day the most plausible charge which can be brought against the working of the Act of Union is that Ireland under it fails to obtain the full benefit of the British constitution, and that in spite of her hundred representatives she is not for practical purposes represented at Westminster in the same sense as is Middlesex or Midlothian. A Parliament again is less capable than a King of compensating for the evils of tyranny by the benefit of good administration, and here we come across a matter hardly to be understood by any one who has not with some care compared the action and the spirit of English and of continental administrative systems. It is hardly an exaggeration to assert that even now we have in the United Kingdom nothing like what foreigners mean by an administration. We know nothing of that official hierarchy which on the Continent represents the authority of the State.* Englishmen are accustomed to consider that institutions under which the business of the country is carried on by unconnected local bodies, such as the magistrates in quarter session, or the corporations of boroughs, controlled in the last resort only by the law courts, ought to be the subject of unqualified admiration. Foreign observers might, even as regards England itself, have something to set off against the merits

---

* See Dicey, 'Law of the Constitution' (Second Edition), pp. 181–210; and compare 1 De Beaumont, 'L'Irlande Sociale,' &c., pp. 253–299.

of a system which is, if the apparent contradiction of
terms may be excused, no system at all, and might point
out that in continental countries the administration may
often be the intelligent guide and protector of the weak
and needy. The system complimented by the name of
self-government, even if as beneficial for England as
Englishmen are inclined without absolute proof to
believe, is absolutely unsuitable for a country harassed
by religious and social feuds, where the owners of land
are not and cannot be the trusted guides of the people.
An impartial official is a better ruler than a hostile or
distrusted landowner, and any one who bears in mind the
benefits conferred by the humanity and justice of Turgot
on a single province of France may, without being any
friend of despotism, hold that in the last century Ireland
suffered greatly from a scheme of government which did
not allow of administration such as Turgot's. In some
respects the virtues of Englishmen have been singularly
unfavourable to their success in conciliating the goodwill
of Ireland. It will always remain a paradox that the
nation which has built up the British Empire (with vast
help, it may be added, from Ireland) has combined extraordinary talent for legislation with a singular incapacity for consolidating subject races or nations into
one State. The explanation of the paradox lies in the
aristocratic sentiment which has moulded the institutions
of England. An aristocracy respects the rights of individuals, but an aristocracy identifies right with privilege,

and is based on the belief in the inequality of men and of classes. Privilege is the keynote of English constitutionalism ; the respect for privileges has preserved English freedom, but it has made England slower than any other civilized country to adopt ideas of equality. This love of privilege has vitiated the English administration in Ireland in more ways than one. The whole administration of the country rested avowedly down to 1829, and unavowedly to a later period, on the inequality of Catholics and Protestants, and Protestant supremacy itself meant (except during the short rule of Cromwell)* not Protestant equality, but Anglican privilege. The spirit which divided Ireland into hostile factions prevented Englishmen who dwelt in England from treating as equals Englishmen who settled in Ulster. When in 1782 the Volunteers claimed Irish independence, and the American colonists renounced connection with the mother country, similar effects were produced by the same cause. In each case English colonists revolted against England's sovereignty, because it meant the privilege of Englishmen

---

* Cromwell's reputation as a statesman suffers even more than that of most great men from the indiscriminating eulogy of admirers. The merit of his Irish policy was not his severity to Catholics, but his equity to Protestants. If he did not acknowledge the equality of man, he at any rate acknowledged what English statesmanship before and after his time refused to admit—the equality of Englishmen, at least when Protestants. His policy handed down to us a legacy of justifiable hatred on the part of Irish Catholics. But it is the fault not of the Protector, but of his successors, that his policy did not ensure to England the loyalty of every Protestant in Ireland.

who dwelt in Great Britain to curtail the rights and hamper the trade of Englishmen who dwelt abroad. For the iniquitous restrictions on the trade of Ireland, which are morally by far the most blameworthy of the wrongs inflicted by England upon Irishmen, were not precisely the acts of deliberate selfishness which they seem to modern critics. The grievance under which Ireland suffered was in character the same as the grievances in respect of trade inflicted on the American colonies. Yet but for the insane attempt to subject the colonists to direct taxation by the English Parliament the War of Independence might have been long deferred. Even the sufferers from a vicious commercial policy did not see its essential iniquity, and it is hardly a subject for wonder that a generation of Englishmen who supposed themselves to gain greatly by controlling or extinguishing the colonial or the Irish trade should not have recognised the full iniquity of a policy which in itself hardly seemed intolerable to many of those colonists who endured the wrong. Still less can we be surprised that Englishmen a century ago, amid a world where the idea of human equality was not as yet recognised, should have failed to perceive what many Englishmen it may be suspected will hardly admit at present, that to most men equality, *i.e.* the treatment of all subjects by their government on similar principles, seems a form of justice, and that the multitude will tolerate restrictions on their freedom far more easily than offences against their sense of equality.

No one will care to deny that French Governments have at all periods been far more despotic than the Government of England; but few persons who have given the matter a thought can deny that France has shown a power quite unknown to Englishmen of attaching to herself by affection countries which she has annexed by force. Strasburg was stolen from Germany, yet Strasburg soon became French in heart. Belgium and the Rhine Provinces would gladly have remained parts of the Napoleonic Empire. Savoy annexed in 1859 showed no disposition to separate from France in 1870. The explanation of these facts is not far to seek. When France annexes a country she may govern it well or ill, but she governs it on the same principles as the rest of the French dominions. Englishmen found it for centuries impossible to govern Englishmen in Ireland or Englishmen in Massachusetts exactly as if they were Englishmen in Middlesex. It is not uninstructive that every French Assembly since the Revolution has included Deputies from the colonies; no colony has ever sent a member to the Parliament at Westminster.

Secondly,—The English connection has inevitably, and therefore without blame to anyone, brought upon Ireland the evils involved in the artificial suppression of revolution.

The crises called revolutions are the ultimate and desperate cures for the fundamental disorganisation of society. The issue of a revolutionary struggle shows what is the true sovereign power in the revolutionised state. So strong is the interest of mankind, at least in any European country, in favour of some sort of settled rule, that civil disturbance will, if left to itself, in general end in the supremacy of some power which by securing the safety, at last gains the attachment, of the people. The Reign of Terror begets the Empire; even wars of religion at last produce peace, albeit peace may be nothing better than the iron uniformity of despotism. Could Ireland have been left for any lengthened period to herself, some form of rule adapted to the needs of the country would in all probability have been established. Whether Protestants or Catholics would have been the predominant element in the State; whether the landlords would have held their own, or whether the English system of tenure would long ago have made way for one more in conformity with native traditions; whether hostile classes and races would at last have established some *modus vivendi* favourable to individual freedom, or whether despotism under some of its various forms would have been sanctioned by the acquiescence of its subjects, are matters of uncertain speculation. A conclusion which, though speculative, is far less uncertain is, that Ireland if left absolutely to herself would have arrived like every other country at some lasting settlement of her difficulties. To the establishment of such a reign of order the British connection has been fatal; revolution has been suppressed at the price of permanent disorganisation, the descendants of colonists and natives have not coalesced into a nation, and a country which has never known independence has never borne the burdens or learnt the lessons of national responsibility. Disastrous as this result has been, it is impossible to say who it was that at any given point was to blame for it. Had France been attached to and dependent upon a powerful neighbour, this sovereign state must have checked the cruelties and the injustice of the Reign of Terror. But the forcible extinction of Jacobinism by an external power would, we can hardly doubt, have arrested the progress and been fatal to the prosperity of France. Ireland, in short, which under English rule has lacked good administration, has by the same rule been inevitably prevented from attempting the cure of deeply-rooted evils by the violent though occasionally successful remedy of revolution.

Thirdly,—From the original flaw in the connection between the two countries has resulted, almost as it were of necessity, the religious oppression, which, recorded as it has been in the penal laws, has become the opprobrium of English rule in Ireland.

The monstrosity of imposing Anglican Protestantism upon a people who had not reached the stage of development which is essential for even the understanding of Protestant dogma, and who if left to themselves would have adhered to Catholicism, conceals from us the strength of the pleas to be urged in excuse of a policy which to critics of the nineteenth century seems at least as absurd as it was iniquitous. Till towards the close of the seventeenth century all the best and wisest men of the most civilised nations in Europe believed that the religion of a country was the concern of the Government, and that a king who neglected to enforce the " truth"—that is, his own theological beliefs—failed in his obligations to his subjects and incurred the displeasure of Heaven. From this point of view the policy of the Tudors must appear to us as natural as to themselves it appeared wise and praiseworthy. That the people of England should have been ripe for Protestantism at a time when the people of Ireland had hardly risen to the level of Roman Catholicism was to each country a grievous misfortune. That English Protestants of the sixteenth and seventeenth centuries should in common with the whole Christian world have believed that the toleration of religious error was a sin, and should have acted on the belief, was a cause of immense calamities. But inevitable ignorance is not the same thing as wickedness.*

Fourthly,—To the same source as religious persecution is due the whole crop of difficulties connected with the tenure of land.

When James I. determined that the old Brehon law was to be abolished, and an appeal to the law of England to be brought within the reach of every Irishman, he and

---

* The penal laws against the Catholics in England were as severe as those in Ireland. Their practical effect and working was however very different in the two countries. See 1 Lecky, ' History of England,' pp. 268–310.

his ministers meant to introduce a beneficial reform. They hoped that out of the old tribal customs a regular system of landowning according to the English tenure would be developed. In forcing on this change, English statesmen felt convinced not only that they were reformers, but that they were promoters of justice. To a generation trained under the teaching of lawyers like Coke, and accustomed to regard the tenure which prevailed in England as good in itself, it must have appeared that to pass from the irregular dominion of uncertain customs to the rule of clear, definite law, was little less than a transition from anarchy and injustice to a condition of order and equity. They acted in precisely the spirit of their descendants, who are absolutely assured that the extension of English maxims of government throughout India must be a blessing to the population of the country, and shape their Egyptian policy upon their unwavering faith in the benefits which European control must of necessity confer on Egyptian fellahs. If, however, it is probable that King James meant well to his Irish subjects, it is absolutely certain that his policy worked gross wrong. His scheme only provided for the more powerful members of the tribes, and took no account of the inferior members, each of whom in his degree had an undeniable if somewhat indefinite interest in the tribal land. Sir John Davis, who carried out the plan, seems to have thought that he had gone quite far enough in erecting the sub-chiefs into freeholders. It never occurred to him

that the humblest member of the tribe should, if strict
justice were done, have received his allotment out of the
common territory ; and the result of his settlement ac-
cordingly was that the tribal land was cut up into a
number of large freehold estates which were given to the
most important personages among the native Irish, and
the bulk of the people were reduced to the condition of
tenants at will.* An intended reform produced injustice,
litigation, misery, and discontent. The case is noticeable,
for it is a type of a thousand subsequent English attempts
to reform and improve Ireland. The rulers of the country
were influenced by ideas different from those of their
subjects. Ignorance and want of sympathy produced all
the evils of cruelty and malignity.

Bad administration, religious persecution, above all a
thoroughly vicious system of land tenure, accompanied by
such sweeping confiscations as to make it at any rate a
plausible assertion that all the land in Ireland has during
the course of Irish history been confiscated at least thrice
over,† are admittedly some of the causes, if they do not
constitute the whole cause, of the one immediate difficulty
which perplexes the policy of England. This is nothing
else than the admitted disaffection to the law of the land
prevailing among large numbers of the Irish people. The

* See Walpole, 'Short History of the Kingdom of Ireland,' p. 176.
† See a speech of Lord Clare made in defence of the Bill for
Establishing the Union with England, and republished by the Irish
Loyal and Patriotic Union.

existence of this disaffection, whatever be the inference to be drawn from it, is undeniable. A series of so-called Coercion Acts passed both before and since the Act of Union give undeniable evidence, if evidence were wanted, of the ceaseless, and as it would appear almost irrepressible, resistance in Ireland offered by the people to the enforcement of the law. I have not the remotest inclination to underrate the lasting and formidable character of this opposition between opinion and law, nor can any jurist who wishes to deal seriously with a serious and infinitely painful topic question for a moment that the ultimate strength of law lies in the sympathy, or at lowest the acquiescence, of the mass of the population. Judges, constables and troops become almost powerless when the conscience of the people permanently opposes the execution of the law. Severity then produces either no effect or bad effects, executed criminals are regarded as heroes or martyrs, and jurymen or witnesses meet with the execration, and often with the fate, of criminals. On such a point it is best to take the judgment of a foreigner unaffected by prejudices or passions, from which no Englishman or Irishman has a right to suppose himself free :

"*Quand vous en êtes arrivés à ce point, croyez bien que dans cette voie de rigueurs tous vos efforts pour rétablir l'ordre et la paix seront inutiles. En vain, pour réprimer des crimes atroces, vous appellerez à votre aide toutes les sévérités du code de Dracon ; en vain vous ferez des lois cruelles pour arrêter le cours de révoltantes cruautés ; vaine-*

*ment vous frapperez de mort le moindre délit se rattachant à
ces grands crimes ; vainement, dans l'effroi de votre im-
puissance, vous suspendrez le cours des lois ordinaires,
proclamerez des comtés entiers en état de suspicion légale,
violerez le principe de la liberté individuelle, créerez des cours
martiales, des commissions extraordinaires, et pour produire
de salutaires impressions de terreur, multiplierez à l'excès
les exécutions capitales."**

* 1 De Beaumont, 'L'Irlande Sociale,' p. 251. It is of primary
consequence that Englishmen should realise the undoubted fact, that
agrarian conspiracies and agrarian outrages, such as those which baffle
the English Government in Ireland, are known to foreign countries.
For centuries the question of tenant-right, in a form very like that in
which it arises in Ireland, has been known in the parts of France near
Saint-Quentin under the name of the *droit de marché*. In France,
as in Ireland, tenants have claimed a right unknown to the law, and
have enforced the right by outrage, by boycotting, by murder. The
Dépointeur is the land grabber, and is treated by French peasants
precisely as the Irish land grabber is treated by Irish peasants. See
Calonne, ' La Vie Agricole, sous l'Ancien Régime,' pp. 66–69. Precisely
the same phenomena have appeared in parts of Belgium, where for
centuries there has been, in respect of land, the conflict to which we are
accustomed in Ireland, between the law of the Courts and the law of
the people. " From the commencement of the year 1836 to the end
of 1842 there had been " [in consequence of this conflict] " forty-three
acts of incendiarism, eleven assassinations, and seven agrarian outrages
entailing capital punishment," all within a limited part of Belgium.
See Parliamentary Reports on Tenure of Land in Countries of Europe,
1869, p. 118–123. In Belgium decisive measures of punishment at last
put an end to agrarian outrages. What should be specially noted is that
in France and Belgium crimes in character exactly resembling the
agrarian outrages which take place in Ireland had, it is admitted, no
connection whatever with national, or even it would seem with general
political feeling.

No advocate of Home Rule can find a clearer statement of the condition of things with which on his view the Imperial Parliament is morally incompetent to deal than in these words of De Beaumont's; but before we hastily draw any inference from an undoubted fact, let us examine into the exact nature of the fact. The opposition of Irish opinion to the law of the land is undoubted, but the opposition is not now, and if we appeal (as under the present argument we are appealing) to the teaching of history never has been general opposition to law, or even general opposition to English law. The statistics of ordinary crime are (it is said) no higher in Ireland than in other parts of the United Kingdom. A pickpocket or a burglar is as easily convicted in Ireland as elsewhere; the persons who lamentably enough are either left unpunished, or if punished may count on popular sympathy, are criminals whose offences, atrocious and cruel as they constantly are, are connected in popular opinion with political, and at bottom, it must be added, with agrarian questions. For more than a century there has existed an hereditary conspiracy against the rights of the landowners. The White Boys of 1760, the Steel Boys of 1772, the Right Boys of 1785, the Rockites of a few years later, the Thrashers of 1806, the White Boys who re-appear in 1811, 1815, 1820, the Terralts of 1831, the White Feet of 1833, the Black Feet of 1837; * later Ribbon men under different names, the Boycotters or the assassins who have added a terrible sanction to the

* See 1 De Beaumont, ' L'Irlande Sociale,' &c., p. 251.

commands of the Land League or of the National League, have each and all been, in most cases avowedly and in every case in fact, the vindicators or asserters of the just or unjust popular aversion to the rights of landlords given by the law and enforced by the courts of the land. It would be folly to assert that all popular opposition to the law in Ireland had been connected with agrarian questions. But if we look either to the experience of past generations, or to the transactions passing before our eyes, we can hardly be mistaken in holding that the main causes of disaffection have been either questions connected with religion, or rather with the position of Roman Catholics, or disputes connected with the possession of land.

The feeling of nationality has played a very subordinate part in fomenting or keeping alive Irish discontent. The Repeal agitation, in spite of O'Connell's legitimate influence, collapsed. No one can read Sir Gavan Duffy's most interesting account of the Young Ireland movement without perceiving that just because it was strictly a nationalist movement it took very little hold upon the people. The Home Rule movement never showed great strength till it became avowedly a Land League, of which the ultimate result should be, by whatever means, to make the tenants of Ireland owners of their land. To this add that in the judgment of foreign critics, and of thinkers like Mill, the popular protest against the maintenance in Ireland of a tenure combining the evils both of large estates and of minute subdivision of farms is founded upon justice. De

Beaumont at any rate teaches that to transform Irish
tenants into peasant proprietors would be the salvation of
the country:—

"*Plus on considère l'Irlande, ses besoins et ses difficultés
de toutes sortes, et plus on est porté à penser que ce change-
ment dans l'état de sa population agricole serait le vrai
remède à ses maux. . . .*

"*J'aurais mille autres raisons pour appuyer cette opinion;
je m'arrête cependant. Un lecteur anglais trouvera mes
arguments incomplets. Tout autre qu'un Anglais les jugera
peut-être surabondants.*" *

This opinion may be well-founded or ill-founded; but
no wise statesman will reject it without the maturest
consideration.

History, then, if fairly interrogated, gives this result:
Historical causes have generated in Ireland a condition of
opinion which in all matters regarding the land impedes
that enforcement of law which is the primary duty of
every civilized government.

From this fact Home Rulers draw the inference that
the law is hated because it is foreign, and that England
should surrender to Irishmen the effort to enforce legal
rights, since this duty is one which can be performed by
a native and cannot be performed by any English or
foreign authority.

This conclusion is clearly not supported by the premisses.

* 2 De Beaumont, 'L'Irlande Sociale, Politique et Religeuse.'
Septième édition, pp. 135 and 137.

If the source of popular discontent be agrarian, then the right course is to amend the land laws while improving the administrative system, and enforcing justice between man and man.

A Home Ruler may, however, if hard driven, say that my interpretation of history is erroneous, and that a hatred to English law, and to all things English, and not a special dislike to the land law, is the sentiment which prevails over every other feeling of the Irish people. It is difficult to me to see how this view can be seriously maintained. Let us grant however for a moment that Home Rulers are right, and that millions of Irishmen are inspired with the passion of nationality. Even on this supposition the Home Rule doctrine stands in a bad way. If the demand of the Irish people be like that of the Italian people— a demand for recognised nationality—then the demand must be satisfied, if at all, not by Home Rule, but by independence. The most eminent among English Home Rulers believes that the law is hated in Ireland because it comes before the Irish people in a foreign garb. Mr. Froude in substance agrees in this matter with Mr. Gladstone, since he holds that "the real grievance is our presence in Ireland at all." But the eminent statesman and the distinguished historian draw a different inference from the same premisses. Mr. Gladstone infers that Ireland can be satisfied by semi-independence. Mr. Froude infers that if we are to meet Irish wishes we must let Ireland be free. Mr. Froude's logic will be to most persons far more intelligible than the logic of the Liberal leader. Here, at any rate, we come to the true issue suggested by the phenomena of Irish history. Is Irish discontent due in the main to agrarian or to political causes? On the answer to this enquiry depends, as far as the argument we have in hand goes, the line of right policy in Ireland. But neither answer favours the contention of Home Rulers.*

The argument from Irish history gives rise to, or, more properly speaking, contains in itself two further distinct lines of reasoning in favour of Home Rule, each of which supplements the other. The first of these aims at showing that to leave Ireland to herself is the only method by which to restore order throughout the country: this I have termed "the argument from the good effects of self-government." The other deduces from the necessity for Coercion Acts the conclusion that England cannot maintain order in Ireland: this I have termed "the argument from the necessity for Coercion Acts." These two lines of reasoning are simply an amplification of points suggested by the Home Rule argument from Irish history, and are of necessity there-

---

* A Home Ruler may in this matter take up one position which is consistent. He may say that England can allow to be carried out through the agency of an Irish Parliament a policy which no English Parliament could itself adopt. To put the matter plainly, an English Parliament which cannot for very shame rob Irish landlords of their property may, it is suggested, create an Irish Parliament with authority to rob them. This position is consistent, but it is disgraceful. To ascribe it to a fair opponent would be gross controversial unfairness.

fore open to the same criticisms to which that argument
is obnoxious.   They have, however, each a certain value
of their own, and have made an impression on the English
public: they can each also be met by more or less special
replies.   The argument, therefore, from the good effects of
self-government and the argument from the necessity for
Coercion Acts each deserve separate statement and consideration.

The argument from the virtues of self-government.—Self-
4. Argument from self-government. dependence is the source of self-reliance and of
self-help.   Leave Ireland to herself, and Ireland
will (it is argued) develop the sense of responsibility and the power of self-government.   Mr. Parnell
or Mr. Davitt as Irish Prime Minister will be able to
perform with ease feats beyond the reach of any English
Cabinets.   He will dare to be strong because he knows he
is popular: he will punish conspirators with a severity
unknown to modern English governments; he will feel
that anarchy is the bane of his country, and he will not
tolerate disorder.   Boycotters, Moonlighters, Dynamiters
or Assassins will find that they are called upon to meet a
force of which they have had before no experience.   They
will discover that they are engaged in a contest with the
will of the people, and deprived, as they will be, of the
moral sympathy which has hitherto given them comfort
and encouragement, will yield obedience to a law which
is the expression of the national will.   Self-government

in Ireland means strong government, and strong government is the one cure for Irish misery.

This train of reflection has, unless I am mistaken, convinced many English Radicals that the installation of an Irish Ministry at Dublin will be the dissolution of every secret society throughout Ireland, and thus gained over to the cause of Home Rule men who detest anarchy even more than they love liberty.

This belief in the virtues of self-government is confirmed by the teaching of American critics, who hold that the recent experience of the United States presents a clue by which Englishmen may find a path out of the labyrinth of their present perplexities. Transactions known to every citizen of the States show conclusively that the hatred of law which in Ireland fills Englishmen with amazement has arisen among a people who, whatever their faults, cannot be charged with those inherited vices which English opinion freely and gratuitously imputes to Irish nature. In Connecticut, in New York, in Georgia, throughout all the Southern States, open or secret combinations, supported by public opinion and enforcing its decrees by violence and murder, have with success defied the law courts. Social conditions, and not the perversities of Irish character, are seen to be the true cause of phenomena which, if they are now a feature of Irish life, have appeared in countries where not an Irishman was to be found, and where the Irish had no appreciable influence. To this fact, which appears to me not to admit of question,

Americans add the consideration that lawlessness when supported by public opinion has in America been successfully met, not by coercion, but by yielding to public sentiment. Hence they draw the conclusion that the proper mode of terminating the conflict between law and widespread sentiment is to yield to opinion, and, by conceding something of the nature of Home Rule, to turn law-breakers into law-makers. The application of this dogma to Ireland is obvious: the crucial instance by which its truth is supposed to be established is the treatment of the conquered South by the victorious North. From the termination of the War of Secession up to 1876 the fixed policy of the Northern Republicans was to maintain order in the South by the use of Federal troops. This policy began and ended in failure: in 1876 the troops were withdrawn; the endeavour to enforce law by means of the Federal armies was given up—as if by magic, chaos gave place to order. Local self-government has given peace to the United States, why should it not restore concord to the United Kingdom ? *

It has been freely admitted in the foregoing pages† that

---

* A reader who wishes to see the American view put in its best and strongest form should read Mr. E. L. Godkin's article on "American Home Rule," *Nineteenth Century,* June, 1886, p. 793. I entirely disagree with the general conclusion to which the article is intended to lead, but I am anxious to acknowledge the importance of the information and the arguments which it contains.

† See pp. 87–89, *ante.*

the historical connection between England and Ireland
has brought upon the weaker country the evils
involved in the suppression of internal revolution by external force. This admission contains the
main ground for the argument in favour of Home Rule
drawn from the good effects of self-government, but is not
in reality a sound foundation on which to place the
suggested conclusion.

Criticism.

For the argument under consideration, even after the
concession that Ireland has suffered from not having been
left to herself, is vitiated by more than one flaw.

Home Rule, as it is again and again necessary to point
out, is not national independence, nor anything like
independence. Home Rule gives Ireland at most semi-
independence—that is to say, it leaves Ireland at least
half dependent upon England. It is vain to argue that
the position of the member of a confederacy or of a
colonial dependency will give to Irishmen the sense of
independence and responsibility which belongs to a self-
governing nation.

Grant, however (though the assumption is a hazardous one), that the creation of an Irish government and
an Irish Parliament would of itself give to Ireland, even
though she were still in many respects dependent on
England, such a new sense of power and of responsibility
as would enable her to create for herself a strong
executive. This concession is not enough to make out the
argument in favour of Home Rule. Laws ought to be not

only strong but just, and Englishmen must consider whether rulers who had come to the head of affairs solely because they represented the strongest among many Irish factions or parties would be able to rule with justice. The " Jacobin Conquest " installed a strong executive in power, but England could not be an accomplice in inaugurating a reign of terror. The connection which under any form of Home Rule would bind together the parts of the present United Kingdom would be, it may be suggested, a guarantee against the supremacy of an Irish Robespierre or Danton. Granted : but if so, Home Rule would restrain an Irish revolution. The strongest, in other words the most reckless leaders, would be prevented from coming to the front. Ireland would not follow her own course, and since she would not be in truth self-governed she would not reap the good fruits of self-government.

Nor, in truth, does the American version of our argument give much help to Home Rulers.

In more than one instance popular sentiment has in the United States defied the law of the land. Nothing can be a better example of such defiance than the anti-rent war which raged in New York between 1839 and 1846.* The struggle exhibited all the recklessness of a no-rent agitation in Ireland, with none of the excuses which can be urged in palliation of outrage by half-starving tenants ; it

* See " American Home Rule," *Nineteenth Century,* June, 1886, pp. 793, 803, 804.

produced a "reign of terror which for ten years practically suspended the operations of law and the payment of rent throughout the district" which was the field of the anti-rent movement; it ended in a nominal compromise which was a real victory for the anti-renters. In this instance, be it remarked, no sentiment of nationality or State right came into play. The law was hated, not because it was "foreign," but because it enforced the obligation of an unpopular contract. Landlords, it is now all but admitted, are not entitled to the full rights of citizens. The triumph therefore of the anti-renters at New York may command a certain amount of sympathy. The popular sentiment which in 1833 induced the people of Connecticut to boycott Miss Prudence Crandall cannot be brought under the sanction of any "higher law." Her crime was that she chose, obeying the dictates of her conscience, to open a school for Negro girls in Connecticut. She was subjected to every annoyance and insult which the most reckless boycotter could invent. Legislation itself was turned against her, and the State failed utterly in the duty of protecting one of the most meritorious, and now, one is happy to think, one of the most honoured among the women of America. The Lyman Riots at Boston, as indeed every stage in the noble struggle of the American Abolitionists against popular injustice, tell the same tale, namely, that law in the United States has once and again failed to assert its due supremacy over injustice backed by public approval. This melancholy failure may possibly support the proposition that England cannot enforce the law in Ireland. It far more conclusively shows that even in countries deeply imbued with the spirit of legality self-government has no necessary tendency to produce just government or just legislation.

Let us, however, examine with care the lessons to be drawn from the treatment of the Southern States of America by the North.

The natural and most obvious moral of modern American history is that the majority of a nation have both the right and power to coerce a minority who claim to break up the unity of the State. The most distinguished English Liberals, such as Bright and Mill, held, and as I conceive on sound grounds of reason and justice, that the Southern States were neither legally nor morally justified in their claim to secede from the Union; but no fair-minded man can deny that a plausible constitutional case could be made out in favour of Secession, nor that the citizens of the Southern confederacy demonstrated their wish and determination to secede by far more cogent evidence than the return of eighty-six Secessionists to Congress. The primâ facie arguments which may be alleged in favour of Secession were tenfold stronger—unfounded as I hold them to have been—than the primâ facie arguments in favour of Ireland's right to Home Rule. Moreover, in studying the history of the United States, an Englishman is at the present moment more concerned with the results than with the justification of the suppression of the Southern rebellion. The policy of the North attained its object: the Union was restored, and its existence is now placed beyond the reach of peril. The abolition of slavery took away the source of disagreement between the Northern and Southern States, and the tremendous exhibition of the power of the Republic has finally, it is supposed, destroyed the very idea of Secession. There is certainly nothing in all this which discourages the attempt to maintain the political unity of Great Britain and Ireland. We are told, however, to forget the force employed to suppress Secession, and to recollect only the policy of the Republicans after the close of the Civil War. That policy was a failure as long as it involved the denial to the Southern States of their State autonomy, and became a success from the moment when it recognised to the full the sacredness of State rights. This, or some statement like this, represents the mode in which the annals of the Union must be read if they are to be interpreted in favour of Home Rule. The reading is a strained interpretation of events which are known to every one. The North, once and for all, settled that the matters which lay at the bottom of the Civil War should be settled in the manner which conform to Northern notions of justice and of expediency. The abolition of slavery, and the final disposal of the alleged right to Secession, gave to the North all the requisite securities against attacks on the unity of the Republic. The Republicans, influenced in part by considerations of party,

but partly (it must in fairness be admitted) by the feeling
that it was a duty to secure for Negro citizens the full
enjoyment of the civil and political rights given them,
under the constitutional amendments supported for years
the so-called Carpet Bag Governments, that is to say, the
rule of Northern adventurers who were kept in office
throughout the South by the Negro vote. The Federal
Government, in short, up to 1876 gave by its arms
authority in the South to the unscrupulosity of Northern
scoundrelism supported by the votes of Negro ignorance.
Such a policy naturally produced bitter irritation among
the Southern Whites. Its reversal as naturally restored
to the Whites at once power and contentment. Whether
this reversal was as satisfactory to the Blacks is less clear.
In any case, it is hard to see how the restoration of the
Southern States to their natural place in the Union tells
in favour of giving Ireland a position quite inconsistent
with the existing constitution of the United Kingdom.
The case stands thus : Northern Republicans insisted that
every State in the South should submit to the supremacy
of the United States on every point which directly or
indirectly concerned the national and political unity of
the American people. Having secured this submission
the Republican party restored to the Southern States the
reality as well as the name of State rights; and allowed
the same and no more than the same independence to
South Carolina as is allowed to New York. No doubt
something was sacrificed; this " something " was a matter

which did not greatly concern the citizens of the North. It was the attempt to secure to the Black citizens of the South the political rights given them by the constitution. The sacrifice may have been necessary; many of the wisest Americans hold that it was so. But we may suspect that even amongst those who, as a matter of policy, approve the course pursued by the Federal Government in the South since 1876, qualms are occasionally felt as to some of its results. The able writer who sets American Home Rule before Englishmen as an example for imitation says with the candour which marks his writings : " I do not propose to defend or explain the way in which " the Native Whites " have since then " (1876) kept the Government " in their hands by suppressing or controlling the Negro vote. This is not necessary to my purpose."* It is however necessary for the purpose of weighing the effect of American experience to bear this "suppression" constantly in mind ; it has deprived the Negroes of political rights which possibly they had better never have received, and has falsified the result of Presidential elections. When we are told that the South votes solid for a Democratic President, we must remember that in the Southern States the Negro vote is " controlled " ; and that in reckoning the number of votes to which a State is entitled in virtue of its population, the Negro voters of the South are counted for as much as the uncontrolled White voters of the North. Whether this state of things

* *Nineteenth Century,* June, 1886, p. 801.

will always be contentedly borne by the Northern States
is a matter on which a foreigner can form no opinion.   It
is a condition of affairs which does not conduce to respect
for law, and the satisfaction with which thoughtful
Americans regard a policy founded on the tolerance of
illegality confirms the belief suggested by other circumstances, that deference to opinion tends in the United
States to undermine respect for law; it certainly does not
tend to show that self-government has much connection
with justice.

The argument, in short, from the good effects of self-
government appears, when examined, either to be an argument which tells far more strongly in favour of Separation
than of Home Rule, or else to be an argument which
shows only that England might gain some immediate
advantage from shutting her eyes to injustice committed
by an Irish government.

The argument from the necessity for Coercion Acts.—

5. Argu-   Coercion Acts are (according to popular appre-
ment from   hension) enactments suspending the operation
Coercion
Acts.   of the ordinary law, and conflicting therefore
with the principles of the English Constitution.   Order
has been maintained in Ireland since the Union (we are
told) mainly by means of Coercion Acts.   The English
democracy, it is argued, cannot acquiesce any longer in
these violations of the Constitution; but since order must
somehow be maintained in Ireland, and Coercion Acts

must no longer be passed, the English democracy must surrender the duty of maintaining the law into the hands of the Irish people, who, as is assumed by Home Rulers, can exact obedience to the law of Ireland without the use of exceptional legislation.

A lawyer irritated by the folly of popular declamation is tempted to dismiss all objections to Coercion Acts, together with all arguments founded upon such Criticism. objections, with one peremptory remark—namely, that since a law is merely a rule which men are compelled to obey by the power of the State, and Coercion is but another name for compulsory obedience to the law, to object to Coercion is in reality to object to law itself, or in effect to the existence of political society. The temptation to cut down a popular delusion by some such summary criticism as this is great, but it is a temptation which at all costs must be resisted. Vague ideas, which have obtained general currency, are, in spite of their inaccuracy, the outgrowth for the most part of reasonable feeling. Whoever wishes to meet, and, if need be, dispel the antipathy to Coercion Acts, must try to understand what is the meaning which sensible men attach to the word " Coercion," what is the conviction represented by the dislike to Coercion Acts, how this dislike may be lessened, and, for the purpose with which these pages are written, how far the disapproval of Coercion Acts provides a reason in favour of Home Rule.

Of all the terms which at the present moment confuse public judgment, none is more vague and misleading than the word "Coercion" when applied to every stringent attempt to enforce in Ireland obedience to the law of the land.

Coercion means and includes two different though closely connected ideas which the laxity of popular thought fails to distinguish.

First.—Coercion means any attempt to enforce a law among people whose moral sympathies are at variance with the law itself. In this sense Coercion is opposed to that enforcement of ordinary law with which we are all familiar. Thus, to punish a Ritualist for not conforming to the judgment of the Privy Council, to enforce vaccination at Leicester, to compel a Quaker to pay tithes, to eject an Irish tenant from the farm he has occupied, to drag him into Court and seize his goods if he does not pay his rent, to punish severely resistance to the Sheriff's officer, or to the bailiff who gives effect to the rights of an Irish landlord, are in popular estimation proceedings which according to the nature of the law put in force are stigmatised as persecution or Coercion. They certainly differ from the compulsion by which common debtors are compelled to pay their debts, or thieves are prevented from picking pockets or breaking into houses. The difference lies in this. Where the enforcement of the law is called "Coercion," not only does the criminal think himself in the right, or at any rate think the law a wrongful law, but also the society to which he belongs holds that the law-breaker is maintaining a moral right against an immoral law. The anti-vaccinator is deemed a martyr at Leicester, the farmer who will not pay his rent is thought a patriot at Cork. Where the enforcement of the law is not popularly deemed coercion the law-breaker does not suppose himself to be in the right, and still less do his associates think him morally praiseworthy. A thief does not in general hold any theory about the rightness of larceny, and there is no society in the United Kingdom at least which denies the moral validity of the Eighth Commandment.

Secondly.—Coercion means the enforcement of law by arbitrary and exceptional methods which tend to diminish the securities for freedom possessed by ordinary citizens. Thus the suspension of the Habeas Corpus Act, the abolition of trial by jury, the introduction of peculiar rules of evidence to facilitate convictions for a particular class of crimes, a suspension (speaking generally) of what would be called in foreign countries " constitutional guarantees," in order to secure obedience to particular laws, would be called coercion.*

An enactment, then, which in ordinary language is called a Coercion Act, has one or both of the two following characteristics. It is an Act which either enforces some

* Contrast the Coercion Acts of 1881 and 1882 respectively. For list of Coercion Acts see " Federal Union with Ireland," by R. B. O'Brian, *Nineteenth Century*, No. 107, p. 35.

I

rule of law (*e.g.*, the law that tenants must pay their rent, or that trades-unionists must not molest artisans who accept lower wages than the scale prescribed by the union), which does not command the moral assent of the society or people among whom it is enforced, or else constrains obedience to law by some exceptional and arbitrary mode of procedure. Now the general prejudice against an Act which has either or both of these characteristics is within certain limits justifiable on grounds of good sense. Laws derive three-fourths of their force not from the fears of law-breakers, but from the assent of law-keepers; and legislation should, as a rule, correspond with the moral sentiment of the people. The maxim *quid leges sine moribus*, though it should always be balanced by the equally important maxim *quid mores sine legibus*, is one which no legislator dares neglect with impunity, and a law permanently at variance with wide moral feeling needs repeal or modification. It is also true that exceptional and arbitrary legislation is, simply because it is exceptional and arbitrary, open to suspicion. If it be desirable that personal liberty should be protected by the writ of Habeas Corpus, a suspension of the Habeas Corpus Act is on the face of it an evil. If it is not desirable that officers of the army should suddenly and without legal training exercise the power of judges, the establishment of martial law is in itself a great, though it may be a necessary calamity. Legislation which has received the odious name of Coercion has frequently (though not always) exhibited one or both of the characteristics which render it fairly obnoxious to that designation. The objection, therefore, to Coercion Acts is on the face of it not unreasonable. What are the inferences which the objection supports is, of course, quite a different matter, and shall be considered in its due place.

It is most important, however, to note that the valid opposition to so-called Coercion Acts may and ought to be greatly mitigated by careful adherence to two maxims which are obvious, but are often neglected.

A Coercion Act, in the first place, should be aimed, not at the direct enforcement of rules opposed to popular opinion, but at the punishment of offences which, though they may be indirectly connected with dislike of an unpopular law or with opposition to rights (for instance, of landowners) not sanctioned by popular opinion, are deeds in themselves condemned by the human conscience. Deliberate breaches of contract, insults to women and children, the murder or torture of witnesses who have given truthful evidence in support of a conviction for crime, brutal cruelty to cattle, may be methods of popular vengeance, or the sanctions which enforce an agrarian code ; but one may feel certain that the man who breaks his word, who tortures or murders his neighbour or who houghs cattle, knows himself to be not only a criminal, but a sinner, and that the law, which condemns him to punishment, though it may excite temporary

I 2

outcry, can rely on the ultimate sanction of the popular conscience.

A Coercion Act, in the second place, should as far as possible be neither a temporary nor an exceptional piece of legislation.

An Act which increases the efficiency of the criminal law should, like other statutes, be a permanent enactment. The temporary character of Coercion Acts has needlessly increased their severity, for members of Parliament have justified to themselves carelessness in fixing the limits of powers conferred upon the Executive under the insufficient plea that these powers were intended to last but for a short time. It has also deprived them of moral weight. An Act which is a law in 1881, but will cease to be a law in 1882, has neither the impressiveness nor the certainty which gives dignity to the ordinary law of the land. Coercion Acts, again, should be general—that is, should apply, not to one part, but to the whole, of the United Kingdom. Powers needed by the Government for constant use in Ireland must occasionally be wanted in England, or, if they do not exist there already, in Scotland. It were the strangest anomaly for the law to sanction a mode of procedure which convicts a dynamiter in Dublin, and not to give the Government the same means for the conviction of the same criminal for the same offence if he has crossed to Liverpool. The principle forbidding exceptional or extraordinary legislation suggests that Coercion Acts should in the main give new stringency

to the criminal procedure, and should not invade the
liberties of ordinary citizens. The object of a Coercion
Act is to facilitate the punishment of wrongdoers, not
to restrict the liberty of citizens who have not broken
the law. This is a point legislators are apt to neglect.
The distinction insisted upon will be understood by any
one who compares the Act for the Better Protection of
Person and Property in Ireland, 44 Vict. c. 4, of 1881,
with the Prevention of Crime (Ireland) Act, 1882, 45 &
46 Vict. c. 25. They were each denounced as Coercion
Acts : the earlier enactment was in many ways the
more lenient of the two; yet in principle the Act of
1881 was thoroughly vicious, whilst in principle the Act
of 1882 was, as regards its most effective sections,
thoroughly sound. The Act of 1881 in effect gave the
Irish executive an unlimited power of arrest : it established
in theory despotic government. The Act of 1882 was in
principle an Act for increasing the stringency of criminal
procedure. The one could not be made permanent, and
applied to the whole United Kingdom, without depriving
every citizen of security for his personal freedom. The
main enactments of the other might extend through the
whole of Great Britain and Ireland, and produce only the
not undesirable effect of making the whole United Kingdom a less pleasant residence than at present for criminals
or conspirators.

An Act which should be permanent, which should apply
to the whole United Kingdom, which should deal, not in-

deed exclusively but in the main, with criminal procedure,
could hardly contain injudicious, harsh or tyrannical
provisions. The passing of one such good Criminal Law
Amendment Act would, though its discussion occupied a
whole Session, save our representatives in Parliament an
infinite waste of time, and would make unnecessary half-
a-dozen Coercion Acts for Ireland. To enlarge the power of
examining persons suspected of connection with a crime,
even though no man is put upon his trial; to get rid of every
difficulty in changing the venue; to give the Courts the right
under certain circumstances of trying criminals without the
intervention of a jury; to organise much more thoroughly
than it is organised at present in England the whole
system of criminal prosecutions; to enable the Executive to
prohibit public meetings which might provoke a breach of
the peace, would in many cases be an improvement on the
criminal law of England itself, and would in several instances be simply an extension to the whole United
Kingdom of laws which exist without exciting any disapproval in some one division of it.* Without special
experience it would be presumptuous to assert that these
or similar changes in criminal procedure would suffice for

* In England the Courts can change the venue for the trial of a
criminal. In Scotland the Lord Advocate can always (I am told) bring
any case he chooses to trial before the High Court of Justiciary in
Edinburgh, and the same thing could be done by the Court on the
application of the prisoner. In Scotland, again, any Sheriff or Chief
Magistrate of a Burgh could prohibit a meeting, however lawful, which
he thought likely to endanger the peace. The provisions of the last
Irish Coercion Act, Prevention of Crime (Ireland) Act, 1882, 45 & 46

the enforcement of the law in Ireland during a period of disturbance. That such improvements in procedure would go a good way to make special Coercion Acts unnecessary, is in the highest degree probable. There is, moreover, nothing objectionable or anomalous in increasing as time goes on the stringency of criminal procedure. The law against crimes is the protection of men who are not criminals. Civilisation raises our estimate of the protection which good citizens ought to receive from the State; it also places new means of attack in the hands of cheats and ruffians. An elaborate criminal code is as necessary for a civilised society as are elaborately trained armies and scientific arms both of defence and of offence.

No adherence, however, to sound maxims of criminal jurisprudence would, it must be frankly admitted, entirely take away, though it might greatly mitigate, the justifiable distaste for Coercion Acts. The necessity for these Acts points to discord in Ireland between the law of the land and the law of the people; they are the outward and visible sign of internal discontent and disloyalty; they give good ground for supposing that the law or some part of it requires amendment, and to many persons laws which admit the existence of a bad social condition will appear to be themselves odious. But the

---

Vict. c. 25, s. 16, giving power to a magistrate where an offence had been committed to summon and examine witnesses, even though no person is charged with the offence, formed, I believe, part of the draft criminal code for England.

necessity for amending bad laws or vicious institutions is
no reason why just laws, or any law which cannot rightly
be repealed, should not be enforced. The fallacies of protection afforded no reason for not punishing smugglers,
though the existence of smuggling gave good ground for
considering whether the customs law did not require revision. There seems to the thoughtless crowd, whether
rich or poor—and all men are thoughtless about most things,
and many men about all things—to be a certain inconsistency between reform and coercion ; there is something
absurd in the policy of "cuffs and kisses." But the inconsistency or absurdity is only apparent. The necessity
for carrying through by legal means an agrarian revolution
—and the passing of the Irish Land Act was in effect an
admission by the English Parliament, that this necessity
exists—is a solid reason for the strict enforcement of justice.
Reform tends, as its immediate result, to produce lawlessness. A wise driver holds his reins all the tighter because
he is compelled to drive along the brink of a precipice.
Whether Coercion Acts, which it must be remembered
have been known before now in England, and were known
in Ireland during the era of her Parliamentary independence, and which are the sign of the difficulty of enforcing
the law, are or are not to be tolerated as a necessary
evil, depends on the answer to the inquiry, whether the
Government of the United Kingdom can by just administration, and by just legislation, remove the source of Irish
opposition to the law ? Answer the question affirmatively,

and the outcry against coercion becomes unmeaning; answer the question negatively, and you produce an argument which tells with crushing power in favour not of Home Rule, but of Separation.

The argument from the inconvenience to England. *— Apologies for Home Rule drawn from foreign experience, from the deference due to the popular will, or from the historical failure of England to govern Ireland with success, have about them 6. The argument from inconvenience. when employed by English members of Parliament a touch of unreality; they are reasons meant to satisfy the hearer, but do not convince the speaker. When however we come to the argument for Home Rule drawn from the inconvenience of the present state of things to England generally, and to English members of Parliament in particular, we know at once that we are at any rate dealing with a real tangible serious plea which has (if anything) only too much weight with the person who employs it. There is nothing in the whole relation of England to Ireland about which politicians are so well assured, as that the presence of a body of Parnellites at Westminster is an unutterable nuisance, and works intolerable evil. Of the reality of their conviction we have the strongest proof. The sufferings of Irish tenants, the difficulties or the wrongs of Irish landlords, the evils of coercion, the terror of assassi-

* See for an admirable statement of this argument, "Alternative Policies in Ireland," in the *Nineteenth Century* for February, 1886.

nation, but slightly ruffled the composure with which
English statesmen faced the perplexities of the Irish
problem. They first began to think that the demand for
Home Rule might have something in it when the refusal
to erect a Parliament at Dublin meant the continuance of
obstruction in the Parliament at Westminster. The
terror of obstruction has to speak the plain truth, done
more to effect the *bonâ fide* conversion of English M.P.'s
into advocates of Home Rule than any other single
influence.

What then is the harm which a body of eighty or
ninety Irish members can work in Parliament? This is
the answer. They may (it is said) in the first place delay,
obstruct, and render impossible the carrying through of
important measures; London may go without a munici-
pality; widowers may wait for years without being able to
marry their deceased wives' sisters; we may not during
this generation get the blessing of a good criminal code, if
Mr. Parnell and his followers sit in Parliament prepared
to practise all the arts of obstruction. The Irish members,
in the second place, perturb and falsify the whole system of
party government. The majority of Great Britain wish to
be ruled say by Lord Salisbury; the Parnellites do not
care whether Lord Salisbury or Mr. Gladstone is Premier,
but they do care for making the English Executive feeble,
and ridiculous. They will, therefore, by the practice of a
very little art, seize some opportunity of putting Lord
Salisbury in a minority, and turning him out of office.

Mr. Gladstone comes back into what is ironically called power. The same game begins again. The Parnellites coalesce with the Tories, we have a change of Cabinet, and possibly a dissolution. Nor are changes of Ministry the whole of the evil. The high tone of party politics is degraded. English or Scottish members of Parliament are but men; they are liable to be tempted; the Parnellites have the means of offering temptation; and temptation, members of Parliament intimate to us, will in the long run be too great for their virtue. The presence, in short, at Westminster of eighty-six gentlemen who do not respect the dignity or care for the efficiency of Parliament is absolutely fatal to the success of Parliamentary government, and to the character of Parliamentary statesmanship. We must, it is inferred, let the Parnellites have a Parliament of their own in Ireland, or else we shall soon cease to have any Parliament worth keeping in England.

The force of this line of argument, as far as it goes, cannot be denied. The presence in the House of Commons of politicians disloyal to Parliament causes immense inconvenience; but to anyone not a member of the House of Commons, it appears singular that men of sense should think the inconveniences of obstruction a sufficient ground for breaking up the Constitution. The whole thing is a question of proportion. The nation suffers a good deal from obstruction, but the suffering is not of a kind to justify revolution. A toothache is a bad

Criticism.

thing, but a severe toothache hardly suggests suicide; and though life might not be worth having, if toothache were to last for years, the thoughts of putting an end to one's existence are removed by the knowledge that an aching tooth can be drawn by a dentist. Now the more obvious evils of obstruction can clearly be removed by changes of procedure. Members of Parliament appear to think that to alter the rules of the House of Commons—to curtail and limit the power of debate—to confer, if necessary, upon the Speaker, or upon the bare majority of members present, authority to bring every debate summarily to a close—is something like overthrowing the monarchy a thing not to be dreamt of by the wildest of innovators. Plain men outside the walls of Parliament can assure our representatives, that the world would bear with infinite calmness the imposition of stringent restrictions on the overflow of Parliamentary eloquence. If even the great debate on Home Rule had been finished say in a week, the outer world would have been well pleased; and measures such as the Government of Ireland Bill happily do not come before Parliament every year. The more subtle evils arising in part at least from the presence of the Irish members must be met by more searching remedies. Parnellite obstruction has revealed rather than caused the weakness of government by Parliament. The experience, not of England only, but of other countries, shows the great difficulty of working our present party system of government in a representative assembly which is divided into more than two parties. The essential difficulty lies in the immediate dependence of a modern ministry for its existence on every vote of the House of Commons. If you see the difficulty, you can also see various means by which it may be removed. In more than one country,. and notably in the United States and in Switzerland— states, be it remarked, in which popular government flourishes—the Executive, though in the long run amenable to the voice of the people, and though in Switzerland actually appointed by the legislature, is not like an English Cabinet, dependent on the fluctuating will of a legislative assembly. If it were necessary to choose between modifications in the relation of the Executive to Parliament and the repeal of the Act of Union, most Englishmen would think that to increase the independence of the executive—a change probably desirable in itself— was a less evil than a disruption of the United Kingdom, not only in itself a gigantic evil, but one which may well lead to others. A modification, however, in the practice would, for the moment at least, save the real principles of Parliamentary government. Were it once understood that a Ministry would not retire from office except in consequence of a direct vote of want of confidence in the House of Commons, the political power of the Parnellite, or of any other minority, would be greatly diminished. Meanwhile, members of Parliament may be reminded that it is on them that the duty lies of removing the obstacles which from time to time impede the working of Parlia-

mentary machinery, and that the existence of temptation
to political turpitude is not an admitted excuse for
yielding to it. In one way or another a majority of 584
members must, if they choose, be able to make head
against the minority of 86. Their failure already excites
astonishment; the time is coming when it will excite
contempt. The English people, moreover, have the
remedy in their own hands. By giving to either of the
great parties an absolute majority they can terminate all
the inconveniences threatened by Parnellite obstruction.
The remedy is in their hands, and recent experience
suggests that they will not be slow to use it.

A survey of the arguments in favour of Home Rule
suggests the following reflections:

The arguments, taken as a whole, do undoubtedly show
that the present state of things is accompanied by considerable evils or inconveniences. They show what no one
who has given a thought to the matter ever doubted, that
the relation between England and Ireland is unsatisfactory.
They are, as far as they go, objections to the maintenance
of the Union, but neither the feelings which favour Home
Rule, nor the reasons by which they are supported, tell in
reality in favour of Home Rule policy. They scarcely
tend to show that Home Rule would cure the evils
complained of; they certainly do not show, they only
assume, that Home Rule in Ireland would not be injurious

to England. They are, in short, arguments in favour of Irish independence ; every one of them would be seen in its true character if the Irish demand should take the form of a claim that Ireland should become an independent nation. Meanwhile, even on the Home Rule view, the case stands thus. The present condition of things excites Irish discontent, and involves great evils ; we have before us but three courses :—maintenance of the Union ; the concession of Irish independence ; the grant of Home Rule to Ireland. The Home Ruler urges that the last is the best course left open to us. To decide whether this be so or not requires a fair examination of the possibilities which each course presents to England.

CHAPTER V.

THE MAINTENANCE OF THE UNION.

EIGHTY-SIX years have elapsed since the conclusion of the

The failure of the Union; its nature.

Treaty of Union between England and Ireland. The two countries do not yet form an united nation. The Irish people are, if not more wretched (for the whole European world has made progress, and Ireland with it), yet more conscious of wretchedness; and Irish disaffection to England is, if not deeper, more wide-spread than in 1800. An Act meant by its authors to be the source of such prosperity and concord as followed though slowly, upon the Union with Scotland, has not made Ireland rich, has not put an end to Irish lawlessness, has not terminated the feud between Protestants and Catholics, has not raised the position of Irish tenants, has not taken away the causes of Irish discontent, and has therefore not removed Irish disloyalty. This is the indictment which can fairly be brought against the Act of Union. It is, however, of importance to notice that the main charges to which the Act of Union is liable are negative. It has not removed (its foes, say that it has not mitigated) great evils ; but the mass of ills for which the Union is constantly made chargeable were in existence before the days of Pitt or Cornwallis. Destitution, sectarian animosities, harsh evictions met by savage outrages, the terror of secret societies, the stern enforcement of law, representing to the people anything but justice, are phenomena of Irish society, which, as they existed before the Irish Volunteers established the Parliamentary independence of their country, and continued to exist in Ireland when subject to no laws but those passed or upheld by an Irish Parliament, cannot be attributed to the Act of Union. That enactment introduced a purely political change. It could not, except very indirectly, either increase or remove evils which it did not affect to touch. To two charges its authors are indeed, with more or less of justice, liable ; they committed the intellectual error of supposing that a change or improvement in the form of the Constitution would remove evils due to social and economical causes ; they committed the moral error of thinking that a beneficial enactment might allowably be passed by means which outraged all the best moral feeling of Ireland. Their mistakes are worth notice. England is again told that a Constitutional change is the remedy for Irish misery. Ethical considerations (in this case the moral rights of a loyal minority and the legal rights of Irish landlords) are, it is again intimated, to be held of slight account compared with the benefit to Ireland and to England which is to be expected from an experiment in

K

Constitution-making. To impartial observers it may appear that the proposed policy of 1886 threatens to reproduce in its essence the errors and the vices of the policy of 1800. Be this as it may, the reflection that the ill results of the Act of Union are mainly negative suggests the conclusion that the good results (if any) of its repeal would probably be negative also, and clears the way for the question with which we are immediately concerned, namely, What are the actual and undoubted evils to England of maintaining a legislative union with Ireland ?

The nature and extent of these evils has been considered in criticising the arguments in favour of Home Rule. A bare enumeration of them therefore may here suffice.

The evils of maintaining the Union.

First.—The Union hampers and complicates English policy, and this even independently of the existing agitation for Home Rule. The tenacity of England during the war with America, her triumphant energy during the revolutionary struggle, were due to a unity of feeling on the part, at any rate, of her governing classes, which even under the most favourable circumstances can hardly exist in a Parliament containing, as the Parliament of the United Kingdom always must contain, a large body of Irish Roman Catholics. If it be urged that the presence of Roman

1. Complication of English policy.

Catholics is due to the Catholic Emancipation Act, and not to the Act of Union, the remark is true but irrelevant No maintainer or assailant of the Union is insane enough to propose the repeal of the Emancipation Act.

Secondly.—The refusal of Home Rule involves a long, tedious, and demoralising contest with opponents who will use, and from their own point of view have a right to use, all the arts of obstruction and of Parliamentary intrigue. The battle of the Constitution must be fought out in Parliament, and if it is to be won, Englishmen may be compelled to forego for a time much useful legislation, to modify the rules of party government, and, it is possible, even the forms of the Constitution.

2. Obstruction.

Thirdly.—If the Union is to be maintained with advantage to any part of the United Kingdom, the people of the United Kingdom must make the most strenuous, firm, and continuous effort, lasting, it may well be, for twenty years or more, to enforce throughout every part of the United Kingdom obedience to the law of the land. This effort can only be justified by the equally strenuous determination (which must involve an infinity of trouble) to give ear to every Irish complaint, and to see that the laws which the Irish people obey are laws of justice, and (what is much the same thing) laws which in the long run the people of Ireland will feel to be just. To carry out this

3. Strict government in Ireland.

K 2

course of action is difficult for all governments, is perhaps specially difficult for a democratic government. To maintain the Union is no easy task, though it has yet to be proved that any form of Home Rule will give more ease to the people of England; nor can the difficulty be got rid of, though it may be somewhat changed, by abolishing the Irish representation in Parliament, or by treating Ireland as a Crown colony. Such steps, which could hardly be termed maintenance of the Union, might, as expedients for carrying through safely a course of reform, be morally and for a time justifiable. Their adoption is, however, liable to an almost insuperable objection. Democracy in Great Britain does not comport with official autocracy in Ireland. Every government must be true to its principles, and a democracy which played the benevolent despot would suffer demoralisation.

The Act of Union has been the aim of so much random invective that its good fruits (for it has borne good no less than evil fruits) are in danger of being forgotten. It ended once and for all an intolerable condition of affairs, and its scope will never be understood unless its enactments are read in the lurid light cast upon them by the rebellion of 1798. The hateful means used to obtain an apparently good end have cast a slur on the reputation of more than one high-toned statesman. Humanity, in the case of Cornwallis at least, had far more share than ambition in his determi-

Good results of the Union.

nation to abolish the Irish Parliament. His anxiety in
1798 to save Catholics and rebels from oppression was as
keen and as noble as the anxiety of Canning in 1858 to
protect the natives of India from the resentments excited
by the Mutiny. Every reason which in our own day after
the disturbances of 1865 made it necessary to abolish the
ancient constitution of Jamaica told in 1800 in favour of
abolishing the still more ancient Parliament of Ireland.
If statesmen, bent on restoring at least the rule of law
and peace in a distracted country, fancied that the
corruption of the legislature might be counted a low price
to pay for protecting the mass of the population from the
rule or the vengeance of a faction, they committed a grave
moral error. But their mistake was more pardonable
than it seems to modern critics, and the lesson which it
teaches—that you cannot base a just policy upon a foundation of iniquity—is one which the modern censors of Pitt
may well lay to heart. However this may be, the transactions which discredited the passing of the Act of Union
give no ground for repealing it, and, except to a rhetorician
in want of an *argumentum ad hominem*, it will never
appear that the philosophic historian who maintains that
the Treaty of Union was ill-conceived and premature,
contradicts the political philosopher who contends that to
repeal the Union would be not to cancel but to aggravate
the evils of an historical error. The considerations which
recommend or require the maintenance of the Union are
often forgotten, but are obvious.

The support of the Union is, after all, let controver-

Reasons for maintaining Union. sialists say what they like, the policy which in fact holds the field, and it is (strange though the assertion may appear) on the advocates of innovation, not on the supporters of things as they are, that lies the burden of making out their case. A fundamental alteration in the constitution of the realm is in itself no light matter, and any man who has eyes to see or ears to hear may easily convince himself that the creation of an Irish Parliament must be the beginning, not the end, of a revolution. Dublin is not the only city in the United Kingdom where has met a Parliament claiming to represent an independent nation ; at Edinburgh an Assembly has sat which not only occasionally denied, but during the whole of its existence never admitted, the sovereignty of the Parliament at Westminster ; and in the present state of the world it is inconceivable that Irish autonomy—if such be the proper term—should not excite or justify claims for local independence which would unloose the ties which bind together the huge fabric of the

Strengthens English Crown. British Empire. The Union again of England and Ireland has increased, as its relaxation would of necessity diminish, the power of the central government. That the Treaty of Union has, disappointing and even harmful as some of its results have been, formed a guarantee against successful rebellion, hardly admits of question. The difference between the abortive revolt of 1848 or the Fenian disturbances of 1866, and

the desperate insurrection of 1798, affords some measure
of the strength which the legislative unity of the kingdom has added to the English Crown. If it be suggested
that the disloyalty, which has prompted sedition during
this century, was less deep than the animosities which
armed the insurgents of '98, the suggestion may be true,
but it incidentally shows that under the Union some
progress, however slight, has been made towards national
harmony, and recalls the important fact that at the
present day the wealth and the energy of Protestant Ireland firmly support the legislative unity of the kingdom.
Consider again what are the facilities possessed, say, by
the State of New York, by the kingdom of Bavaria, or by
the Cape Colony for interfering with or arresting the
action of the central power to which the State, kingdom,
or dependency is subject, and you perceive at once how
ample must, from the very necessity of the case, be the
opportunities possessed by a semi-independent Irish executive representing a semi-independent Irish Parliament for
embarrassing the action of the Government in London.
This will appear more clearly from a detailed examination
of the different forms which may be assumed by Home
Rule.   One remark, however, may with advantage be made
at this point of our argument, since it holds good of every
possible scheme for repealing or modifying the Union.
Powers conferred upon an Executive and a Parliament at
Dublin must, from the nature of things, be a deduction
from the powers which can be exercised by the Parliament

and Ministry at Westminster. This is a principle the truth of which is independent of the wishes or fancies either of Englishmen or of Irishmen. "The more you have of the more," runs a quaint Spanish proverb, "the less you have of the less." The saying is of mathematical certainty, but, in the excitement of controversy, men constantly forget the depth and variety of the maxim's application.

To the existence of the Union and to the power which

Enables it to maintain freedom. it confers upon the Executive, is due the possibility of curbing the violence of religious and political zealots by the interposition of an authority endowed at once with overpowering strength and obvious impartiality. In Belfast even a Nationalist must, if he is a peaceable citizen, feel that the withdrawal of the Queen's troops would not conduce to his comfort. Under a system of Home Rule (it will perhaps be said) one body of fanatics or the other would, with or without the aid of the army, gain the upper hand and restore order. Grant the truth, perhaps open to doubt, of this suggestion, it is at best a plea, not for Home Rule but for separation, since no civilised government could (whilst England and Ireland formed, under any terms whatever, parts of the same political community) suffer Belfast to become the scene of a free fight, which should decide by the ordeal of battle, whether Protestants should tyrannise over Catholics, or Catholics coerce Protestants by a reign of terror. A reign of order moreover is not equivalent to

the reign of justice. Still less is it equivalent to the
establishment of that personal freedom which can only
exist under the equal rule of equal law, and is the blessing which every government worthy the name is bound
to confer upon its subjects.

An impartial foreigner again would probably hold, as
indeed De Beaumont (unless I misunderstand his teaching)
did, to the end of his life, actually hold, that the existing
connection between England and Ireland is dictated, by
the state of the world, by the circumstances of the times,
by the very nature of things. We are living in 1886, not
in 1782: the nineteenth century is not the age for small
States or for weak States. Such an observer, however,
would also see much that is hidden, by the dust of battle,
from the combatants in a desperate political conflict.
What is really needed to meet the real wants, of which the
cry for Home Rule is a more or less factitious expression,
is, he would note, much more a change in the spirit of
Englishmen than an alteration in the constitution of
England. If Englishmen could learn to speak and think
of Irishmen with the respect and consideration due to
fellow-citizens, if they could cease to jeer at Irishmen now
as not much more than a century ago they used to jeer at
Scotchmen, the Union would soon become something
more than a mere work of legal ingenuity. A change of
feeling would make it easy for English politicians and
English voters to perceive that the local affairs of Ireland
ought to be managed in the Parliament of the United

Kingdom in accordance with the opinion of the Parliamentary representatives of Ireland, just as Scotch affairs are managed at Westminster in accordance with the opinions of Parliamentary representatives of Scotland. Towards this reform in the practice, which need not change anything in the law of our constitution, Mr. Bright has already pointed the way. And Mr. Bright's moral intuitions have more than once endowed him with a prophetic insight denied to our other statesmen, into the future of English policy. Meanwhile those who urge the maintenance of the Union have a right to insist upon the possibilities which it contains of reconciling the strength of the Empire with due regard to the local interests and local sentiment of Ireland.

The Union, lastly, whilst it increases the power of the whole United Kingdom, provides the means for carrying out, and for carrying out with due regard to justice, any reform, innovation, or if you please revolution, required for the prosperity of the Irish people. The duty, it has been laid down, of an English Minister is to effect by his policy all those changes in Ireland which a revolution would effect by force. The maxim comes from a strange quarter, but the doctrine of Disraeli sums up on this matter the teaching of Mill and De Beaumont, and it is absolutely sound if you add to it the implied condition that an English Minister, whilst aiming at the ends of a wise revolutionist, must pay a respect to the demands of justice not always evinced by

And carry out just reforms.

the revolutionary spirit. But to put in force a policy of
just revolution, nothing is so necessary as the combination
of resistless power with infinite wealth. This is exactly
what the government of the United Kingdom can, and no
Irish government could, supply. Mr. Gladstone and his
followers fully admit this, and the Land Purchase Bill was
the sign of their conviction that the policy of Home Rule
itself needs for its success and justification the power to
draw upon the wealth of the United Kingdom. Let the
United Kingdom, it is said in effect, pay fifty millions,
that, without any injustice to Irish landlords, Irish tenants
may be turned into landowners, and may then enjoy the
blessings of Home Rule, freed from all temptation to use
legislative power for purposes of confiscation. The advice
may in one sense be sound, but prudence suggests that if
the fifty millions are to be expended, it were best first to
settle the agrarian feud, and then to see whether the
demand for Home Rule would not die a natural death.
French peasants were Jacobins until the revolution
secured to them the soil of France. The same men when
transformed into landed proprietors became the staunch
opponents of Jacobinism. It is in any case the interest of
England to see whether, say in a generation, the existing
or further changes in the tenure of land may not avert
all necessity or demand for changes in the constitution. Interest here coincides with duty. No scheme
(either of Home Rule or of Irish independence) has
been proposed, nor, it may be said with confidence,

ever can be proposed, which, disguise the matter as you will, does not savour of treachery to thousands of Irishmen who have performed the duties and claim to retain the rights of citizens of the United Kingdom. The worst delusion of the revolutionary spirit is the notion that justice to the people may be based upon injustice to individuals. Protestants have not more, but neither have they less, claim to protection from the State than Catholics. Even landowners are not of necessity wrong-doers. Rent is a debt, and it may occasionally be the duty, even of a tenant, to pay his creditor. An insolvent debtor has, however excusable or pitiable his position, no absolute moral right to improve his own position by torturing or murdering any solvent neighbour who may be inclined to pay his own debts. To maintain the Union is to maintain the effort to perform the obligations of the country, and to compel all citizens of the country to perform the duties imposed by law. The effort is an arduous one, the more so since it must be combined with the equally strenuous endeavour to see that in Ireland, as in every part of the United Kingdom, the demands of the law be made to coincide with the demands of morality and of humanity. Still *pactum serva* is a good maxim for nations no less than for individuals : there may be a higher law than the rule of keeping one's promise, but before a man or a government incurs even the appearance of bad faith, it were well to see whether the so-called higher law of conscience may not in reality be the lower dictates of indolence or cowardice.

Neither nations nor individuals are bound in duty to do impossibilities. The limit of power is the limit of responsibility, but if England can no longer enforce justice in Ireland, there will still be the grave question whether this fearful result of past misdoing or error does not suggest and justify Separation rather than Home Rule.

CHAPTER VI.

SEPARATION.

ENGLISHMEN are so firmly and with such good reason
convinced that the independence of Ireland
would be fatal to the greatness and security
of Great Britain, that they rarely attempt to
weigh accurately the grounds of reason producible
in support of a conviction which has acquired the
character of a political instinct. The evils, however, to
England which may be reasonably anticipated from the
political separation of the two countries, may be summed
up under three heads.

Evils of Separation.

First.—The acquiescence by England in Irish independence, would be a deliberate and complete surrender of the
objects at which English statesmanship has, under one
form or another, aimed for centuries. Such a surrender
would, in addition to its material effects, inflict an amount
of moral discredit on England which would itself be the
cause of serious dangers. That a powerful nation should
(except under the force of crushing defeat) assent to an
arrangement which would decrease its resources and

authority must inevitably appear to all the world to be, and probably would be in reality, such a sign either of declining strength or of declining spirit as must in a short time provoke the aggression of rivals and enemies. Abdication of royal or imperial authority is with States no less than with individuals the precursor of death. Loss of territory, indeed, in consequence of defeat, is in itself only in so far damaging as defeat may imply a want of capacity to resist attack, or as the diminution of territory may involve loss of resources. Thus the surrender of Lombardy by Austria, of Alsace by France, of Schleswig-Holstein by Denmark, the acquiescence of Holland in the independence of Belgium, or, to come nearer home, the treaty by which England acknowledged that the struggle to retain her American colonies had ended in failure, each and all of them brought only such discredit upon the defeated country as is the direct conse-quence of want of success. None of these transactions had anything like the disastrous results which the con-cession of Irish independence would entail on England. The Austrians, the French, the Danes, and the Dutch had, as the whole world admitted, struggled manfully to main-tain their power. They were beaten as one party or other to a fight must be beaten, but they did not betray any of those failings which encourage further attack. The close of the conflict with our colonies assuredly did not leave England disgraced before the world. The obstinacy of George III., the splendid resistance made by a nation assailed at once by a combination of enemies (any one of whom alone would have seemed a formidable foe), the victories of Rodney, the defence of Gibraltar, not only saved but increased the renown of England, and were warnings which no foreigner could disregard, that the loss of the American colonies, though it might diminish the Empire, had not quenched the spirit or undermined the strength of Great Britain. No one can suppose that a peaceful retreat from the difficulties and responsibility of providing for the Government of Ireland would leave to England that reputation for courage and endurance which, even in the midst of defeat, was retained by the generation which acknowledged the independence of America. Peaceable surrender may avert material loss; it cannot maintain moral character. One thing only would render the concession of Irish independence compatible with Englishmen's respect for themselves, or with the respect of other nations for England. This condition would be the obvious, and, so to speak, patent conviction on the part of the whole English people, that the grant of independence to Ireland was the fulfilment of a duty demanded by justice. No such conviction exists, nor is it ever likely to come into existence. Even were so great a change of English sentiment to take place that a majority of the people became ready, on grounds of expediency, to break up the connection between Great Britain and the neighbouring island, it would still be hard to persuade the nation that there was not vile treachery.

in refusing to stand by and support that part of the Irish
people which wished to retain the connection with England. The treachery would approach to infamy if it
should appear that England, for the sake of her own
comfort, left English subjects who had always obeyed the
law and relied on the honourable protection of the
United Kingdom at the mercy of conspirators whose
lawlessness had taken the form of cruelty and tyranny,
and whose vindictiveness was certain to punish as criminality former acts of loyalty or obedience to English
sovereignty. High-toned self-sacrifice which results in
breach of faith to associates is considered by the world at
large as a particularly odious form of hypocrisy. Nothing
in the treaty between England and the American Colonies
involved more just bitterness of feeling than the partial,
and probably inevitable, desertion of the Loyalists. The
national conscience would condemn rather than approve
the prudential considerations which might, under certain
circumstances, induce Englishmen to consent to see
Ireland an independent nation; such consent would imply
the adoption of views of national interest fundamentally
inconsistent with the maintenance of Imperial power; the
damage resulting from loss of character is difficult to
estimate, but is none the less real because it does not
admit of computation in the terms of the multiplication
table.

Secondly, the independence of Ireland means loss to
Great Britain both in money and in men. The pecuniary

L

loss is, indeed, not quite so serious as might at first sight
be looked for.*   The provisions of the rejected Government of Ireland Bill imply, it would seem, that the
pecuniary gain of the United Kingdom from Ireland in
the way of taxation may, in Mr. Gladstone's judgment, be
estimated at about three and a half millions per annum,
and this may presumably be taken as a not unfair estimate.   The sacrifice of a seventh part of the population of
the United Kingdom is no slight matter.   Its importance
is enhanced by the circumstance, never to be forgotten,
that Great Britain is the centre of an Empire.   The
brutal and stupid jests by which respectable Englishmen
often hint that the bravery, the capacity, and the genius
of Irishmen are of little service to the Empire, and that
their value is more than counterbalanced by the ill results
of Irish discontent and sedition, conceal from unreflecting
minds the extent to which every part of the United
Kingdom has severally contributed to the fortune and
power of the country.   Irish labourers, Irish soldiers, Irish
generals, and Irish statesmen have assuredly rendered
no trifling services to the British Crown.   There is,
however, one valid ground for rating the loss in men to
England, which would result from separation from Ireland
somewhat lower than one would on first thoughts be
inclined to place it.   Even were Ireland an independent
country there is nothing to prevent England from leaving

* See 'Economic Value of Ireland to Great Britain,' by Robert
Giffen, *The Nineteenth Century*, March, 1886, p. 229.

all the advantages of English citizenship open to the
inhabitants of the Irish State. In this matter much is to
be learnt from Germany. Neither Stein, nor Niebuhr,
nor Moltke, were by birth subjects of Prussia, yet Prussia
did not lose the inestimable gains to be derived from
their talents. A generous, a liberal, and a just extension
of the privileges of citizenship might fill the English army
and the English civil service with men drawn from a
State independent of Great Britain. If the independence
of Ireland were proclaimed to-morrow, there would not be
a hundred Irish labourers the fewer in Liverpool or in
London. Connections and relations depending upon
community of language, community of interest, community
of feeling, the ties of kindred, of business, of friendship, or
of affection cannot, happily, be dissolved, or to any great
extent affected, by political revolutions. In any case, it
would depend on the wisdom of Great Britain whether
separation from Ireland should or should not mean the
estrangement of Irishmen.

Thirdly, the independence of Ireland would give England
a foreign, and possibly a hostile, neighbour along the
western coast of Great Britain. We should, for the first
time since the accession of the Stuarts, occupy a position
something like that of a Continental nation, and know
what it was to have a foe, or at best a very cold friend,
upon our borders. In time of war Ireland would be the
abettor or the open ally of, say, the United States, or of
France; Dublin would, unless reconquered, be the outpost

L 2

of the French Republic or of the American Union. In
times of peace things would not stand much better; our
diplomacy would be constantly occupied with the intrigues
carried on in Dublin; the possibility of attack from
Ireland would necessitate the increase of our forces;
increased taxation would be drawn from a diminished
population; we should be compelled to double our army
when we had lost that part of the kingdom which used to
form our best recruiting-ground. Sooner or later England
would be driven, like every Continental State, to accept
the burden of conscription, and with conscription would
come essential changes in the whole habits of English life.
Nor can we count upon this being the end of our calamities. The burden of conscription would deprive us of our
one great advantage over competitors in the struggle for
trade; an overtaxed and overburdened people could not
long maintain their mercantile pre-eminence. This is the
picture which is constantly drawn, in one shape or another,
of the ruinous results to England of the free development
of Irish nationality. No one can undertake to say that
its main features are false. Still, it must be admitted
that the prophets of evil neglect to notice several facts
which ought not to be overlooked. Ireland is a poor
country of about the population of Belgium; it is occupied
by a people far less wealthy than the inhabitants of
England; and, moreover, by a people divided among
themselves by marked differences of race, religion, and
historical tradition. Is it really to be feared that such a

neighbour could, even if both independent and hostile, be half the peril to England that Germany is to France, or France to Italy? Money constitutes now more truly than ever the sinews of war, and it will be a long time before Ireland is a country abounding in money. There is, to say the least, something ignominious in the dread that Englishmen could not hold their own in the face of an Irish Republic, which would certainly be poor, and would probably be a prey to violent factions. . Grant again—and this is granting a good deal—that Ireland might become a province of France, there is still some difficulty in seeing why Englishmen can live without fear within sight of Boulogne, and yet must tremble at the thought of French regiments assembling in Dublin. The command of the sea moreover would, whether Ireland were or were not aided by foreign allies, be a complete protection for England against invasion. If England's naval supremacy were lost, the power of the British Empire would in any case be gone. The vital matter for us is to retain command of the seas. Our capacity for doing this would not be greatly affected by Irish independence. America, further, and France are the only allies to whom Ireland could look for aid. The notion that the United States would consent to receive Ireland under any terms into the Union must appear to any one who has studied American politics the wildest of dreams. It supposes that the Americans would, without any gain to themselves, disarrange the whole balance of their consti-

tution, and by involving themselves in all the complexi-
ties of European politics depart from the path which they
have continuously pursued, and which is marked out to
them by the plainest rules of common sense, and, it is
hardly an exaggeration to say, by the laws of nature. A
people who decline to annex Cuba, and are fully willing to
wait till circumstances bring Canada into the Union and
give the United States possession of Mexico, are not likely
to incorporate Ireland. The alliance of France is a different
matter. Reflection, however, mitigates the dread of its
occurrence. Active alliance with Ireland would mean
war with England, and now for seventy years France and
England have been at peace. This state of things is the
more remarkable because there have during that period
arisen occasions for discord, and because no feeling of
sentimental friendship forbids warfare. The true guarantee for peace between nations which were long deemed
hereditary foes is the immense interest which each
has in abstaining from war. Could the state of things
which existed at the beginning of the century be revived,
thousands of Englishmen and Frenchmen would be ruined.
The security for peace depending upon national interest
would not be diminished were Ireland to-morrow proclaimed an independent republic. That this independence
would facilitate French attack is undeniable, but attack
would not be the more likely to occur. Add to all this
that Irish discontent or sedition would, during a war, help
France as much as Irish independence. Ireland is no

doubt the weak point in the defences of Great Britain.
This no one denies. The only question is whether and to
what extent the independence of that country would
widen the breach in England's defensive system.

Any one who attempts to forecast the probable evils to
England of Irish independence should keep one Possible
recollection constantly before his mind. The advantages
of Separa-
wisest thinkers of the eighteenth century (in- tion.
cluding Burke) held that the independence of the
American Colonies meant the irreparable ruin of Great
Britain. There were apparently solid grounds for this
belief; experience has proved it to be without foundation.

A calm observer can even now see that the complete
dissolution of the connection between Great Britain and
Ireland, disastrous as in many respects such an event
would undoubtedly be, holds out to the larger country the
possibility of two advantages.

Loss of territory might be equivalent in some aspects
to increase of power.

There exists in Europe no country so completely at
unity with itself as Great Britain. Fifty years of reform
have done their work, and have removed the discontents,
the divisions, the disaffection, and the conspiracies which
marked the first quarter or the first half of this century.
Great Britain, if left to herself, could act with all the
force, consistency, and energy given by unity of sentiment
and community of interests. The distraction and the

uncertainty of our political aims, the feebleness and inconsistency with which they are pursued, arise, in part at
least, from the connection with Ireland.   Neither Englishmen nor Irishmen are to blame for the fact that it is
difficult for communities differing in historical associations
and in political conceptions to keep step together in the
path of progress.   For other evils arising from the connection the blame must rest on English statesmen.   All
the inherent vices of party government, all the weaknesses
of the Parliamentary system, all the evils arising from
the perverse notion that reform ought always to be preceded by a period of lengthy and more than half
factitious agitation met by equally factitious resistance,
have been fostered and increased by the inter-action of
Irish and English politics.   No one can believe that the
inveterate habit of ruling one part of the United Kingdom
on principles which no one would venture to apply to the
government of any other part of it, can have produced
anything but the most injurious effect on the stability of
our Government and the character of our public men.
The advocates of Home Rule find by far their strongest
arguments for influencing English opinion, in the proofs
which they produce that England, no less than Ireland,
has suffered from a political arrangement under which
legal union has failed to secure moral unity; these
arguments, whatever their strength, are, however, it must
be noted, far more available to a Nationalist than to an
advocate of Federalism.   English authority in Ireland

would be increased by the possession of that freedom of action which every powerful State exercises in its dealings with a weaker though an independent nation. There is something so repulsive to the best feelings of citizenship in even the hypothetical contemplation of the advantages (such as they are) which would accrue to Great Britain from the transformation of thousands of our fellow-countrymen into aliens, that it is painful to trace out in clear language the strength of the position which England would occupy towards the Irish Republic. But in argument the strict following out of the conclusions flowing from facts is a form of honesty, and however repulsive these conclusions may be, their statement is a matter of duty. Were Ireland independent, England would possess means far more effective for enforcing her will upon her weaker neighbour than are coercion acts, courts, or constables. England could deal not with individuals, but with the State, and she could compel respect for treaties or due regard to English interests by invasion, by a pacific blockade, or by a hostile tariff. There is a special reason for dwelling on the facility with which England could compel the observance of engagements. Morally the most serious of all the objections to England's conceding Irish independence is the indelible disgrace which would rightly fall upon any country which did not provide for the protection of men who had been loyal and faithful citizens. Now the point to be noted is that England's authority, resulting not from law but from power, in an independent Ireland, would greatly enhance her capacity for ensuring the fair treatment of Irish Protestants. The treaty of independence would provide guarantees for their rights, and any breach of these guarantees would be a *casus belli.* The mere threat of a hostile tariff would of itself be a stronger sanction than the most strenuous provisions of an Act of Parliament backed only by the very hypothetical power of compelling a half-independent Executive to obey the judgments of, say, the Privy Council. The guarantees of a treaty are, it may be said, often worthless. This is so; but their worthlessness arises from the weakness of the country in whose favour they are made. In any event they may be worth a good deal more than provisions of an Act of Parliament. The deriders of a paper Union which has lasted for a century have no right to count on the validity of a paper Federation which still awaits creation.

It is, again, possible that the severance of all political connection might open the way to friendship or alliance.

This assertion is no unmeaning paradox. If one could anticipate with any confidence that the acknowledgment of Irish nationality would bring to Ireland happiness and prosperity, it would not be a very bold conjecture that as Ireland flourished and prospered, ill-will to England might rapidly decrease. With nations, as with individuals, to remove all causes of mutual irritation is much the same thing as removing the disposition to quarrel. Not twenty-one years have passed since the last Austrian soldier marched

out of Italy, yet Austria is at this moment less unpopular
with the Italians than France, and Garibaldi's death
evoked tributes of respect at Vienna. For fifteen years
the whole force of European law was employed to keep
Belgium united to Holland; the obvious interests, moreover, of all the inhabitants of the kingdom of the Nether-
lands told in favour of union. Yet year by year the two
divisions of one country became more and more hostile to
each other. Fifty years of separation have, as far as
appearances go, restored, or for the first time created,
feelings of friendliness between the Belgians and the
Dutch. There are to be found Belgian statesmen who
regret the proclamation of Belgian independence. When in
1881 the Americans celebrated at Yorktown the centenary
of British defeat, they went out of their way to display
their goodwill towards Great Britain. Plaudits and toasts,
it may be said, prove nothing except the existence of a
sentiment which, even if it be genuine, is certain to be
evanescent. This is true; but the matter for consideration
is not whether the feeling of friendliness towards Great
Britain which found expression during the festivities at
Yorktown would survive a conflict of interest between
England and America, but whether a condition of feeling
which allows the two nations to look calmly after their
own interests, unblinded by passion or animosity, could
possibly have been produced by the continuance of that
connection between England and America which was
terminated by the surrender of Cornwallis. There is at

least no absurdity in the supposition that this question ought to be answered in the negative, and that Americans and Englishmen are at any rate not enemies just because a hundred years ago they ceased to be fellow-citizens.

Let not, however, the gist of my argument be misunderstood. The possible increase of English power, and the possible growth of goodwill between England and Ireland, are not used as anything like reasons in favour of Separation. They are set down simply as deductions from the immense evils of a policy which no Englishman can regard as other than most injurious to the whole United Kingdom. The reason why it is wise to dwell on this kind of set-off against the ill effects of Separation is that Home Rule, while involving almost all the evils of Separation, will be found on examination not to hold out anything like the same hopes of compensating advantages.

CHAPTER VII,

HOME RULE—ITS FORMS.

THE proposals for giving Ireland Home Rule, in so far as they have taken any definite shape whatever, have assumed four forms :— Forms of Home Rule.

    I. Home Rule as Federalism.

    II. Home Rule as Colonial Independence.

    III. Home Rule as the revival of Grattan's Constitution.

    IV. Home Rule under the proposed Gladstonian Constitution.

How far Home Rule under these forms, or any one of them, is compatible with the interests of the English people must be determined by considering what are the conditions which an acceptable plan of Home Rule must fulfil, and Conditions to be satisfied by plan of Home Rule. by then examining how far any given form of Home Rule satisfies them.

    Any scheme of Home Rule which can conceivably be

accepted by England must, it is admitted, satisfy the following conditions.*

It must in the first place be consistent with the ultimate supremacy of the British Parliament. †

It must in the second place be just; it must provide that each part of the United Kingdom take a fair share of Imperial burdens; that the citizens of each part have equality of rights; that the rights both of individuals and of minorities be safely guarded. ‡

---

* Compare Mr. Gladstone's speech of 8th April, 1886, ' *The Times* Parliamentary Debates,' pp. 130, 131; and Mr. Gladstone's speech of 13th April, *ibid.*, pp. 255, 256.

† Compare *ibid.*, pp. 130, 132.

‡ Compare the following expressions in Mr. Gladstone's speeches:—
" The essential conditions of any plan that Parliament can be asked or could be expected to entertain are, in my opinion, these:—The unity of the Empire must not be placed in jeopardy; the safety and welfare of the whole—if there is an unfortunate conflict, which I do not believe—the welfare and security of the whole must be preferred to the security and advantage of the part. The political equality of the three countries must be maintained. They stand by statute on a footing of absolute equality, and that footing ought not to be altered or brought into question. There should be what I will at present term an equitable distribution of Imperial burdens. Next I introduce a provision which may seem to be exceptional, but which in the peculiar circumstances of Ireland, whose history unhappily has been one long chain of internal controversies as well as of difficulties external, is necessary in order that there may be reasonable safeguards for the minority. I am asked why there should be safeguards for the minority.

*   *   *   *   *   *

" I have spoken now of the essential conditions of a good plan for Ireland, and I add only this—that in order to be a good plan it must be a plan promising to be a real settlement of Ireland. (Speech of

It must in the third place promise finality; it must be in the nature of a final settlement of the demands made on behalf of Ireland, and not be a mere provocation to the revival of fresh demands.

It must, in short, to sum up the whole matter, be, as already insisted upon, a scheme which promises to England at least not greater evils than the maintenance of the Union or than Irish independence.

These conditions constitute the touchstone by which any given plan of Home Rule must be tested. No scheme, however ingenious, can be accepted which lacks any of

---

Mr. Gladstone, 8th April, 1886, ' *The Times* Parliamentary Debates, pp. 130, 131.)

" I laid down, I say, five essential conditions, from which it appeared to me we could under no circumstances depart. These were the essential conditions under which in our opinion the granting of a domestic Legislature to Ireland would be justifiable and wise—first, that it must be consistent with Imperial unity; secondly, that it must be founded upon the political equality of the three nations; thirdly, that there must be an equitable distribution of Imperial burdens; fourthly, that there should be safeguards for the minority; and, fifthly, that it should be in the nature of a settlement, and not of a mere provocation to the revival of fresh demands, which, according to the right hon. gentleman, exceeded all reasonable expectation and calculation." (Speech of Mr. Gladstone, 13th April, 1886, ' *The Times* Parliamentary Debates,' p. 256.) Let it be observed that when Mr. Gladstone speaks of the unity of the Empire he means the sovereignty of Parliament, for in the same speech from which these extracts are taken he says, " The unity of the Empire rests upon the supremacy of Parliament and on considerations much higher than considerations merely fiscal. (' *The Times* Parliamentary Debates,' p. 132.)

these characteristics, namely, the maintenance of Parliamentary sovereignty—justice—finality.

I. *Home Rule as Federalism.*—Federal government is
General the latest invention of constitutional science.
character Several circumstances confer upon it at the
of Fede-
ralism. present moment extraordinary prestige.   It
is a piece of political mechanism which has been
found to work with success in three notorious instances.   In its favour is engaged the pride—may we
not say vanity?—of one of the leading nations of the
earth.   Americans regard Federalism with pardonable
partiality.   They are the original inventors of the best
Federal system in the world, and Federalism has made
them the greatest of all free communities.   A polity under
which the United States has grown up and flourished, and
fought the biggest war which has been fought during the
century, and come out of it victorious, and with renewed
strength, must, it is felt, be a constitution suited for all
nations who aspire to freedom.   There is nothing therefore
surprising in the fact that Federalism is supposed to be
the panacea for all social evils, and all political perplexities,
or that it should be thrust upon our attention as the
device for bringing England and her colonies into closer
connection, and (not perhaps quite consistently) for relaxing the connection and terminating the feud between
England and Ireland.   We should do well, therefore, to
recollect what is the true nature of Federalism.   Federal

government, whatever be its merits, is a mere arrangement for the distribution of political power. It is an
arrangement which requires for its application certain
well-defined conditions.*

There must, in the first place, exist a body of countries,
(such, for example, as the cantons of Switzerland, or the
colonies of America, or the provinces of Canada,) so closely
connected by locality, by history, by race, or the like, as
to be capable of bearing in the eyes of their inhabitants an
impress of common nationality. There must, in the second
place, be found among the people of the countries which it
is proposed to unite in Federal union, a very peculiar state
of sentiment. They must desire union; they must not desire
unity. Federalism, in short, is in its nature a scheme for
bringing together into closer connection a set of states, each
of which desires, whilst retaining its individuality, to form
together with its neighbours one nation. It is not, at any
rate as it has hitherto been applied, a plan for disuniting
the parts of a united state. It may possibly be capable of
this application; experience, however, gives no guidance
on this point,† and loyalty to the central government is to

* Dicey, 'Law of the Constitution,' lecture iv. Parliamentary
Sovereignty and Federalism.

† A singular instance of the attempt to dissolve a country into
States deserves notice. In 1852 a constitution was devised for New
Zealand, under which the country was to be governed by a central
legislature and subordinate provincial governments and councils. This
artificial federation was of short duration; the provincial governments
were in 1875 abolished by an Act of the General Assembly.—Todd,
'Parliamentary Government,' pp. 320–322.

M

the working of a Federal system as necessary as loyalty on the part of individual citizens to their own separate State. When, therefore, it is suggested that Federalism may establish a satisfactory relation between England and Ireland, a doubt naturally suggests itself whether the United Kingdom presents the conditions necessary for the success of the Federal experiment. Whether in the case of two countries, of which the one has no desire for State rights and the other has no desire for union, the bases of a Federal scheme are not wanting, is an inquiry which deserves consideration. Politicians, however, may reject references to abstract theory, and the best way of testing the application of Federalism to the relations between England and Ireland is to make clear to ourselves what are the aims proposed to himself by a genuine Home Ruler, and then trace in outline the characteristics of Federalism, and consider how the Federal system would work in reference to the interests of England.

" My plan of Home Rule for Ireland," writes an eminent Home Ruler, "would establish between Ireland and the Imperial Parliament the same relations in principle that exist between a State of the American Union and the Federal Government, or between any State of the Dominion of Canada and that Central Canadian Parliament which meets in Ottawa."

Aim of Home Rulers.

This statement exhibits both laxity of language and laxity of thought, but it gives a definition of the objects proposed to himself by a genuine Home Ruler which is sufficiently definite for the ends of my argument. Home Rule is, for our present purpose, Federalism. We may, therefore, assume that it involves the adoption throughout the present United Kingdom of a constitution in principle, though not in detail, like that of the United States. The United Kingdom would, if the distinguished Home Ruler's proposals were adopted, be transformed into a confederacy ; the different States, say Great Britain and Ireland, or England, Scotland, and Ireland, would bear to the whole Union the same relation which Virginia and New York bear to the United States ; they would bear towards each other the same relation which Virginia bears to New York, or which they both bear towards Massachusetts. Such a constitution has, it must be at once admitted, no necessary connection with Republicanism. The King or Queen of England for the time being would occupy the position of a hereditary president; this arrangement would, as Mr. Butt seems to have perceived, increase rather than diminish the authority of the Crown. It must, on the other hand, be noted that Federalism necessarily involves the formation of a new constitution, not for Ireland only, but for the whole of the United Kingdom. It is necessary to insist upon this point For half the fallacies of the arguments for Home Rule rest upon the idea that Home Rule is a matter affecting Ireland alone. 'Irish Federalism,' the title of a pamphlet by Mr. Butt, is a term involving something like self-

M 2

contradiction. The misnomer is curious and full of instruction.

Whoever wishes to understand the relation of Federalism to the English Constitution and to English interests must give some attention to the nature of a Federal Union.

A Federal constitution must, from its very nature, be marked by the following characteristics.

Character-istics of Federal-ism. It must, at any rate in modern days, be a written constitution, for its very foundation is the "Federal pact" or contract; the constitution must define with more or less precision the respective powers of the central government, and of the State governments of the central legislature and of the local legislatures; it must provide some means (*e.g.*, reference to a popular vote) for bringing into play that ultimate sovereign power which is able to modify or reform the constitution itself; it must provide some arbiter, be it Council, Court, or Crown, with authority to decide whether the Federal pact has been observed; it must institute some means by which the principles of the constitution may be upheld, and the decrees of the arbiter or Court be enforced against the resistance (if need be) of one or more of the separate States. These are not the accidents but the essential features of any Federal constitution; and are found under the constitution of the Canadian Dominion and of the Swiss Confederacy, no less than under the constitution of the

United States. They all depend on the simple, but often neglected fact, that a Federal constitution implies an elaborate distribution and definition of political powers; that it is from its very nature a compromise between the claims of rival authorities, the Confederacy and the States, and that behind all the mechanism and artifices of the constitution there lies, however artfully concealed, some sovereign power which must have the means both to support the principles of the constitution and, when occasion requires, to modify its terms. Hence almost of necessity flow some further results. Under a federation the law of the land must be divided into constitutional laws (or, in other words, articles of the constitution), which can be changed, if at all, only with special difficulty, say by an appeal to the popular vote or by a constituent assembly, and ordinary laws which may be changed by the central Congress or by the separate assemblies of the States. The powers both of the central Parliament and of the local parliaments, depending as they do upon the constitutional compact, must be limited. Neither the National Assembly of Switzerland nor the Congress of the United States have anything like the sovereign power of the British Parliament: the same thing is obviously true of the Cantonal or State Assemblies. Such are, under one form or another, the essential characteristics of a Federal Government. A confederation of which England and Ireland formed a part would further of necessity exhibit a feature not to be found in the United States. The authority of the Confederacy would in reality mean the power of one State—namely, Great Britain. No artificial distribution of the whole country into separate States would get rid of a fact depending upon laws or facts of nature beyond the reach of constitutional arrangements.

It is now possible to perceive pretty clearly the relation of Federalism to British or English interests.

Advan-
tages of
Federal-
ism to
England.

It would, as compared with the independence of Ireland, present three advantages. There would not be the same obvious and patent failure in the efforts of British statesmanship to unite all the British isles into one country; the continuity of English history would be to a certain extent preserved; the break with the past would be lessened. The Federal Union might, in the eyes of foreign powers, be simply the United Kingdom under another form. The loss, again, to England in material resources would be somewhat less than that involved in separation. Ireland might possibly continue to contribute her share to the Federal Exchequer, though a critic, who reflects upon the expectations expressed by Home Rulers of benefit to Ireland from the expenditure of Irish taxes on Irish objects, will wonder how, unless the taxation of a poverty-stricken country is to be greatly increased, the Irish people could support the expense both of the central and of the local governments. American experience hardly justifies the notion that Federalism is an economical form of Government. It would, and this is no small advantage, make it possible to guarantee, at any rate in appearance, that the executive and legislative authority of the Irish Government should be exercised with due regard to justice. The Federal compact might, and probably would, contain articles which forbade any State Government or legislature to suspend the Habeas Corpus Act, to bestow political privileges upon any church, to pass laws which infringe the obligation of contracts, or to deprive any man of his property without due compensation. The Ten Commandments, in short, and the obvious applications thereof, might be embodied in the fundamental law of the land. Federalism would at lowest preserve a formal respect for justice, and, if the system worked efficiently, would protect individuals and minorities from gross oppression at the hands of the Irish State Government.

These are the benefits Great Britain might derive from Federalism. Let us now examine what are the evils to Great Britain of the proposed constitutional revolution. For whoever either will meditate for a short time on the nature of Federalism, or will examine the mode in which the constitution of the United States—the most successful federation which the world has seen—actually works, will soon perceive that what is miscalled "Irish Federalism" is in reality "British Federalism," and amounts, as I am forced to reiterate again and again, to a proposal for changing the whole constitution of the United Kingdom. It is, in fact, the most "revolutionary" proposal, if the

word " revolutionary " be used in its strict sense, which
has ever been submitted to an English Parliament. The
abolition of the House of Lords, the disestablishment of
the Church, the abolition of the monarchy, might leave
the English constitution far less essentially changed than
would the adoption of Federalism even in that apparently
moderate form in which it was presented by Mr. Butt to
the consideration of the English public.

The definite disadvantages to England of the proposed

Disadvan-
tages of
Federal-
ism to
England.

revolution may be summed up under three
heads :—First, the sovereignty of the Imperial
Parliament would be destroyed and all English
constitutional arrangements would be dislocated
secondly, the power of Great Britain would be diminished ;
thirdly, the chance of further disagreement with Ireland
would certainly not be diminished, and would probably
be increased.

First.—Under all the formality, the antiquarianism, the
shams of the British constitution, there lies latent an
element of power which has been the true source of its
life and growth. This secret source of strength is the
absolute omnipotence,* the sovereignty, of Parliament.
As to the mode in which King, Lords, and Commons were
to divide the sovereign power between themselves there
have been at different times disputes leading to civil war;
but that Parliament—that is, the Crown, the Peers, and

* See Dicey, ' Law of the Constitution,' 2nd ed., pp. 35–79.

the Commons acting together—is absolutely supreme, has
never been doubted. Here constitutional theory and
constitutional practice are for once at one. Hence, it has
been well said by the acutest of foreign critics that the
merit of the English constitution is that it is no constitution at all. The distinction between fundamental
articles of the constitution and laws, between statutes
which can only be touched (if at all) by a constituent
assembly, and statutes which can be repealed by an
ordinary Parliament—the whole apparatus, in short, of
artificial constitutionalism—is utterly unknown to Englishmen. Thus freedom has in England been found compatible at crises of danger with an energy of action
generally supposed to be peculiar to despotism. The
source of strength is, in fact, in each case the same. The
sovereignty of Parliament is like the sovereignty of the
Czar. It is like all sovereignty at bottom, nothing else
but unlimited power; and, unlike some other forms of
sovereignty, can be at once put in force by the ordinary
means of law. This is the one great advantage of our
constitution over that of the United States. In America,
every ordinary authority throughout the Union is
hampered by constitutional restrictions; legislation must
be slow, because the change of any constitutional rule
is impeded by endless difficulties. The vigour which is
wanting to Congress is indeed to a certain extent to be
found in the extensive executive power left in the hands
of the President; but it takes little acuteness to perceive

that in point of pliability, power of development, and freedom of action, English constitutionalism far excels the
Federalism of the United States. Nor is it less obvious
that the very qualities in which the English constitution
excels that of the United States are essential to the
maintenance by England of the British Empire. Home
Rulers, whether they know it or not, touch the mainspring
of the British constitution. For from the moment that
Great Britain becomes part of a federation, the omnipotence of Parliament is gone. The Federal Congress might
be called by the name of the Imperial Parliament. It
might possibly be made up of the same elements, be
elected by the same electors, and even in the main consist
of the very same persons as the existing Parliament of the
United Kingdom; but its nature would be changed, and its
power would be limited on all sides. It might deal with
Imperial expenditure, with foreign affairs, with peace and
war, with other matters placed within its competence; on
every other point the British Congress would, like the
American Congress, be powerless. Nor would all the
powers taken from the Congress be necessarily given to
the local assemblies. Every analogy points the other
way. If the example of the United States is to be
followed, articles of the constitution would limit the power
both of the Imperial Congress and of the local representative assemblies. This limitation of authority could not
be measured by what appeared on the face of the constitution. Some council, tribunal, or other arbiter—let us, for

the sake of simplicity, call it the Federal Court—would have authority to determine whether a law was or was not constitutional, or, in other words, whether it was or was not a law. Let no one fancy that the restraint placed on the power of ordinary legislation by the authority of a Federal Court, which alone can interpret the constitution, is a mere form which has no practical effect. The history of the United States is on this point decisive. De Tocqueville, Story, and Kent are far safer and better instructed guides than authors who " cannot conceive how any conflict of authority could arise which could not be easily settled by argument, by conference, by gradual experience;" and who seem to hold that to deny the existence of a difficulty is the same thing as providing for its removal. The following are a few of the instances in which the American judiciary have in fact determined the limits which bound the powers, either of Congress or of the State legislatures. The judiciary have ruled that a State is liable to be sued in the Federal Courts; that Congress has authority to incorporate a bank ; that a tax imposed by Congress was an indirect tax, and therefore valid ; that the control of the militia really and truly belongs to Congress, and not, as in effect contended by Connecticut and Massachusetts, to the governors of the separate States. The Federal judiciary have determined the limits to their own jurisdiction and to that of the State Courts. The judiciary have pronounced one law after another invalid, as contrary to some article of the constitution—*e.g.*, either

by being tainted with the vice of *ex post facto* legislation,
or by impairing the obligation of contracts. These are a
few samples of the mode in which a Federal Court limits
all legislative authority. If any one wishes to see the
extent to which the power of such a Court has gone in
fact, he should study the decisions on the Legal Tender
Act, which all but overset or nullified the financial legislation of Congress during the War of Secession. If he wishes
to see the effect of applying the constitution of the United
States, or anything like that constitution, to Great Britain
and Ireland, he should consider what is implied in the
undoubted fact that the Land Act of 1870 and the Land
Act of 1881 would, whether passed by the central or by
any local legislature under such a constitution, be at once
treated as void.* If I am told that we might adopt
Federalism without adopting the details of the American
constitution, my reply is, not only that the remark comes
awkwardly from innovators who wish to place Ireland in
the position of Massachusetts, but that the very gist of my
argument is that the existence of some arbiter (whether it
be named Crown, Council, or Court), who may decide
whether the constitution has or has not been violated, is
of the essence of Federalism, while the existence of such an
arbiter absolutely destroys the sovereignty of Parliament.
Nor do the inferences to be drawn from the action of the

---

* If passed by Congress it would be invalid as being *ultra vires*; if
passed by a State legislature it would be invalid as impairing the
obligation of contracts. See 'Constitution of the United States,'
Art. 1, s. 8, and Art. 1, s. 10, cl. 1.

Federal Court, and a study of the American constitution
as it actually exists, end here.   In the decisions of the
Court we may trace the rise of question after question—
that is, of conflict after conflict—as to the respective rights,
of the Federation and the individual States.   From the
history and from the immobility of the constitution, we
may perceive the extent to which the existence of a
Federal pact checks change, or, in other words, reform.
Every institution which can lay claim to be based upon an
organic law acquires a sort of sacredness.   Under a system
of Federalism, the Crown, the House of Peers, the
Imperial Parliament itself, when transformed into a
Federal Assembly, would be almost beyond the reach of
change, reform, or abolition.   Nor is it the Legislature of
Great Britain alone which would suffer a fundamental
change.   The relations between the Executive and the
country would undergo immense modification.   The
authority of the Crown might be enhanced by the
establishment of a Federal Union: the King would
become, in a very special sense, the representative of
national or Imperial unity, and the weakening of Parliament might lead to the strengthening of the monarch.
However this might be, it has, it is submitted, been now
shown that Federalism would dislocate every English constitutional arrangement.

Secondly.—The changes necessitated by Federalism
would all tend to weaken the power of Great Britain.
That this is so has been already to a great degree estab-

lished, in considering the mode in which Federalism destroys the sovereignty of Parliament. But a system of Federalism would assuredly weaken the Government quite as much as the Legislature. The Executive, as the organ of the Federal Union, would be hampered by new conditions utterly unknown to an English Ministry. The language of Federalists exhibits a curious and ominous silence or ambiguity as to the disposal of the armed forces. Is the army to be a British army, with authority at the will of the Federal Government to enter every part of the new Union, or is Ireland to have an independent force of her own? This, again—and every specific criticism is open to the same retort—may be called a detail, but it is a detail which touches the root of the whole matter. If the Federal, that is in effect the English, Government is to retain the same control over the whole army as at present —if Ireland is not to own a local force under the control of local authorities—then the language as to Irish independence used by Irish Nationalists is singularly misleading. If, on the other hand, order is to be maintained, or not maintained, by a native army under the guidance of Irish commanders, then it passes the wit of man to see by what means the rights of the central government are to be enforced in any case of disagreement between the Imperial and the Irish Parliament. With the memory of the Irish volunteers before his mind, an historian, such, for example, as Mr. McCarthy, will hardly assert that the difficulty raised is one of which he cannot conceive the existence. For my part, I heartily join in the admiration he, no doubt, feels for the patriots of 1782, but no man in his senses will maintain that the moral of that year is that a local Irish army cannot under any circumstances, prove an embarrassment to the central Government. The general tone, even more than the precise language of Irish Federalists, all but forbids the supposition that they are prepared to secure the supremacy of the Federal Government by giving it the sole control of the only armed force which is to exist in any part of the Union. They probably hope that some sort of compromise may be found with regard to a matter in which, as theory and experience alike prove, compromise is all but impossible. Under certain circumstances, and in certain cases, and subject to certain conditions, the use of the armed force throughout Great Britain and Ireland is, we may suppose, to be left in the hands of the Federal Executive; under other circumstances, and under other conditions, the local forces are probably to be controlled by the local or State Government. Whether such an arrangement would continue in working order for a year, is more than doubtful. Assume, however, that somehow it could be got to work, the fact still remains that a scheme, intended to secure local liberty, would certainly ensure Imperial weakness. The need, moreover, for bestowing some element of strength on a Federal Executive as a counterpoise to its many elements of weakness leads almost of necessity to a result which has scarcely received due notice. The

executive authority must be placed beyond the control of
a representative assembly.   Neither in the United States,
nor in Switzerland, nor in the German Empire, can the
Federal administration be displaced by the vote of an
assembly.   Federalism is in effect incompatible with
Parliamentary government as practised in England.   The
Canadian Ministry (it may be urged) can be changed at
the will of the Dominion Parliament, and the common
Ministry of Austria-Hungary is responsible to the Delegations.   This is true; but these exceptions are precisely
of the class which prove the rule which they are cited to
invalidate.   The Cabinet system of the Dominion is a
defect in the Canadian Constitution, and could not work
were not Canada, by its position as a dependency, under
the guidance of a power beyond the reach of the Dominion
Parliament.   What may be the real responsibility to the
Delegations of the common ministry of Austria-Hungary
admits of a good deal of doubt.   No one, who will not
be deceived by words, believes the responsibility to be
at all like the liability of Mr. Gladstone or Lord Salisbury to be dismissed from office by a vote of the House of
Commons.   The Emperor-King is, as regards the Austro-
Hungarian Monarchy, the permanent and unchangeable
head of the State.   Turn the United Kingdom into a
Federal State, and Parliamentary Government, as Englishmen now know it, is at an end.   This may or may not
be an evil, but it is a revolution which ought to give
pause to innovators who deem it a slighter danger to

innovate on the Act of Union than to remodel the procedure of the House of Commons.

The central Government would again, merely from that division of powers which is of the essence of Federalism, be as feeble against foreign aggression as against local resistance. · Home Rule, it is constantly said, has at least this advantage, as compared with Irish independence, that it prevents any alliance between Ireland and a foreign enemy. This gain might turn out rather nominal than real. Neither the United States nor France could, of course, send an Embassy to any State comprised within the British Union ; but, if war impended, they might and would attempt to gain the favour of the Irish Ministry, or the Irish party who controlled the Irish Parliament, or exercised the authority of the local Government of Ireland. Suppose that when war was about to be proclaimed between the British Federation and France, the Irish Parliament objected to hostilities with the French Republic. Can it be denied that the local Parliament and the local Executive could, by protests, by action, or even by inaction, give aid or comfort to the foreign enemy ? The local legislature would, in the supposed case, be aided by a minority of the central Parliament or Congress. Obstruction would go hand in hand with sedition. Loyalty to the Union was strong throughout the Northern States during the War of Secession ; but the tale used certainly to be told that, had Meade been defeated at Gettysburg, the leaders of the New York democracy would have

N

attempted "to carry the State out of the Union." Moreover, Great Britain would perhaps find it easier to control
the action of an independent than of a confederated
Ireland. Blockades and embargoes are, as already pointed
out, modes of persuasion applicable to foreigners, but
inapplicable to citizens ; the Government of the Union
found it harder to check the latent disloyalty of South
Carolina than it would have found it to deal with the
open enmity of Canada. This topic is too odious and too
far removed from the realm of practical politics, to need
more than the allusion required for the completeness of
my argument.

Federalism, in short, would mean the weakness of
Great Britain, both at home and abroad. As the head of
a Confederacy, England, as the head also of the British
Empire, would meet undiminished responsibilities with
greatly diminished power.

Thirdly.—Federalism is at least as likely to stereotype
and increase the causes of division between England and
Ireland as to remove them.

A Federal Government is, of all constitutions, the most
artificial. If such a government is to be worked with
anything like success, there must exist among the citizens
of the confederacy a spirit of genuine loyalty to the
Union. The "Unitarian" feeling of the people must
distinctly predominate over the sentiment in favour of
"State rights." To require this is to require a good deal
more than that mere general submission to the Govern-

ment which is requisite for the prosperity of every State, whatever be the nature of its polity. In a Federation every citizen is influenced by a double allegiance. He owes fealty to the central Government; he owes fealty also to his Canton or State. National allegiance and local allegiance divide and perplex the feelings even of loyal citizens. Unless the national sentiment predominate, the Federation will go to pieces at any of those crises when the interest or wishes of any of the States conflict with the interest or wishes of the Union. So keen an observer and profound a critic as De Tocqueville believed that both the American and the Swiss Federations would make shipwreck on this rock. He was mistaken; he did not allow for the rapid development of national sentiment. But his error was pardonable. The leaders of the Sonderbund did prefer the interest of Lucerne to the unity of Switzerland. Lee and Jackson were disloyal to the Union, because they were loyal to Virginia. Leading officers of the United States army, soldiers educated at Westpoint, trained the armies of the Confederates. They were men of unblemished honour; they were, some of them, not originally zealous in the cause of secession, but they believed that their duty to their State—to Virginia, to South Carolina, or to Georgia—was paramount over their duty to the Government at Washington. If Virginia had stood by the Union, General Lee might, in all probability, have been the conqueror of those Confederate States, of which he was the hero. Ireland has had far graver causes for disaffection towards the English Government than any of the reasons alleged for the secession of Virginia; but Irish officers and Irish soldiers have always been perfectly loyal to England. The reason of the difference is obvious; the officers of the English army have never been distracted by the difficulties of divided allegiance. Make Ireland one of the States of a Confederacy, and these difficulties will at once arise. Irish officers and Irish soldiers, members of the Irish State—paid by and to a certain extent under the command of the Irish Government—can hardly be blamed if in times of civil differences, leading it may be to civil war, they should feel more loyalty to their State than to the Union. This Union, be it remembered, would in such a case be nothing but Great Britain under a new and less impressive title, while the State would be Ireland.

The existence and nature of the Federal bond is calculated to supply both the causes and occasions of such differences.

Home Rulers, it is clear, form already most exaggerated hopes of the benefits to be conferred on Ireland by Home Rule; and, further, in their own minds (naturally enough) confound Federalism with national independence.

"Give Ireland," writes Mr. Finch,* "the management of her own affairs, and you will see called into her service the ablest and most capable of her sons; while, as things now stand, the intellect of Ireland is shut out from all

* *Contemporary Review*, vol. xli., p. 908.

share in the administration. With careers at home worthy of the best and ablest of the people, much of the wealth which is now drained off from Ireland without any return, will be expended in developing the industrial resources of the country; industry will revive, and with the revival of industry will come employment for the people. 'It is the difficulty of living by wages in Ireland,' says Sir G. C. Lewis, 'which makes every man look to the land for maintenance.' With employment for the people, half the difficulty of the land question will be solved. If, then, we wish to promote the moral and material welfare of the Irish people, let us make them masters of their own affairs."

" I have indicated what I believe," writes Mr. O'Neill Daunt,* " to be the radical disease of Ireland : the want of a domestic legislature racy of the soil, and acting in harmony with the national sentiment. God has created Ireland with the needs of a separate nation, and with the needs are associated the rights. 'Our patent to be a State, not a shire,' said Goold in 1799, ' comes direct from Heaven. The Almighty has in majestic characters signed the great charter of our independence. The great Creator of the world has given our beloved country the gigantic outlines of a kingdom.'

" If Ireland had been left the unfettered use of the natural materials of wealth in her soil and in her people, and of the facilities of internal and external commerce

* *Contemporary Review*, vol. xli., p. 921.

supplied by her physical configuration and her geographical position—if her interests were protected by a Parliament sitting in her capital, securing the expenditure at home of her annual revenue, both public and private, rendering impossible that destructive hæmorrhage of her income by which she is impoverished, aiding the development of her industries, and resisting all aggression on her commercial and political rights—in a word, if the Irish Constitution had not been treacherously undermined and overthrown, we should now have been the best support of the Empire, instead of being its scandal and its weakness."

Politicians who write thus expect far more from national independence than nationality itself can give. More than fifty years have elapsed since Spain expelled the foreign invader; but Spain has not yet succeeded in expelling ignorance, prejudice, superstition, or oppression. But whatever be the miracles of nationality, Ireland would not, under Federalism, be a nation. Rhode Island has all the freedom demanded for his country by an eminent Home Ruler, whose expressions I have cited. He surely does not consider the inhabitants of Rhode Island to be a nation.

Whatever else Home Rule might give to Ireland, one gift it assuredly would not bring with it. It would not endow the country with wealth. To Irish enthusiasm and patriotism illusions on this matter are pardonable. In the English advocate of Home Rule they are unpardonable.

Ireland is, and must, under any form of government conceivable, for a length of time remain a poor country. Capital knows nothing of patriotism or sentiment. Commerce has no partiality for the masses. Credit cherishes no trust towards the people. The one prediction which we may make with confidence is that a measure of Home Rule would not increase Irish capital, and would shake Irish credit. The rumour of Home Rule has already, it is said disturbed the course of business in Ireland. From the nature of things, then, the establishment of Federalism would lead to bitter disappointment. The country would not enjoy the dignity of independence; it would not enjoy the comfort of wealth. Every Irishman would feel that he had been cheated of his hopes, and this he would feel not because he is an Irishman, but because he is a man. It is human to expect far more from even the most beneficial of revolutions than any political change can bring. The unity of Italy was well worth all the price it cost. The unity of Germany gave intense gratification to natural feelings of national pride. Yet there are probably many even in the Italian Kingdom who sigh for the light taxes of the Bourbon or the Pope, and Germans who glory in the greatness of the Empire flee by thousands to the United States that they may escape the burden of conscription. The disappointment which naturally attends a great change would in the case of Ireland be specially bitter. To what cause would the disappointment be attributed? The answer is easy to find. If taxation

increased—as it probably would; if wealth did not increase—as it certainly would not; if the sense of semi-
independence did not produce the hope, the energy, the
new life, the regeneration which enthusiasts consider to
be the natural result of nationality—if anything, in short,
failed to go according to the hopes of men who had formed
hopes which a miracle itself could . hardly satisfy—the
blame for the non-fulfilment of groundless anticipations
would rest upon the Confederacy—that is, in other words,
upon England.   To suppose this, is not to attribute
special unreasonableness to Irishmen.   If Italy had been
forced to accept, instead of her longed-for independence,
the local self-government which might be conceded to the
State of an Austrian Federation, we may be quite sure
that the Grist Tax, the Sicilian Banditti, the intrigues of
France in Tunis, the perversity of the Pope, the poverty
of Italian workmen, the factiousness of Italian politicians,
every evil, in short, real or imaginary, under which Italy
now suffers, or has suffered since 1870—would have
been attributed to her connection with a Union pre-
sided over by the Austrian Emperor.   National independence, like every other form of independence, has at
least this merit, that it compels men to take their fate
into their own hands, and to feel that they themselves
or the circumstances of the world are the causes of
their misfortunes.   Semi-independence makes it easy for
men to attribute every mishap to the absence of absolute
freedom.

If the existence of a Federal constitution would of itself supply the cause for discontent, it is of the very nature of such a constitution to supply the occasions of dispute. Nothing can prevent the rise of burning questions about Federal and State rights. Is nullification or secession, or the refusal to pay Federal taxes a State right? If these questions arise, by whom are they to be settled? Suppose they are referred to a Federal Court, say the Privy Council, is it reasonable to fancy that Irishmen or Englishmen, for that matter, will acquiesce in the decision of grave political issues (say the right of the Federal Government to proclaim martial law at Dublin, or the validity of the Land Act) by any tribunal? For when political issues are referred to the decision of a Court the difficulty is great of enlisting public opinion in favour of its decrees. The theory of the constitution and the expectation of the people is that references to the judges will be events of rare occurrence, and that the Bench, when it acts at all, will act only as interpreter of the constitutional pact. Things are certain to turn out far otherwise. The intervention of the tribunals will in one form or another be constantly invoked, and will be invoked to determine the most burning questions of the day. The Constitution of the United States would be unintelligible without reference to a long line of determined cases; its principles are to be found quite as much in the decisions of the Supreme Court as in its Articles. Swiss Constitutionalists have greatly enlarged, as years have gone on, the originally

limited powers of the Federal tribunal. The statesmen who
drafted the Act constituting the Canadian Dominion fancied
they could in effect avoid the necessity for judicial interpretation, but a long series of reports proves the futility
of their expectation. Each day increases the mass, and it
must be added the importance, of the judgments by which
the Privy Council determines questions of constitutional
law for the Colonies. Moreover, even laymen soon perceive
that interpretation means legislation. It is technically
correct to say that the Supreme Court of the United
States acts only as interpreter of the Constitution, but we
must not be deceived by fictions. The Supreme Court
has legislated as truly, and perhaps more effectively than
Congress. It has achieved, and from the nature of things
was compelled to achieve, a feat forbidden to Congress ; it
has added to or enlarged the Articles of the Constitution.
The good fortune of the United States gave to them in
Judge Marshall a profound and statesmanlike lawyer, and
the judgments of the great Chief Justice have built up the
existing Constitution. He may be counted, if not among
its founders, at any rate as its main architect. In this
instance judicial authority was combined with political
wisdom, and Marshall's opinion was, it is said, rejected by
the Court in but two cases, and had it in these instances
been followed, would have improved the Constitution.
Unfortunately, while one may often secure the fairness
one cannot ensure the wisdom of the Bench. Judges err ;
a final Court of Appeal must often give decisions which

are or are supposed to be erroneous, *i.e.*, not a just deduction from the facts and principles which the Court is
called upon to consider.   No historian will, it is likely,
now defend the doctrine of the House of Lords about
marriage laid down in *Reg.* v. *Millis.*   Competent authorities question some of the most important ecclesiastical
judgments given by the Judicial Committee of the Privy
Council.   The decision in the *Dred Scott Case,* whether
right or wrong, did not approve itself to some eminent
lawyers in the United States.   One of the decisions of the
Supreme Court in the *Legal Tender Cases* must have been
wrong; whether the last was sound is open to debate.   It
is when a Court gives what is thought to be an erroneous
decision on matters exciting the feelings of large classes
that the difficulty of obtaining acquiescence in its judgments is palpable.   The judges decided, and it is quite
possible decided rightly, that Ship Money was a legal
exaction, and that the Crown's dispensing power was
authorized by law.   Popular opinion branded the judges
as sycophants and traitors.   Chief Justice Taney and his
colleagues decided in effect, and from a legal point of view
may have been right in deciding, that slavery was recognised by the Constitution of the United States.   Their decision was denounced by many of the best men in the Union
as infamous.   The Privy Council have laid down doctrines
on matters of ritual which are held to be erroneous by a
large body of the clergy, and Ritualists have gone to
prison rather than treat the judgment of the Privy Council

as of moral validity. Clergymen are not perhaps the most reasonable of mankind, but they are not more unreasonable than political enthusiasts. How then is it possible to expect that a Federal tribunal would command an obedience not yielded willingly to the laws of the Imperial Parliament? Englishmen, indeed, might, it is possible, acquiesce in the ruling of Federal judges, and this for two reasons: they are a legally-minded nation; and (what is of far more consequence) a Federal Court must represent in the main the opinions of the Federal Government—that is, of Great Britain. But it is idle to suppose that Mr. Parnell and Mr. Parnell's followers would find it easier to respect an Imperial or Federal tribunal than to bow to the will of the Imperial Parliament.

Home Rulers would, moreover, soon discover a reason for resistance to the Federal Court or the Federal Government, which from their point of view would be a perfectly valid reason. The Federal Government would, in effect, be the Government of England; the Federal Court would in effect be a Court appointed by the English Government. In a Confederacy where there are many States, the Government of the Federation cannot be identified with even the most powerful of the States; it were ridiculous to assert that the Government at Washington is only the Government of New York under another name. Where a Confederacy consists in reality, if not in name, of two States only, of which the one has at least four or five times the power of the other, the authority of the Confederacy means the authority of the powerful State. "Irish Federalism," if in reality established, would soon generate a demand from Ireland, not unreasonable in itself under the circumstances of the case, that the whole British Empire should be turned into a Confederacy, under the guidance of a general Congress. Thus alone could Ireland become a real State, the member of a genuine Confederation. Hence arises a new danger. Apply Federalism to Ireland and you immediately provoke demands for autonomy in other parts of the United Kingdom, and for constitutional changes in other parts of the British Empire. Federalism, which in other lands has been a step towards Union, would, it is likely enough, be in our case the first stage towards a dissolution of the United Kingdom into separate States, and hence towards the breaking-up of the British Empire. This is no future or imaginary peril; the mere proposal of Home Rule, under something like a Federal form, has already made it an immediate and pressing danger. Sir Gavan Duffy, by far the ablest among the Irish advocates of Home Rule, predicts that before ten years have elapsed there will be a Federation of the Empire.[*] A majority of Scotch electors support the policy of Mr. Gladstone, and forthwith a most respectable Scotch periodical puts forward a plan of Home Rule for Scotland. Canon MacColl

---

[*] 'Mr. Gladstone's Irish Constitution,' *Contemporary Review*, May, 1886, p. 616.

already suggests that we should make tentatively an experiment capable of development into a permanent system on the lines of the American Constitution, and make it not only in Ireland, but also perhaps gradually in Scotland, and even in Wales.* It is unnecessary to discuss Canon MacColl's argument at length. When he asks † "why should a system which imparts strength to America, to Austria, and to Germany, disintegrate and ruin the British Empire," he raises an inquiry which does not admit of an answer, since it assumes the identity of things which are radically different. The system which may or may not impart strength to Austria is no more the system which imparts strength to America, than the system which imparts strength to England is the same as the system which does or does not impart strength to Russia. To lump under one head every policy which can by any straining of the terms be brought under the heads of "Federalism" or "Home Rule," is neither more nor less absurd than to classify together every Constitution which can be called a monarchy.

A significant indication has now appeared of the nearness of the danger of Imperial disintegration. Mr. Gladstone's own method of interpreting his own past utterances makes it the duty of his critics to weigh well not only his direct

---

* 'Arguments for and against Home Rule,' by the Rev. Malcolm MacColl, M.A., p. 71.

† *Ibid.*

statements, but his suggestions; and there is, I think, no
possible unfairness in construing the language of his
pamphlet on the Irish Question as an intimation that he
already entertains, if he does not favour, the idea of
applying the Federal principle to Scotland and to Wales.*
Federalism is the solvent which, if applied to one part
of the United Kingdom, will undo the work not only of
Pitt, but of Somers, of Henry VIII., and of Edward I.
Meanwhile, the one prediction which may be made with
absolute confidence is that Federalism would not generate
that goodwill between England and Ireland which, could
it be produced, would, in my judgment at least, be an
adequate compensation even for the evils and the inconveniences of the Federal system.

To the view of Federalism here maintained there exist
one or two objections, so obvious that without some
reference to them my argument would lack completeness.

Federalism, it is urged, has succeeded in Switzerland
and in America; it may, therefore, succeed in the United
Kingdom.

If the general drift of my argument does not sufficiently
answer this objection, two special replies lie near at hand.
In the case both of Switzerland and of America, a Federal
Constitution supplied the means by which States, conscious of a common national feeling, have approached to

* 'The Irish Question,' by the Right Hon. W. E. Gladstone,
pp. 36, 37.

political unity. It were a rash inference from this fact, that when two parts of one nation are found (as must be asserted by any Home Ruler) not to be animated by a common feeling of nationality, a Federal Constitution is the proper means by which to keep them in union. The more natural deduction from the general history of Federalism is, that a confederation is an imperfect political union, transitory in its nature, and tending either to pass into one really united State, or to break up into the different States which compose the Federation.

If, again, the example either of America or of Switzerland is to teach us anything worth knowing, the history of those countries must be read as a whole. It will then be seen that the two most successful confederacies in the world have been kept together only by the decisive triumph through force of arms of the central power over real or alleged State rights. General Dufour in Switzerland, General Grant and General Sherman in America, were the true interpreters and preservers of the constitutional pact. This undoubted fact hardly suits the theories of Irish Federalists.

Nor ought we to stop at this point. Citizens of the Union filled with justifiable pride at the success of the American Constitution assume that a Federal Government is in itself absolutely the best form of government, that in any country where it can be adopted it must be an improvement on the existing institutions of the land, and that as compared with the constitutional monarchy of England federalism exhibits no special faults from which English constitutionalism is free. This assumption is perfectly natural; it resembles that absolute faith in the virtues of the British Constitution which reached its culminating point when Burke's intimate friend and pupil, Gilbert Elliot, himself no mean states-man, went to Corsica to keep going a miniature copy of English Parliamentary institutions.* But in each case a faith which is natural will also be pronounced by any candid judge to be unfounded. Federalism has in its very essence, and even as it exists in America, at least two special faults. It distracts the allegiance of citizens, and what is even more to the present point, it does not provide sufficient protection for the legal rights of unpopular minorities. There is not, and never was, a word in the Articles of the Constitution forbidding American citizens to criticise the institutions of the State. An American Abolitionist had as much right to denounce slavery at Boston, or for that matter at Charlestown, as an English Abolitionist had to denounce slavery in London or Liver-pool. It were ridiculous to maintain that the right was one which either Lloyd Garrison or his disciples were able to exercise. Mr. Godkin† has repeated with perfect fairness the tale of the persecutions suffered by Prudence Crandall in Connecticut because she chose in exercise of

* See Life and Letters of Gilbert Elliot, vol. 2, pp. 354, 355.
† 'American Home Rule,' by E. L. Godkin, *Nineteenth Century* June, 1886, pp. 793, 802.

her legal and moral rights to educate young women of colour. Mr. Godkin apparently draws, as I have already pointed out, from the fact an inference—which I confess myself not well able to follow—against all attempts to enforce an unpopular law. The more natural conclusion is that the Federal Government was not able to protect the rights of individuals against strong local sentiment. This moral at any rate has an obvious application to any scheme of Federalism for Ireland.

The experience of Canada, again, is adduced to prove that a Federal constitution is compatible with loyalty to the British Crown. Why should an arrangement which produces peace, prosperity, and loyalty across the Atlantic not be applied to Ireland?

The answer is, that the case of Canada is as regards Federalism irrelevant. Canada is not part of a British Federation. The Dominion as a whole is simply a colony, standing essentially in the same relation to England as Victoria or New South Wales. The laws of the Parliament that meets at Ottawa need the Royal sanction, or, in other words, may be vetoed, or rather not approved, by the English Ministry of the day. The Act itself on which the existence of the Canadian constitution depends is an Act of the British Parliament, and cannot be modified by any other authority. The British Parliament is supreme in Canada as throughout the British dominions; and Canada sends no representatives to the British Parliament. The provinces, no doubt, which

compose the Dominion are under an Act of Parliament
a Federation; but the dangers and difficulties of Federalism
are to a great extent avoided by the supremacy of the
British Crown. These difficulties, however, do arise. If
any one will study the " Letellier case," he will soon
perceive that Canada has exhibited the germ of the conflict between the central authority of the Dominion and
the " State right" of the provinces; he will also perceive
that the conflict was determined by a reference to the
English Ministry, who in effect gave judgment in favour
of the Dominion. The example of Canada suggests, if anything, that some Irish difficulties might be solved by
turning Ireland into a colony without representatives in
the Imperial Parliament.

We have now the materials for comparing, as regards
the interests of England, the effects of Irish independence
with the effects of Home Rule as Federalism. The case
as between the two stands thus :—

The national independence of Ireland entails on England
three great evils—the deliberate surrender of the main
object at which English statesmanship has aimed for
centuries, together with all the moral loss and disgrace
which such surrender entails; the loss of considerable
material resources in money, and still more in men; the
incalculable evil of the existence in the neighbourhood
of Great Britain of a new, a foreign, and, possibly, a
hostile State. For these evils there are, indeed, to be
found two real though inadequate compensations—namely,

the probability that loss of territory might restore to England a unity and consistency of action equivalent to an increase of strength, and the possibility that separation might be the first step towards gaining the goodwill, and ultimately the alliance of Ireland. It is, however, hardly worth while to calculate what might be the extent of the possible deductions from evils which no English statesman would knowingly bring on Great Britain. By men of all parties and of all views it is practically conceded that England neither will nor can, except under compulsion, assent to Irish independence.

Federalism, on the other hand, has the appearance of a compromise. It does not avowedly break up the unity of Great Britain and Ireland; it does not wholly deprive England of Irish resources; it does not, directly at least, lay Great Britain open to foreign attack. Federalism has, however, special evils of its own. It revolutionizes the whole Constitution of the United Kingdom; by undermining the sovereignty of Parliament, it deprives English institutions of their elasticity, their strength, and their life; it weakens the Executive at home, and lessens the power of the country to resist foreign attack. The revolution which works these changes holds out no hope of reconciliation with Ireland. An attempt, in short, to impose on England and Scotland a constitution which they do not want, and which is quite unsuited to the historical traditions and to the genius of Great Britain, offers to Ireland a constitution which Ireland is certain to dislike, which has none of the real or imaginary charms of independence, and ensures none of the solid benefits to be hoped for from a genuine union with England.

If this be the true state of the case, thus much at least is argumentatively made out : Federalism offers to England not a constitutional compromise, but a fundamental revolution; and this revolution, however moderate in its form or in the intention of its advocates, does not offer that reasonable chance of reconciliation with the mass of the Irish people which might counterbalance the evils of Separation, while it is at least as much opposed to the interests of Great Britain as would be the national independence of Ireland. This conclusion is a purely negative one, but it is, as far as British statesmen are concerned, the *reductio ad impossibile* of the case in favour of Home Rule in so far as Home Rule takes the form of Federalism.

II. *Home Rule as Colonial Independence.*—The modern Colonial policy of England has, or is thought to have, achieved two results which impress popular imagination : —it has relieved English statesmanship from an unbearable burden of worry and anxiety ; it has (as most people believe) changed Colonial unfriendliness or discontent into enthusiastic or ostentatious loyalty. Some politicians, therefore, who are anxious to terminate the secular feud between England and Ireland, and to free Parliament from the presence, and therefore from the obstructiveness,

of the Home Rulers, readily assume that the formula of
"Colonial independence" contains the solution of the
problem how to satisfy at once the demand of Ireland for
independence and the resolution of Great Britain to
maintain the integrity of the Empire. This assumption
rests on no sure foundation, but derives such plausibility
as it possesses from the gross ignorance of the public as to
the principles and habits which govern the English State
system. A mere account of the constitutional relations
existing between England and a self-governed colony is
almost equivalent to a suggestion of the reasons which
forbid the hope that the true answer to the agitation for
Home Rule is to be found in conceding to Ireland institutions like those which satisfy the inhabitants of New
South Wales or Victoria. To render such a statement at
once brief and intelligible is no easy matter, for, among
all the political arrangements devised by the ingenuity of
statesmen, none can be found more singular, more complicated, or more anomalous than the position of combined
independence and subordination occupied by the large
number of self-governing colonies which are scattered
throughout the British Empire. Victoria, which may be
taken as a type of the whole class, is, for most purposes
of local and internal administration, and for some purposes which go beyond the sphere usually assigned to
local government, an independent, self-governing community. Victoria is at the same time, for all purposes in
theory and for many purposes in fact, a merely subor-

dinate portion of the British Empire, and as truly subject to the British Parliament as is Middlesex or the Isle of Wight.

Let us try in the first place to realize—for this is the essential matter as regards my present argument—the full extent of Victorian independence.

Victoria enjoys a Constitution after the British model. The Governor, the two Houses, the Ministry, reproduce the well-known features of our limited monarchy. The Victorian Parliament further possesses in Victoria that character of sovereignty which the British Parliament possesses throughout the dominions of the Crown, and is (subject, of course, to the authority of the British Parliament itself) as supreme at Melbourne as are Queen, Lords, and Commons at Westminster. It makes and unmakes Cabinets; it controls the executive action of the Ministry; who, in their turn, are the authorized advisers of that sham constitutional monarch, the Colonial Governor. The Parliament, moreover, recognizes no restrictions on its legislative powers; it is not, as is the Congress of the United States, restrained within a very limited sphere of action; it is not, as are both the Congress and the State Legislatures of the Union, bound hand and foot by the articles of a rigid Constitution; it is not compelled to respect any immutable maxims of legislation. Hence the Victorian Parliament—in this resembling its creator, the British Parliament—exercises an amount of legislative freedom unknown to most foreign representative assemblies. It can, and does, legislate on education, on marriage and

divorce, on ecclesiastical topics, on the tenure of land, on
finance, on every subject, in short, which can interest the
Colony.   It provides for the raising of Colonial forces; it
may levy taxes or impose duties for the support of the
Victorian administration, or for the protection of Colonial
manufactures.   It is not forbidden to tax goods imported
from other parts of the Empire; it is not bound to abstain
from passing *ex post facto* laws, to respect the sanctity of
contracts, or to pay any regard to the commercial interests
of the United Kingdom.   It may alter the Constitution
on which its own powers depend, and, for example,
extend the franchise or remodel the Upper House.   To
understand the full extent of the authority possessed by
the Victorian Parliament and the Victorian Ministry—
which is, in fact, appointed by the Parliament—it should
be noted that, while every branch of the administration
(the courts, the police, and the Colonial forces) is, as in
England, more or less directly under the influence or the
control of the Cabinet, the Colonies have, since 1862,
provided for their own defence, and, except in time of
war, or peril of war, are not garrisoned by British troops.*
It is, therefore, no practical exaggeration to assert that
Victoria is governed by its own Executive, which is
appointed by its own Parliament, and which maintains
order by means of the Victorian police, supported, in case
of need, by Victorian soldiers.   An intelligent foreigner,

* See Todd, 'Parliamentary Government in the British Colonies,'
pp. 274-303, and especially p. 281, as to the position of the colonial
troops in Victoria. .

therefore, might reside for years in Melbourne, and conceive that the supremacy of the British Government was little more than nominal. In this he would be mistaken. But should he assert that, as to all merely Colonial matters, Victoria was in practice a self-governed and independent country, his language would not be accurate, yet his assertion would not go very wide of the truth.

The local independence, however, of an English colony is hardly more noteworthy than are the devices by which a colony is retained in its place as a subordinate portion of the British Empire, and anyone who would understand the English Colonial system must pay hardly less attention to the subordination than to the independence of a country like Victoria.

The foundation of the whole scheme is the admission of the complete and unquestioned supremacy of the British Parliament throughout every portion of the royal dominions. No Colonial statesman, judge, or lawyer ever dreams of denying that Crown, Lords, and Commons can legislate for Victoria, and that a statute of the Imperial Parliament overrides every law or custom repugnant thereto, by whomsoever enacted, in every part of the Crown dominions. The right, moreover, of Imperial legislation has not fallen into disuse. Mr. Tarring *

---

* See Tarring, 'Chapters on the Law relating to the Colonies,' pp. 79–85. As examples of Imperial Statutes which affect the Colonies may be taken the Foreign Enlistment Act, 1870, the Coinage Act, 1870, and the Territorial Waters Jurisdiction Act, 1878.

enumerates from sixty to seventy Imperial statutes,
extending from 7 Geo. III. c. 50 to 44 & 45 Vict. c. 69,
which apply to the Colonies generally, and to this list,
which might now be lengthened, must be added a large
number of statutes applying to particular colonies. The
sovereignty of Parliament, moreover, is formally recorded
in the Colonial Laws Act, 1865 (28 & 29 Vict. cap. 63),
which itself may well be termed the Charter of Colonial
legislative authority. This essential dogma of parliamentary sovereignty, moreover, is not proclaimed as a
merely abstract principle—it is enforced by two different
methods. Every court, in the first place, as well in
Victoria as elsewhere throughout the British dominions,
is bound to hold void, and in fact does hold void, enactments which contravene an Imperial statute, and from
Colonial courts there is an appeal to the Privy Council.
The Colonial Governor, in the second place, though from
one point of view he is a constitutional monarch acting
under the advice given him by his Ministers, bears also
another and a different character. He is an Imperial official
appointed by the Crown—that is, by the English Cabinet,
which represents the wishes of the Imperial Parliament—and he is, as such representative of the Imperial
power, bound to avert if possible the passing of any Bill,
and when he cannot avert the passing, then to veto any
Act of the Colonial Legislature, which is disapproved of by
the Home Government as opposed either to Imperial law
or to Imperial policy. Thus, a Victorian Act, even when
sanctioned by the Governor, must pass through another

stage before it finally becomes law. It must receive the
assent of the Crown, or, in other words, the assent of the
English Secretary of State for the Colonies, and, unless
this assent be either actually or constructively given, it
does not come into force.* The matter to be carefully

* See Dicey, 'Law of the Constitution,' pp. 105, 106.

The somewhat complicated principles which govern what is popularly called the right of veto on Bills passed by Colonial Legislatures,
are thus stated in the ' Rules and Regulations' published for the use of
the Colonial Office, Chapter III., Legislative Councils and Assemblies,
Rules 48–55 :—

"48. In every Colony the Governor has authority either to give
or to withhold his assent to laws passed by the other branches or
members of the Legislature, and until that assent is given no such
law is valid or binding.

"49. Laws are in some cases passed with suspending clauses; that
is, although assented to by the Governor they do not come into
operation or take effect in the Colony until they shall have been
specially confirmed by Her Majesty, and in other cases Parliament
has for the same purpose empowered the Governor to reserve Laws
for the Crown's assent, instead of himself assenting or refusing his
assent to them.

"50. Every Law which has received the Governor's assent (unless
it contains a suspending clause) comes into operation immediately
or at the time specified in the Law itself. But the Crown retains
power to disallow the Law; and if such power be exercised at any
time afterwards, the Law ceases to have operation from the date at
which such disallowance is published in the Colony.

"51. In Colonies having Representative Assemblies the disallowance
of any Law, or the Crown's assent to a reserved Bill, is signified by
Order in Council. The confirmation of an Act passed with a suspending clause is not signified by Order in Council unless this mode
of confirmation is required by the terms of the suspending clause
itself, or by some special provision in the constitution of the Colony.

"52. In Crown Colonies the allowance or disallowance of any Law
is generally signified by despatch.

noted is that the Crown, or, in other words, the English
Ministry, which represents the House of Commons, has, as

"53. In some cases a period is limited, after the expiration of which
Local Enactments, though not actually disallowed, cease to have the
authority of Law in the Colony, unless before the lapse of that time
Her Majesty's confirmation of them shall have been signified there;
but the general rule is otherwise.

"54. In Colonies possessing Representative Assemblies, Laws purport to be made by the Queen or by the Governor on Her Majesty's
behalf or sometimes by the Governor alone, omitting any express
reference to Her Majesty, with the advice and consent of the Council
and Assembly. They are almost invariably designated as Acts. In
Colonies not having such Assemblies, Laws are designated as Ordin-
ances, and purport to be made by the Governor with the advice and
consent of the Legislative Council (or in British Guiana of the Court
of Policy).

"55. In West Indian Islands or African Settlements which form part
of any general Government, every Bill or Draft Ordinance must be
submitted to the Governor-in-Chief before it receives the assent of the
Lieutenant-Governor or Administrator. If the Governor-in-Chief shall
consider any amendment indispensable, he may either require that
amendment to be made before the Law is brought into operation, or he
may authorize the officer administering to assent to the Bill or Draft
on the express engagement of the Legislature to give effect to the
Governor-in-Chief's recommendation by a supplementary Enactment."

The effect of these Regulations may be best understood by taking the
following supposed case as an example of their operation.

The Houses of the Victorian Parliament pass a Bill legalising the
marriage of a widower with his deceased wife's sister.

i. The Governor refuses his assent. The Bill is lost and never
becomes law.

ii. The Governor assents to the Bill on the 1st of January. It
thereupon becomes an Act, and law in Victoria.

iii. The Crown disallows the Act on the 1st of April. The disallowance is published in Victoria on the 1st of May. From the
1st of May the Act ceases to be law in any part of the British Do-

far as law goes, complete power of controlling the legislation even of colonies like Victoria. This power is both positive and negative. If the Victorian Parliament fails to pass some enactment necessary, in the opinion of the British Parliament, for the safety of the Empire, then the Parliament at Westminster can pass an Act for Victoria supplying the needful provisions. If on the other hand the Victorian Legislature passes a bill, (*e.g.* expelling Chinese from the Colony,) which the Home Government representing the British Parliament deems opposed to Imperial interests, then the Government can either direct the Governor to refuse his assent to the law, or cause the Crown to disallow it, and thus in any case make it void. When we add to all this that there are many occasions, to which we can here only allude, when a Colonial Governor can, and does, act so as to hinder courses of action which conflict with English interests or policy, it becomes clear enough that, as far as

---

minions, but marriages made under it between the 1st of January and the 1st of May are valid.

iv. The Crown allows the Bill. It thereupon becomes an Act which continues in force in Victoria until it be repealed either by the British Parliament or by the Victorian Parliament.

v. The Bill contains a clause that it shall not come into force unless and until allowed by the Crown within two years of its passing. It is not so allowed, it never comes into force, or in other words never becomes law.

The point to be noted is that the Crown, or in reality the Colonial Office, has and often exercises the power of placing a veto upon any Colonial law whatever.

constitutional arrangements can secure the reality of sovereignty, the Imperial Parliament maintains its supremacy throughout the length and breadth of the British Empire. It is of course prefectly true that Parliament having once given representative institutions to a colony, does not dream of habitually overriding or thwarting Colonial legislation. But it were a gross error to suppose that Colonial recognition of British sovereignty is a mere form. It is in the main cheerfully acquiesced in by the people of Victoria, because they gain considerable prestige and no small material advantage from forming part of the Empire. They have no traditional hostility to the mother country; they have every reason to deprecate separation, and—a matter of equal consequence—they believe that, if they wished for independence, it would not be refused them. England stands, in short, as regards Victoria, in a position of singular advantage. She could suppress local riot, or cause it to be suppressed, and she would not try to oppose a national demand for separation. Hence a complicated political arrangement is kept in tolerable working order by a series of understandings and of mutual concessions. If either England or Victoria were not willing to give and take, the connection between England and the Colony could not last a month. The policy, in short, of Colonial independence is, like most of our constitutional arrangements, based on the assumption that the parties to it will act towards one another in a spirit of compromise and good-will, and, though

at the present moment the pride of England in her
Colonial empire, and the appreciation on the part of our
colonies of the benefits, moral and material, of the supremacy of Great Britain, keep our scheme of Colonial
government in working order, it is well to realize, that
this system is not so invariably successful as might be inferred from the optimism which naturally colours official
utterances. The names of Sir Charles Darling and of Sir
George Bowen recall transactions which show, that a
community as loyal as Victoria may adopt a course of
policy which meets with the disapproval of English
statesmen. The recent and deliberate refusal of the
citizens of Melbourne to endure the landing on their
shores of informers whose evidence had procured the
punishment of an outrageous crime, combined with the
fact that the populace of Melbourne were abetted in a
gross, indubitable, patent breach of law by Colonial
Ministers, who were after all, technically speaking,
servants of the Crown, raises serious reflections, and
suggests that, even under favourable circumstances,
Colonial independence is hardly consistent with that
enforcement throughout the Crown's dominions of due
respect for law which is the main justification for the
existence of the British Empire.* A student, moreover,
who turns his eyes towards dependencies less favourably
situated than Victoria, soon perceives how great may, at

* Compare ' Victorian Parliamentary Paper,' 1883, 2 S., No. 22, and
the *Times* of September 27, October 2, 5, 10, 12, 15 and 18, 1883.

any moment, become the difficulty of working an artificial and complicated system of double sovereignty. In Jamaica the hostility of the Whites and Blacks led to riot on the part of the Blacks, followed by lawless suppression of riot on the part of the Governor, who represented the feelings of the Whites, and the restoration of peace and order ultimately entailed the abolition of representative government. At the Cape the pressure of war at once exposed the weak part of the constitutional machine. The pretensions of the Cape Ministry to snatch from the hands of the Governor the control of the armed forces met with successful resistance; but the question then raised as to the proper relation between the Colonial Ministry and the army, though for a time evaded, is certain sooner or later to re-appear, and will not always admit of an easy or peaceable answer.*

Any reader interested in my argument should supplement this brief statement of the relation actually existing between England and her self-governing colonies by a perusal of Mr. Todd's most instructive 'Parliamentary Government in the British Colonies.' But the statement, brief and colourless though it be, is sufficient for its purpose; it shows that the proposal to give to Ireland the institutions of a colony is open to two fatal objections.

1st.—The concession to Ireland of Colonial independence would entail upon England probable peril and certain disgrace.

* See Todd, 'Parliamentary Government in the Colonies,' p. 283.

The peril is obvious. An Irish Cabinet armed with the authority possessed by a Victorian Ministry would forthwith provide for the self-defence of Ireland, and an Irish army, obeying an Irish Executive and commanded by Irish officers, would be none the less formidable because it might in name be identified with an armed police, or, like the troops raised at the Cape or in Victoria, enjoy the ominous title of Volunteers. If the Colonial precedent were strictly carried out, British troops ought, from the time Ireland obtained an independent Parliament, to be withdrawn from the country. The acknowledged danger of foreign invasion, and the unavowed probability of Irish insurrection, would make the retirement of the English army impossible. But the presence of British forces—and forces, be it remarked, intended in reality as a check on the action of the local Government—would of itself place Ireland in a position utterly unlike the situation of Victoria, and would also involve both the Imperial and the local Government in endless difficulties and controversies. If any one doubts this, let him read the correspondence between Mr. Molteno * and Sir Bartle Frere, and substitute for the Premier of the Cape Colony the name of Mr. Parnell, and for Sir Bartle Frere the name of any Lord-Lieutenant who might be unfortunate enough to hold office in Ireland after Mr. Parnell became Premier of an Irish Cabinet. Suppose, however, that by some miracle of management or good luck the Irish and English forces

* Todd, p. 283.

P

acted well together, and that the satisfaction given by a state of things approaching to independence prevented for the moment all attempts at separation, England might escape peril, but she would assuredly not avoid deserved disgrace. An Irish Parliament, returned in the main by the very men who support the National League, would assuredly pass laws which every man in England, and many men throughout Ireland, would hold to be unjust, and which, whether in themselves unjust or not, would certainly set aside Imperial legislation, which England is bound by every consideration of honour and justice to uphold. There is no need to demonstrate here what has been demonstrated by one writer after another, and, indeed, hardly needs proof, that at the present day an Irish Parliament would certainly deprive Irish landlords, and possibly deprive Irish Protestants, of rights which the Imperial Parliament would never take away, and which the Imperial Government is absolutely bound to protect.* If the English Government were to be base enough to acquiesce in legislation which the Imperial Parliament would never itself have countenanced, then England would be dishonoured ; if Bill after Bill passed by the Irish Legislature were prevented from becoming law by veto after veto, then English honour might be saved, but the self-government of Ireland would be at an end, nor would England gain much in credit. The English Ministry can, as long as the connection with a colony endures, arrest

* See, *e.g.*, a letter by Mr. Lecky in the *Times* of January 13, 1886.

Colonial legislation. But the Home Government cannot for any effective purpose interfere with the administrative action of a Colonial Executive. Given courts, an army, and a police controlled by the leaders of the Land League, and it is easy to see how rents might be abolished and landlords driven into exile without the passing by the Irish Parliament of a single Act which a Colonial Secretary could reasonably veto, or which even an English court could hold void under the provisions of the Colonial Laws Act. It is indeed probable that wild legislation at Dublin might provoke armed resistance in Ulster. But a movement which, were Ireland an independent nation, might ensure just government for all classes of Irishmen would, if Ireland were a colony, only add a new element of confusion to an already intolerable state of affairs. Imagine for a moment what would have been the position of England if Englishmen had been convinced that Riel, though technically a rebel, was in reality a patriot, resisting the intolerable oppression of the Dominion Parliament, and you may form some slight idea of the feeling of shame and disgrace with which Englishmen would see British soldiers employed to suppress the revolt of Ulster against a Government which, without English aid, would find it difficult to resist or punish the insurgents. The most painful and least creditable feature in the history of the United States is the apathy with which, for thirty years, the Northern States tolerated Southern lawlessness, and even now indirectly support Southern oppression.

2nd.—If Colonial independence would be found, in Ireland, inconsistent with the protection of England's interests and with the discharge of England's duties, it would also fail to produce the one result, which would be an adequate compensation for many probable or certain evils—namely, the extinction of Irish discontent.

It is by no means certain, indeed, that Colonial independence would be accepted, with genuine acquiescence, by any class of Irishmen.   Certainly the demand for Grattan's Parliament lends no countenance to the supposition, that the people of Ireland would accept with satisfaction a political arrangement which is absolutely opposed in its character to the Constitution of 1782.*   . Suppose, however, for the sake of argument, that the Irish leaders and the Irish people accepted the offer of Colonial independence ; we may be well assured that this acceptance would not produce good-will towards England, and this not from the perversity of the Irish nature, of which we hear a great deal too much, but from difficulties in the nature of things, of which we hear a great deal too little.   The restrictions on the authority of the Irish Parliament would, one cannot doubt, be, as safeguards for the authority of the Imperial Government, absolutely illusory.   But they would cause intense irritation.   Irish leaders would wish, and from their own point of view, rightly wish, to carry through a revolutionary policy.   The Imperial Government would attempt, and, from an English point of view,

* See pp. 221, 222, *post.*

rightly attempt, to arrest revolution. Every considerable legislative measure would give ground for negotiation and for understandings—that is, for dissatisfaction and for misunderstandings. There would be disputes about the land laws, disputes about the army, disputes about the police, disputes about the authority of Imperial legislation, disputes about the validity of Irish enactments, disputes about appeals to the Privy Council. To say that all these sources of irritation might embitter the relation between England and Victoria, and that, as they do not habitually do so, one may infer that they will not embitter the relation between England and Ireland, is to argue that institutions nominally the same will work in the same way when applied to totally different circumstances. Victoria is prosperous; Ireland is in distress. Victoria takes pride in the Imperial connection; large bodies of Irishmen detest the British Empire. Victoria has never aspired to be a nation; the best side of Irish discontent consists in enthusiasm for Irish nationality. Above all this, there has never been any lasting feud between England and her Australian dependencies; the main ground in favour of a fundamental change in the constitutional relations of Ireland and England is the necessity of appeasing, at almost any cost, traditional hatred and misunderstanding generated by centuries of misgovernment and misery. If, as many believe, the source of this misery, so far as it can be touched by law at all, is a vicious system of land tenure, it is vain to imagine that the misfortunes of Ireland can be cured by any mere change of constitutional forms. Grant, however, for the sake of argument, that the passion of nationality is the true ground of the demand for Home Rule ; grant, also, in defiance of patent facts, that the autonomy of a dependency satisfies the sensibilities of a nation ; still it is idle to fancy that a system based, like our scheme of Colonial government, on friendly understandings and the habitual practice of compromise, can regulate the relations of two countries which are kept apart, mainly, because they cannot understand one another, and can neither of them admit the necessity of mutual concessions. Moreover, a scheme of nominal subjection combined with real independence has one vital defect; it does not teach the lessons which men and nations derive from dependence on their own unassisted and uncontrolled efforts. No one learns self-control who fancies he is controlled by a master.*

The scheme, in short, of Colonial independence, though less absolutely impracticable than any form of Federalism, has, as a solution of our Irish difficulties, two fatal defects : it gives Ireland a degree of independence more dangerous to England than would be the existence of Ireland as a separate nation; it bestows on Ireland a kind of self-government which presents neither the material advantages derived from the Union, nor the possible, though

---

* See a letter in the *Spectator* of January 2, 1886, on ʻHome Rule or Separation,ʼ by Mr. J. Cotter Morison.

hypothetical, gains which might accrue to her from the self-control and energy supposed to flow from the inspiring sentiment of nationality. Still the Colonial system remains in spite of its immense defects as a scheme of Home Rule for Ireland, out and out the least objectionable of the models which have been proposed to us for our imitation, and this for several reasons. To grant to Ireland, if she be prepared to accept it, the position of Victoria is not to impair the supremacy of Parliament; if we copied faithfully the Victorian polity, every Irish member of Parliament would permanently depart from Westminster, there would be no more need for having at Westminster a representative of Dublin than there is for having at Westminster a representative of Melbourne, the Irish Parliament would depend for its very existence on an Act of the Imperial Parliament, and the British Parliament would be able without consulting any Irish representative to modify, override, or abolish all or any part of the Act constituting the Irish Parliament. In this there would be no breach of faith, for the Constitution would bear on its face that the Act of Parliament on which it depended could be changed by the British Parliament as lawfully as can the Act 18 & 19 Vict. c. 55, which calls into existence the Victorian legislature. The legal authority and the ease with which the British Parliament could suspend or abolish the Irish Constitution would have two good results: the one that Great Britain would have a sanction by which to enforce the adherence of the Irish government to just principles of legislation and of administration; the other that the readiness with which this sanction could be applied would, it is not unlikely, make its application needless. England, again, would not by the concession of Colonial independence dislocate her own Constitution : she would only be extending to Ireland a scheme of government already existing in other parts of the Empire, and would find herself possessed of officials accustomed to make a Colonial Constitution work. Nothing would be changed: there would only be one Colony the more, and the Colonial Office would find no insuperable difficulty in undertaking the government of Ireland in the same sense in which the Office undertakes the government of Victoria. The position, it may be objected, would be a very poor one for Ireland. With this objection I entirely agree: my very contention is that for Ireland, no less than for England, it is best that Ireland shall form part of the United Kingdom. Home Rulers think otherwise: they prefer the local autonomy of Victoria to a share in the United Kingdom. They may probably, however, say that taxation involves representation, and that if Ireland is to take the disadvantages she must also receive the immunities of a colony. Here fair-minded men will hold that the Home Rulers are right. The maxim, indeed, that taxation involves representation, need not deeply impress any one who remembers that throughout the United Kingdom the property of every woman is taxed, and that no woman has a share in Parliamentary representation. But a formula which is not logically defensible may yet be the embodiment of a just claim. If the very hazardous experiment of placing Ireland in the position of Victoria is to be tried, it must be tried fairly and with every circumstance which may increase its chances of success. Ireland on assuming the position of a colony should, like other colonies, be freed from Imperial taxation. England can afford the sacrifice of three or four millions a year, and she would obtain a valuable *quid pro quo* in the increased homogeneity of the British Parliament. Ireland too would gain something. A country impoverished, in part at least through bad government, might think it no hard bargain to gain at once local independence and exemption from a heavy weight of taxation. The absence of anything like a tribute to Great Britain would be an immense advantage, for it would remove one cause of certain discontent, and would for once place England before the Irish people at any rate in the light of a liberal ally. Let me not be misunderstood. I do not recommend Home Rule under any form whatever: what I do assert is that of all its forms the Colonial form is the least injurious to British interests, and that the experiment of placing Ireland in the situation of Victoria cannot be carried out either with fairness nor with any chance of success, unless Englishmen let Ireland, like Victoria, be exempt from Imperial taxation. If any English taxpayer says that the price is too high to pay for the success of an experiment of which I do not myself recommend the trial, I am not concerned to consider whether he is right. My only concern is to insist that the sacrifice of three or four millions per annum is an essential feature of this particular scheme of Home Rule, and that persons who say the sacrifice is too great have only added one more to the many arguments which lead to the conclusion that under no form whatever can Irish Home Rule be accepted by England.

III. *Home Rule as the revival of Grattan's Constitution.*—

Objection to Constitution of 1782, not faults of Irish Parliament.

The cry for Home Rule sometimes takes the form of a demand that Ireland should reacquire the Constitution of 1782. The true answer to this demand is not to be found, where Englishmen often seek for it, in attacks on Grattan's Parliament. That body exhibited some grave defects common to the English Parliament of the day; it had also many faults of its own to answer for; but it displayed with all its demerits, virtues which still cast a halo round its memory in the eyes of Irish patriotism, and serve to redeem many of its admitted faults in the judgment of impartial history. It produced great men. Flood, Grattan, Curran, and Fitzgibbon were none of them faultless statesmen, but they were leaders of whom any people have a right to be proud. Grattan's Parliament, moreover, though it represented a class, represented a class of Irishmen, and we may even say the best class of Irishmen. It was lastly, with all its defects, a Parliament of men who knew Ireland

and belonged to Ireland, and after its lights cared for the country. It was in a true sense a national Parliament. When we consider further that the Parliament was abolished against the wish of the best men in Ireland, that it was abolished by arts which have brought lasting and just discredit on the men who carried through the Act of Union, we can well understand why as calm and as well-informed judges as Mr. Lecky hold to the belief—certainly in nowise in itself unreasonable—that the Treaty of Union was, to say the least, premature, and that England and Ireland would have gained much if, for a generation or two more, the interest and repute of Ireland had been guarded by an Irish Parliament. The argument that the Irish Parliament because it was corrupt, or because it represented a class, was rightly abolished, proves too much. The English Parliament, under Walpole, was at least as open as the Irish Parliament in the time of Grattan, to each of these charges, yet, long before legislation had removed the flagrant anomalies of the unreformed House of Commons, the English Parliament had cast off its worst vices; and few persons will maintain that England would have gained if during the time of Walpole Parliamentary government had been abolished. Be this as it may, vituperation of Grattan's Parliament, is for our present purpose, as irrelevant as it is unjust and injudicious.

The true reason for declining to consider the demand for

the Constitution of 1782 is, that to concede it is in the
strictest sense of the word an impossibility.
Grattan's Constitution not only is dead, but can
look for no resurrection. The social, the political,
the religious, we might almost say the physical conditions
under which Grattan's Parliament existed have vanished,.
never to return. "It cannot be too clearly understood,"
writes Mr. Lecky, "that the real meaning of the separate
Irish Parliament of the eighteenth century was that the
efficient government of the country was placed in the
hands of its Protestant gentry, qualified by the fact that
the English Government possessed a sufficient number of
nomination boroughs to exercise a constant controlling
influence over their proceedings. The existing Grand
Juries and the Synod of the disestablished Church are the
bodies which now represent most faithfully the independent elements in Grattan's Parliament. That Parliament
consisted exclusively of men who were bound to the
English connection by the closest ties of interest and
sentiment [and] who were pre-eminently the representatives.
of property."* We may deplore that such a Parliament
was doomed to destruction when it might possibly have
been saved by reform. But, to any one who has eyes to
see, it is as clear as day that with Protestant ascendancy,.
with the prestige of the Established Church, with the
leading position of Irish landlords, with the submission of
Irish tenants, with the power of control exercised by the

Side note: True ob-
jection,
restoration
impossible.

* *The Times*, May 5, 1886.

English Government, with the necessary dependence of the English Colony upon the connection with England, Grattan's Constitution with all its possibilities or impossibilities has vanished for ever. You can no more restore the Parliament of 1782 in Ireland than you can restore the unreformed Parliament of 1832 in England. In either case to reproduce the form would not renew the spirit of an ancient institution, and the attempted revival of an anomaly would turn out the creation of a monstrosity.

One consideration suggested by the memory of Grattan's Parliament is well worth attention. With the curious laxity of thought about constitutional changes which marks modern British statesmanship, language is often used which implies that to ask for Grattan's Parliament is equivalent to asking for Colonial self-government as in Victoria. No two things are in reality more different. It is no exaggeration to say that the Constitution of 1782 presented, in its principles, the exact antithesis to the modern Constitution of Victoria. Grattan's Constitution rested on the absolute denial of British Parliamentary sovereignty. The keynote of his policy was the Parliamentary independence of Ireland; its aim was to make Ireland an independent nation connected with England only by goodwill, by common interest, and by what has been called the "golden link" of the Crown. The statement, indeed, that between the date of Irish Parliamentary independence and the date of the Union England and Ireland were governed under two Crowns,

is not much better than a piece of rhetorical antiquarianism.* It is, however, undoubtedly true that from
1782 to 1800 the British Parliament had no more right
to legislate for Ireland than at the present day it has to
legislate for New York, and no appeal lay from any
Irish Court to any English tribunal. But if under the
Constitution of 1782 Ireland was in one sense an independent nation, she could not under that Constitution
be called a self-governed country. The Irish Executive
was controlled by George the Third and his English
Ministers, and the passing of the Act of Union was proof,
if evidence were needed, that England possessed potent,
though unavowed, means for controlling the decision of the
Irish Legislature. The Constitution, it may be added, bore
exactly the fruit to be expected from its anomalous
character. It stimulated national feeling; this was its
saving merit. It did not secure supremacy to the will of
the Irish nation; this, as appeared in 1800, was its fatal

---

* Under the political arrangements connecting the two countries, it
was practically impossible that the two crowns could by legal means
be separated without the assent of the British Parliament. George III.
was necessarily a member both of the British and of the Irish Parliaments; and it is inconceivable that as King of Ireland he should have
assented to a bill passed by the Irish Houses of Parliament which was
strenuously opposed by the British Houses of Parliament. The mad-
ness of the King raised a case not provided for by the Constitution, and
the accidental difference of opinion between the British and Irish
Houses of Parliament, as to the Regency, has been treated as possessing more importance than, from a constitutional point of view,
belonged to it.

flaw. Compare with this the Constitution of Victoria. The Victorian Constitution is based on complete acknowledgment of English Parliamentary sovereignty. But the amplest recognition of British authority is balanced by the unrestricted enjoyment of local self-government. Hence Victoria manages her own affairs, but Victorians are not inspired with the sense of constituting a nation.

IV. *Home Rule under the Gladstonian Constitution.** — No legislative proposal submitted to Parliament has ever received harder measure than the Government of Ireland Bill. Its introduction aroused the keenest political battle which during half a century has been fought in England. The Bill therefore became at once the mark of hostile and (what is nearly the same thing) of unfair criticism at the hands of opponents. This was to be expected; it is the necessary result of the system which makes tenure of office depend on success in carrying through or resisting proposed legislation. What did take place but was not

Gladstonian Constitution—its character.

* See Appendix for the Government of Ireland Bill. It is there printed in extenso. The clauses which mainly concern the points discussed in the following pages are printed in italics. Readers who wish to understand my comments on the Gladstonian Constitution, should study the Bill itself. I am anxious to call attention to its words, because I am quite aware that on more than one point the interpretation put by me upon its provisions will be disputed by supporters of Mr. Gladstone's policy. My interpretation is, I believe, sound, but it would be unfair not to give my readers the opportunity of judging for themselves as to its soundness.

to be expected was, that the Government of Ireland Bill
met with harsh criticism at the hands of its friends. The
Opposition wished to prove that the principle of the Bill
was bad, by showing that it led to disastrous and absurd
results. They therefore directed their assaults upon the
details of a measure which they disliked, in reality, not
because of the special provisions which they attacked, but
because of the principle to which these provisions gave
effect. Ministeralists on the other hand were only too
ready to surrender any clause in the Bill as a matter of
detail, provided only they could persuade Parliament to
sanction the principle of the measure, and thereby affirm
the policy of giving Ireland an Irish Executive and an
Irish Parliament. Nor was this course of action dictated
solely by the exigencies of Parliamentary strategy.
Ministerialists saw the flaws in the Bill as plainly as did
the Opposition, and no man (it may be conjectured), from
the Premier who devised, down to the draughtsman who
drew, the Government of Ireland Bill, would have wished
it to become an Act in the form in which it stood on the
7th day of June, 1886. The supporters, moreover, of the
Government emphasized their dislike to the details of the
particular measure, because to attack a detail of the
machinery by which it was proposed to give Ireland Home
Rule countenanced in the critic's own mind the assumption that some mechanism could be invented which
might carry out the principle of creating an Irish
Parliament without violating the conditions on which

alone the idea of any such measure could be entertained by any English statesman. Opponents, in short, of the Government of Ireland Bill attacked its details out of hostility to its principle; its defenders tried to win approval for its principle by conceding or insisting upon the defects of its details.* The result was unfortunate. The Bill was never either by its opponents or its friends regarded in the light in which it ought to be viewed by a constitutional lawyer. It was never criticised as a whole; it never therefore received full justice. Whoever examines the now celebrated Bill in the spirit of a jurist will see that it constitutes, in spite of many obvious blots both in its special provisions and in its language, a most ingenious attempt to solve the problem of giving to Ireland a legislature which shall be at once practically independent,

* Criticism of particular provisions was made the easier by the fact that hesitations of statesmanship betrayed themselves throughout the Bill in blunders of draughtsmanship. The very heading of the Bill is a misdescription, and involves confusion of ideas. The expressions "status of the Crown," "Executive Government," "Imperial Parliament," are from a legal point of view open to severe criticism; and the substitution of the name "Irish legislature" or "Legislature of Ireland" for the plain intelligible term Irish Parliament, involves something like political cowardice. For errors of this kind, though in one sense errors of draughtsmanship, official draughtsmen are, it must in fairness be remembered, no more responsible than is an amanuensis for the erasures and blots which mar a letter written or re-written to suit the contradictory views of a writer who does not quite know his own meaning and is not anxious to put his meaning into plain words. (See for some excellent criticisms on the Government of Ireland Bill two letters in the *St. James's Gazette* of 20th and 22nd April, 1886, signed H.)

Q

and theoretically dependent, upon the Parliament of
Great Britain; which shall have full power to make laws
and appoint an Executive for Ireland, and yet shall not use
that power in a way opposed to English interests or sense
of justice. The problem (it may be said) admits of no
solution. This may be so, and is indeed my own conviction. But this conviction ought not to prevent the
acknowledgment that the Bill is the rough outline of
an ingeniously attempted solution. If the Bill fails in
achieving its object, the failure arises not from mistakes of
detail, but from the unsoundness of the principle on which
the Bill rests, and shows that the conditions on which
Englishmen can wisely give Home Rule to Ireland are
conditions which no scheme of Home Rule can satisfy.
The idea which lies at the basis of the plan sketched out
in the Government of Ireland Bill is the combination of
the Federal system and the Colonial system of Home
Rule. The right mode of criticising this combination is
first to trace in the barest outline the leading features of
the Bill, treating it much as if it had become an Act, and
had given to Ireland an actual Constitution; and next to
examine how far this Constitution, which may with no
unfairness be called the "Gladstonian Constitution,"
satisfies the conditions which a scheme of Home Rule is
bound to fulfil.

The Gladstonian Constitution establishes a new form of
government in Ireland; it also modifies, or, to use plain
and accurate language, repeals the main provisions of the

Act of Union, and thus introduces a fundamental change into the existing Constitution of England.*

* My statement that the Government of Ireland Bill repeals the main provisions of the Act of Union is made, not because I anticipate that the Bill if passed would lead to a repeal of the Union, but because it is my opinion that the Bill if passed would, as a matter of law, repeal the provisions of that Act, under which the United Kingdom is represented in one and the same Parliament to be styled the Parliament of Great Britain and Ireland. The effect of the Bill would be in very general terms that Ireland would be represented in a Parliament which contained no English or Scotch representatives, and Great Britain would be represented in a Parliament which contained no Irish representatives. Occasionally and for one definite purpose, and no other, namely for the purpose of modifying the terms of the Gladstonian Constitution, a Parliament might be convened which contained representatives from England, Scotland, and Ireland. By what name any one of these assemblies might be called is a matter of indifference; but that, either the British Parliament which contained no Irish representatives, or the Irish Parliament which contained no English or Scotch representatives, or the exceptional and only occasionally convoked body whose one function is to modify a single Act of Parliament, could be considered by any lawyer the "one and the same Parliament" in which the United Kingdom is now represented, is in my judgment all but incredible. If, however, the term " repeal" causes offence or misunderstanding, let us substitute the word " modify," which, however, I believe to be less accurate. The lay reader ought to be reminded that " Statutes may be repealed either by express words contained in later Acts of Parliament, or by implication," and that " a repeal by implication is effected when the provisions of a later enactment are so inconsistent with, or repugnant to, the provisions of an earlier enactment that the two cannot stand together" (Wilberforce, 'Statute Law,' p. 310). My contention is that the Government of Ireland Bill would on becoming law be so inconsistent with portions of 39 & 40 Geo. III. cap. 67, as to amount to a repeal thereof. (For a statement of an opposite opinion, see Mr. Gladstone's pamphlet on the Irish Question, pp. 38, 39.) My opinion that the Government of Ireland Bill repeals

Q 2

The following are for our present purpose its principal features.

As regards the government of Ireland—

The Executive Government of Ireland is vested in the Queen, but is carried on by the Lord-Lieutenant and a Council.* Though the formation and powers of the Executive are under the Constitution left very much at large, we may fairly assume that the authors of the Constitution intend that the Lord-Lieutenant should occupy the position in substance of a Colonial Governor, and rule Ireland through a ministry nominally appointed by the Lord-Lieutenant, but in reality selected by the Irish legislative body. In this matter the Irish Constitution is, like that of Victoria, a copy of the English original.

Its features as regards government of Ireland.

There is created—and this, of course, is the vital provision of the Constitution — an Irish legislature, which I shall take leave hereafter to call by its proper name, the "Irish Parliament," consisting of the Queen and an Irish legislative body, (which we may call a House of Parliament or a Chamber,) made up itself of two orders.†

The Irish Parliament, subject to certain restrictions, has authority to make or repeal any laws for the peace, order, and good government of Ireland; it is in fact in the

---

the Act of Union is now, I am happy to think, supported by the high authority of Lord Selborne. See Lord Selborne's speech at the Conference of Unionist Liberals, reported in *the Times*, 8th Dec., 1886.

* The Government of Ireland Bill, clause 7.

† See the Government of Ireland Bill, clauses 1, 9.

strictest sense what I have termed it, an Irish Parliament. It is the body which indirectly appoints and controls the Executive, and directly legislates for Ireland. It can repeal laws which have been passed by the existing Parliament of the United Kingdom in so far as they are in force in Ireland.

The powers of the Irish Parliament are, it should be noted, indefinite. The Irish Parliament, that is to say, may pass any law which it is not, under the Constitution, forbidden to pass. In this respect it stands not in the position of the American Congress, which can legislate only on certain topics, which are expressly placed within the competence of Congress, but in a position like that occupied by the Parliament of the Canadian Dominion, which can legislate on all topics not expressly excepted from its competence. The difference between a legislature of definite and a legislature of indefinite powers is important. In the one case changes of circumstances may diminish but cannot increase the authority of the legislature; in the other case changes of circumstances may increase but cannot diminish that authority. The Irish Parliament is a body whose authority will, from the necessity of things, tend constantly to increase.

If the authority given to the Irish Parliament is indefinite, it is not unlimited. A large number of exceptions and restrictions are imposed upon its freedom of action. It is hard to name any clear principle on which they rest. Their object undoubtedly is to guard against legis-

lation on subjects such as the armed forces, the coinage,
and the like, which are of Imperial rather than of local
concern. But we can hardly say that the line between
the things which the Irish Parliament can do, and the
things which it cannot do, exactly coincides with the line
which divides Imperial from local legislation. The Irish
Parliament might lawfully pass laws opposed to the whole
tenour of British legislation, such, for instance, as an Act
preventing particular classes of foreigners, or even of
Englishmen, from settling in Ireland. The Irish Parliament could not, on the other hand, pass any law for the
establishment or the endowment of religion. Hence
Ireland could not, in imitation of England and Scotland,
provide herself with an established Church, nor could she
again pass any law relating to volunteers. She could not
therefore take steps for the defence of the country, which
are permissible to Victoria or Canada.

The observance of these limitations on the Parliament's
power of legislation is enforced by a twofold method: first,
by the veto of the Lord-Lieutenant;* secondly, by the
special authority given to the Judicial Committee of the
English Privy Council.†

The Lord-Lieutenant can, after the manner of a Colonial
Governor, refuse the Royal assent to any bill passed by
the Irish House of Parliament.‡ It would rather appear
(though this is by no means certain) that a Bill passed by

* See the Government of Ireland Bill, clause 7.
† *Ibid.*, clause 25.   ‡ *Ibid.*, clause 7.

the Irish Parliament might, even though the Lord-Lieutenant assented thereto, be like the Bill of a Colonial legislature, disallowed by the Crown, or in effect by the English Ministry.*

The Judicial Committee of the English Privy Council, with the addition of certain members, who must be, or have been, Irish Judges, exercises under the Gladstonian Constitution a very peculiar authority in respect of Irish legislation. It becomes both an administrative and a judicial body.

As an administrative body it can give a decision as to the constitutional validity † of any Bill brought before or Act passed by, the Irish Parliament. In its judicial character it is a court of final appeal, with exclusive power to pronounce a decision upon the validity of an Act of the Irish Parliament whenever the validity thereof comes in question in the course of an action. ‡ The decisions of the Privy Council are final; their twofold character as opinions and judgments deserves special attention. The result is that the Judicial Committee of the English Privy Council can always in one way or another pronounce void the proposed or actual legislation of the Irish Parliament if in the judgment of the Privy Council such legislation is unconstitutional.

* As to the disallowance of Colonial bills, see pp. 202–5, *ante.*

† It therefore is intended to exercise an authority different in kind from the power possessed by the Supreme Court of the United States.

‡ See the Government of Ireland Bill, clause 25, sub-clause (*a*), (*b*) and (*c*).

Ireland in return for the advantages gained by her under the Gladstonian Constitution gives up the representation which she now has in each of the two Houses of the Parliament of the United Kingdom. No Irish representative, either Peer or Commoner, sits under that Constitution at Westminster.* The present Parliament of the United Kingdom under whatever name it be described, and whatever be its powers, becomes therefore on the withdrawal of the Irish representatives a British Parliament, and is hereinafter termed by me, for the sake of distinction, the British Parliament. Ireland also contributes annually to the Consolidated Fund of the United Kingdom a sum of over four millions. The Irish customs and excise are made the security for the payment of this contribution; they are, if I understand the Government of Ireland Bill rightly, to be collected by British officials and paid into the British Treasury, but the details of the financial arrangements intended to exist under the Gladstonian Constitution are not within the scope of this work.

The Irish Parliament has no power to modify or alter the provisions of the Constitution under which it exists,† except in one or two cases provided for by the Constitution

* Government of Ireland Bill, clause 24.
† Government of Ireland Bill, clauses 37, 39. On the whole question as to the mode in which the Gladstonian Constitution, or in other words the Government of Ireland Bill, is intended to be altered, readers are specially referred to the terms of the Bill itself. The whole matter is involved in so much controversy that one can hardly make any statement about it which an opponent will not question. The parts of the Bill to be studied are clauses 37 and 39.

itself. The Constitution is alterable in a particular manner therein pointed out, namely by the co-operation of the British Parliament and the Irish Parliament. If we omit certain complications of detail, this co-operation takes place by the Irish representatives being summoned back, and thus added to the British Parliament. The body thus constituted for the alteration of the Gladstonian Constitution is formed of much the same elements as the existing Parliament of the United Kingdom, and is hereinafter called the Imperial Parliament.*

As regards the Constitution of England—

The Gladstonian Constitution, as it will now be seen, does, (whatever the intention of its authors) as a matter of fact seriously affect the Constitution of England, and this in more points than one. *As regards English Constitution.*

First.—The withdrawal of the Irish representation from the Parliament of the United Kingdom constitutes in effect a new body, which in its composition is different from the present Parliament of the United Kingdom, and which since (allowing for changes introduced by the different Reform Acts which have been passed during the century) it corresponds with the Parliament of Great Britain as it existed before the Union with Ireland, may be rightly described by the name I have applied to it, of the British Parliament. This British Parliament has admittedly authority to legislate on every matter which

---

* See Government of Ireland Bill, clause 39.

comes within the competence neither of the Irish Parliament, nor of the body which I have distinguished as the Imperial Parliament, and which, it will be remembered, consists of the British Parliament with the Irish representatives summoned thereto. Whether the British Parliament has or has not any further powers is a moot question which I purposely leave for the moment untouched. What is admitted on all hands is that a Parliament in which Irish representatives have no voice whatever can legislate on every matter affecting England, Scotland, or the British Empire, and also on the topics specially excluded from the competence of the Irish Parliament unless they belong to the one topic, namely, the alteration of the Gladstonian Constitution, reserved for the Imperial Parliament.

Secondly.—The British Parliament, whatever be its theoretical authority, will cease under the Gladstonian Constitution to pass laws for Ireland, and will not impose any taxation on Ireland in addition to the contribution which Ireland is compelled to pay under the Constitution.

Hence, *Thirdly,*—and as a result of the various features in the Gladstonian Constitution which have been already noted, there exist under it three bodies with different functions which, by whatever name they may be each called, ought to be carefully distinguished. They are—

(i.) The British Parliament at Westminster (containing no Irish members), which legislates for Great Britain, and for the whole of the British Empire, except Ireland, but which does not in general at any rate legislate for Ireland.

(ii.) The Irish Parliament at Dublin (containing no British representatives), which legislates for Ireland, but does not legislate for England, Scotland, or for any other part of the British Empire, and does not have any voice whatever in the general policy of the Empire.

(iii.) The Imperial Parliament also sitting at Westminster, and comprising both the British and the Irish Parliament. This body, which in composition corresponds nearly if not exactly with the existing Parliament of the United Kingdom, comes together only on special occasions and only for a special purpose, namely the revision or alteration of the Gladstonian Constitution.

That the existence of these three bodies, each normally exercising the different functions or powers I have attributed to them, constitutes an unmistakable, and I should myself say a fundamental, change in the existing English Constitution with its one sovereign Parliament of the United Kingdom, hardly in my judgment requires or admits of proof. If the change be denied, I have no course but to leave the decision of the question whether such a change can be fairly ignored to the intelligence of my readers.*

* I am quite aware that the account I have given of the proposed Gladstonian Constitution is likely not to be accepted as correct by some of the supporters of the Government of Ireland Bill. That measure by designating both what I have termed the British Parliament and the Imperial Parliament by the one name Imperial Parliament, conceals in my judgment the extent of the alteration which the Bill contemplates. For the sake of clearness of thought I must request my readers to distinguish carefully four different bodies :—

1. The Parliament of the United Kingdom of Great Britain and

The Gladstonian Constitution, if it worked in the way contemplated by its authors—if everything, that is to say, went exactly as it was wished, and everybody acted exactly in the manner in which constitutionally they ought to act—would provide a complicated but, as I have already said, most ingenious solution of the problem

---

Ireland. This is the actually existing Parliament constituted by the Act of Union with Ireland.

2. The British Parliament; that is, the Parliament of the United Kingdom with the Irish representatives removed from it. This body is called under the Government of Ireland Bill the Imperial Parliament. It is a distinctly different body from the Parliament of the United Kingdom. Whether it does or does not inherit the legal powers of the Parliament of the United Kingdom is a separate question afterwards to be considered. All that I now insist upon is that it is a different body.

3. The Irish Parliament, a body admittedly constituted or to be constituted under the Government of Ireland Bill, and therein called the Irish Legislature.

4. The Imperial Parliament, a body in effect consisting of the British Parliament with the addition of the Irish representatives, or in other words of the British Parliament combined with the Irish Parliament. This body can be convoked, as I have pointed out, only for the special purpose of altering the Gladstonian Constitution. It is termed in the Government of Ireland Bill the Imperial Parliament.

What I am most anxious my readers should note is that the bodies 2 and 4 are each termed in the Bill the Imperial Parliament, and thereby not only confused together, but as far as possible each identified with the existing Parliament of the United Kingdom, with which neither really corresponds.

The British Parliament differs from the Parliament of the United Kingdom certainly in constitution, if not also in authority.

The so-called Imperial Parliament nearly corresponds with the Parliament of the United Kingdom in constitution, but differs from it in function and authority.

before us. The British Parliament would sit at Westminster undisturbed by any Irish obstructives, and
legislate for Great Britain and the whole British
Empire in accordance with the wishes of the people of
England and Scotland. Not only would Irish obstruction
vanish, but what is even better, the necessity of considering Irish questions at all would disappear. English
legislators would not be called upon to pay more attention
to the affairs of Ireland than to the affairs of Canada or of
New Zealand. The Irish Parliament would take the
whole burden of legislation for Ireland off our hands, and
Irishmen if they did not like Irish laws would have
nobody to complain of but Irish legislators. But the
Irish Parliament whilst it saved England from all trouble
would, if the Constitution worked properly, give England
no trouble whatever. If Bills were proposed or Acts
passed at Dublin in violation of the Constitution they
would be pronounced void by the Privy Council, and all
Ireland would at once acquiesce in the final decisions of
that exalted tribunal. If on the other hand the Irish
House of Parliament were to pass enactments which
though not unconstitutional were inexpedient, then foolish
proposals would be nullified by the veto of the Lord-
Lieutenant. The contribution from Ireland would be
duly collected and be paid up to the day, since its
collection would lie in the hands of British officials; and
should any difficulty arise, the collectors would be aided
by the Irish Court of Exchequer, the Judges of which

would be appointed by the English Government, and the
judgments of the Court of Exchequer could, if need were,
be enforced by the British Army. This paper federation,
in short, looks as promising as paper Constitutions generally
do. It appears at first sight to combine the merits of
American Federalism and of Colonial independence. To
see, however, whether the Gladstonian Constitution gives
any real promise of fulfilling the hopes which it seems to
hold out, let us examine how far it really fulfils the
conditions on which alone, as we have already pointed
out, Home Rule can possibly be accepted by the people of
Great Britain.

1st Ques-
tion.—Is
sovereign-
ty of Par-
liament
preserved?

1st Question.—Is the Gladstonian Constitution
consistent with the sovereignty or ultimate legislative supremacy of the British Parliament? *

* In reference to the legal effect of the Government of Ireland Bill on
the sovereignty of Parliament, see on the one side the speeches of Sir
Henry James of 13th May, 1886, ' *The Times* Parliamentary Debates,' p.
468 ; of Mr. Finlay, 21st May, 1886, ' *The Times* Parliamentary Debates,'
p. 614 ; and an article by Sir William Anson on the Government of
Ireland Bill and the Sovereignty of Parliament in the *Law Quarterly
Review* for October, 1886. See on the other side Mr. Gladstone's speeches
in Parliament of 8th April, 1886, ' *The Times* Parliamentary Debates,'
p. 125 ; of 13th April, 1886, *ibid.* 255 ; of 10th May, 1886, *ibid.* 404 ;
and of 7th June, 1886, *ibid.* p. 861 ; of Mr. Parnell of 7th June, *ibid.*
p. 847 ; and ' The Government of Ireland Bill,' being a speech delivered
by Mr. James Bryce, M.P., on 17th May, 1886, and published as a
pamphlet. My disagreement with Mr. Bryce's conclusions makes me
anxious to express my great admiration for his speech, which is by far
the best statement I have read of the view undoubtedly held by Mr.

It is well to make clear to ourselves the precise meaning of this enquiry. It is nothing else than this: Do or do not the provisions of the Gladstonian Constitution either legally or morally impair the right of the British Parliament when sitting at Westminster without having summoned a single representative from Ireland to legislate (*e.g.* pass a Coercion Act) for Ireland, and if need be to repeal of its own authority all or any of the provisions of the Gladstonian Constitution, including the very provision under which it is declared in substance that the Constitution shall not be alterable except by the Imperial Parliament, which consists, as already noted, of the British Parliament and the Irish Parliament? To put the same matter in another shape, the enquiry is whether, under the Gladstonian Constitution, the British Parliament does or does not retain the sovereignty now admittedly possessed by the Parliament of the United Kingdom.*

Let us first consider the matter as a pure question of constitutional law.

Gladstone and his followers, that the Bill did not affect the sovereignty of Parliament. The reader should notice that the question throughout between the late Government and its opponents was as to the effect of the Bill on the sovereignty of what I have called the "British Parliament," *i.e.* the body, by whatever name it be called, which consists of the representatives of England and Scotland only, and does not include representatives of Ireland.

* As to the sovereignty of Parliament, see Dicey, 'Law of the Constitution,' pp. 35-79.

The inquiry then is whether a judge in England
As a ques-
tion of con-
stitutional
law. or Ireland resolved to do his duty would or
would not be bound to treat as invalid
an Act passed by the British Parliament
either inconsistent with or, to put the matter more
strongly, actually repealing of such Parliament's own
authority the provisions of the Gladstonian Constitution,
or in other words of the Government of Ireland Bill,
which would then (as we are assuming the Gladstonian
Constitution to be in existence) have become the Irish
Government Act.

Such a judge would have to consider a question to which
English Courts are now quite unaccustomed as regards
Acts passed by the Parliament of the United Kingdom.
The reason why they are unused to solve the particular
kind of question supposed to arise under the new Irish
Constitution is, that as the Parliament of the United
Kingdom is undoubtedly a sovereign body, the validity of
its enactments is in any British Court beyond dispute.
The reason why the problem might under the Gladstonian
Constitution require an answer is, that the question might
arise whether the British Parliament were or were not a
sovereign body.

Our judge would find the question more difficult to
answer than is readily admitted by English lawyers not
versed in any constitution except their own. He would
have to consider the language and effect of the Irish
Government Act in the light of certain propositions

which are now, and at the supposed passing of that Act must have been, true of the Parliament of the United Kingdom.

These propositions may be thus stated, roughly indeed but with sufficient accuracy for our purpose :—

The Parliament of the United Kingdom is admittedly the sovereign of the whole British Empire.

The Parliament of the United Kingdom because it is a sovereign body can make laws for every part of the British Empire, and can legally make or unmake any law, and establish, alter, or abolish any institution (including in that term the Constitution of the Canadian Dominion or of Victoria) existing within the limits of any country subject to the British Crown.

The Parliament of the United Kingdom just because it is a sovereign body cannot, whilst retaining its position as sovereign of the British Empire, be itself bound by any Act of Parliament whatever.

To recur to an instance which is pre-eminently instructive, Parliament conferred in 1867 upon the Dominion of Canada as large a measure of independence as is compatible with a colony's maintaining its position as part of the British Empire. Yet the Parliament of the United Kingdom retains now, as ever, the indisputable legal power to change or abolish the Constitution of the Dominion.

The Parliament of the United Kingdom, just because it is a sovereign body, though it cannot remain a sovereign and place a legal limit on its own powers, can, like any other sovereign, *e.g.* the Czar of Russia, abdicate its sovereignty in

R

reference to the whole, or it may be to part of the Crown's
dominions; and the Parliament of theUnited Kingdom can,
just because it is a sovereign body, do what is at bottom the
same thing as abdicate, namely, merge its own powers in
those of another sovereign body, or, in other words, form, or
aid in forming, a new sovereign for the British Empire.

This proposition has during the Home Rule controversy
been occasionally, in words at least, disputed or questioned
by the supporters of Mr. Gladstone's policy, and language
has been used which seems to imply that a sovereign
power such as the Parliament of the United Kingdom can
never by its own act divest itself of sovereignty. I can
hardly think that the able controversialists who seem to
maintain this doctrine really meant to contend for more
than the admitted principle that a sovereign cannot while
remaining a sovereign limit his sovereign powers. If,
however, it be seriously suggested that the Parliament of
the United Kingdom cannot divest itself of sovereignty,
the suggestion is as a matter of argument untenable, and
this for more than one reason.

An autocrat, such as the Russian Czar, can undoubtedly
abdicate; but sovereignty, whether it be the sovereignty
of the Czar or of Parliament, is always one and the same
quality. If the Czar can abdicate, so can Parliament.
The Czar again could, instead of abdicating in the ordinary
sense of the term, constitute a new sovereign body for the
government of Russia, of which he might himself be a
part. Thus he may undoubtedly give Russia a constitu-

tion like that of England, under which the Czar and
two Houses of Parliament might together become the
sovereign of the Russian State, and no constitutionalist
would dream of maintaining that the new power thus
constituted was the less supreme owing to the fact that
one of its members, namely the Czar, had at one time
been himself the real sovereign of Russia. Here again
what is true of the Czar is true of Parliament. The Parliament of the United Kingdom certainly might become
a part of another sovereign body, or might join in
constituting a sovereign power supreme throughout the
British Empire of which Parliament itself did not form a
part. There is nothing in the theory of sovereignty to
prevent the Parliament of the United Kingdom from
forming a constitution for the whole British Empire under
which the Parliament of the United Kingdom, the Victorian
Parliament, the Parliament of the Canadian Dominion and
so forth should become simply State Parliaments, whilst
the whole British Empire was ruled by some Imperial
Congress sitting, say, either in London or in Victoria. Nor
need we in this matter have recourse to theory. The
present Parliament of the United Kingdom is itself a
monument of the historical fact that sovereign Parliaments
can divest themselves of sovereignty. For the Parliament of the United Kingdom is itself the result of the
abdication of supreme power by sovereign Parliaments.
The Union with Scotland was not, as Englishmen often, I
suspect, fancy, the absorption of the Parliament of Scot-

land in the Parliament of England. The transaction bears, when carefully looked at, a quite different character. Up to the year 1707 there existed an English Parliament sovereign in England, and there existed a Scotch Parliament sovereign in Scotland. These two sovereign bodies in negotiating the Treaty of Union acted with scrupulous, and on the Scotch side with punctilious, independence. Neither sovereign body would consent to be absorbed in the other. What they did agree to was to constitute a new State, namely, the United Kingdom of Great Britain, and each to surrender their separate sovereignty in favour of a new sovereign, namely, the sovereign Parliament of the United Kingdom. The English Parliament no more became supreme in Scotland than the Scotch Parliament became supreme in England. The old Parliament of each country abdicated and lost its identity in the New Parliament of Great Britain. In theory the Treaty of Union between Great Britain and Ireland bore exactly the same character as the Treaty of Union between England and Scotland. But on this point I do not care strongly to insist, because at the present moment every part of Irish history excites controversy. When, however, the excitement of the day has passed by, no one will dispute that 22 Geo. III. c. 53 and 23 Geo. III. c. 28 constituted the renunciation by the British Parliament of sovereignty over Ireland. The difference between the limitation of sovereignty and the surrender of sovereignty has been pressed far enough for my present purpose; no principle of jurisprudence is more certain than that sovereignty implies the power of abdication, and no fact of history is more certain than that a sovereign Parliament has more than once abdicated or shared its powers. To argue or imply that because sovereignty is not limitable (which is true), it cannot be surrendered (which is palpably untrue) is to confuse together two distinct ideas, and is like arguing that because no man can while he lives give up, do what he will, his freedom of volition, therefore no man can commit suicide.

The Parliament of the United Kingdom, further, whilst because it is a sovereign body it cannot impose any legal limit to the exercise of its own power, may so express an intention to use or not to use its power in a particular way as to excite expectations which it will be extremely difficult or hazardous to disappoint, and so may find itself morally fettered as to its subsequent legislative action.

A notorious instance, taken from our constitutional history, illustrates this proposition. The statute 18 Geo. III. c. 12 declares in substance that Parliament will not impose any tax on any colony in North America or in the West Indies. The history of the statute is told by its date—1778. Now no constitutional lawyer will contend that the Parliament of the United Kingdom is legally bound by this Act. If Parliament were to impose an income tax on Jamaica to-morrow the impost would be legal, and could, no doubt, be enforced. But the Declaratory Act of 1778 makes it morally impossible for Parliament to tax any colony. That the impossibility does not arise from a law is clear, because it applies with as much strength to colonies which do not fall as to colonies which do fall within the terms of 18 Geo. III. c. 12. Victoria is not a colony in North America or in the West Indies, but Victoria is at least as well protected from Imperial taxation as is Barbadoes. The so-called Act establishes not a rule of law, but a precept of constitutional morality. It does not theoretically limit, but it practically impedes and interferes with the legislative sovereignty of Parliament.

Our judge with these propositions fully before his mind would scan the terms of the Gladstonian Constitution, or in other words of the Irish Government Act. He would certainly come to the conclusion that the point for his decision was one of great nicety. Against the validity of any Act passed by the British Parliament in contravention of the provisions of the Constitution could be adduced the precise and formal enactment, passed, be it noted, by the undoubtedly sovereign Parliament of the United Kingdom, that the Constitution should be alterable in one way, and in one way only ; * and if it were said that the body which passed this enactment could also repeal it, then the judge might consider that the body in question, namely the Parliament of the United Kingdom, had in effect ceased to exist, and that the successor (if any) to its sovereign powers was not the British Parliament, but the Imperial Parliament, the body which, under any view, had legal

* Government of Ireland Bill, clause 39.

authority to alter the Constitution. No doubt there would be a great deal to be urged on the other side. The attention of the judge would be called to the singular and ambiguous use throughout the Constitution of the term Imperial Parliament, which it might be argued was meant to show that what I have called the British Parliament was to be identified with the Parliament of the United Kingdom. Reference would also be made to the ambiguous saving of powers contained in the 37th section of the Irish Government Act. The high and all-important enquiry as to the authority of the British Parliament sitting at Westminster would come to turn upon the studied ambiguities of one ill-drawn section of an Act of Parliament. There the legal question of the sovereignty of the British Parliament under the Gladstonian Constitution may well be left. It is not within the scope of this work to deal with the draughtsmanship of the Government of Ireland Bill. It is easy to anticipate what would be the practical result of that Bill's ambiguities if it passed into an Act. Irish judges would honestly take one view, English judges would as honestly take another. The Courts of Ireland would maintain that the Constitution could be altered only in the method provided by the Constitution, namely, by the Imperial Parliament. The English Courts would maintain that the Constitution could also be altered by the British Parliament, which was itself the Parliament of the United Kingdom, and possessed the sovereignty inherent in the Parliament of the United

Kingdom.   No Court in either country could satisfactorily terminate the dispute.   Force would no doubt settle what law had left undecided, but to interpret a Constitution by power of arms is in reality to substitute revolutionary violence for forensic discussion.*

---

* I do not, of course, for a moment deny that an Act could te so drawn as to give Ireland an Irish Parliament, to remove the Irish members from the Parliament of the United Kingdom, and at the same time to reserve to the residue of the United Parliament, or Rump, the full sovereignty now possessed by the Parliament of the United Kingdom.   What I do insist upon is, that it is open to question whether the Government of Ireland Bill was so drawn as to achieve these results.   Nor is the question unimportant.   The fundamental ambiguity of the Bill obviously arose from the fact that its authors, whilst wishing to promise in appearance to Ireland that the new Irish constitution should not be changed by a body in which Ireland had no representatives, also wished to soothe the apprehensions of England by tacitly reserving to the British Parliament the power of altering or repealing the Irish constitution without recalling the representatives of Ireland. The consequence is that the Bill proclaims in so many words that its provisions shall be altered in one way only, but by implication, as its authors suppose, provides that its provisions may be altered in another and quite different way.   If this is the intended effect of the Bill it ought to have been made patent on its face.   In constitutional matters, as indeed in all the serious concerns of life, ambiguity and uncertainty of expression is the source both of misunderstanding and of danger.

The question of the sovereignty of the British Parliament might, it should be noted, arise in another and more perplexing form, which received, unless I am mistaken, no attention during the debates on the Irish Government Bill.   Admit for the sake of argument that the British Parliament can legislate for Ireland ; is it equally certain that the Imperial Parliament (*i.e.* the British Parliament with the addition of Irish representatives) cannot claim to legislate for England or for the whole British Empire?   No doubt the Gladstonian Constitution proposes that the Imperial Parliament should be convened only for a limited and definite purpose ; but is it certain that the Imperial Parliament, which

Let us next consider the matter before us, not as a question of constitutional law, but as a question of public morality.

The enquiry then is whether under the Gladstonian Constitution the legislative supremacy of the British Parliament is or is not morally and in fact impaired? It is extremely difficult to see how any candid person can answer this question except by the admission that for all practical purposes, and except on possible but very extreme occasions, the right of the British Parliament to legislate for Ireland is morally not only impaired but destroyed. The supporters of the Government of Ireland Bill have admitted again and again that it constitutes what they term a Parliamentary compact; it embodies, in other words, a solemn contract between Great Britain and the people of Ireland that the British Parliament, whatever be its legal power, shall not legislate about Irish affairs without summoning Irish representatives

As question of public morality.

---

would in its constituent parts be in effect the reunited Parliament of the United Kingdom, might not when convened claim to reassume sovereign power? The addition of a hundred Irish members might turn a minority in the British Parliament into a majority in the Imperial Parliament; can we feel sure that the English minority in the British Parliament would resist the temptation to exalt the authority of a body in which they would be supreme? The enquiry sounds to Englishmen a strange one; but the annals of foreign constitutions suggest that an assembly which, though convoked for a particular purpose, is able from any point of view to consider itself sovereign is with difficulty restrained from asserting supreme power. From this side the Gladstonian Constitution might prove a menace to the supremacy of the British Parliament.

to share in its deliberations. This covenant is made for great and valuable consideration, namely, the withdrawal. of the Irish representatives from the Parliament of the United Kingdom, and the consequent acquisition by the British Parliament of power to legislate not only on every British but on every Imperial concern without consulting the wishes of the Irish people. This is in a moral point of view little less than a treaty ; it is an engagement which England could not break, or incur the imputation of breaking, without dishonour. With all this every man of sense and of honour agrees; but if this be so, it is impossible to see how any one can maintain that this Parliamentary compact does not morally impair, as far as Ireland is concerned, the sovereignty or legislative supremacy of the British Parliament. It may be doubted whether the most earnest Gladstonian really and seriously maintains that under the Gladstonian Constitution the British Parliament sitting at Westminster could or ever would legislate for Ireland in contravention at any rate of the patent and apparent meaning of the Constitution. All that is really maintained is that the British Parliament would retain a legal power of doing that which would never be done by it. There is, however, it is suggested, convenience in retaining a nominal sovereignty which is not intended for real use. Convenience there may be, but there is also immense danger. The Irish Parliament we will suppose acts in a way which is most annoying to England, but the Irish Parliament at the same time takes care not to violate a line of the Constitution. The temptation to use our sovereign authority is great, and likely enough may prove irresistible ; yet if we use it every Irishman, and many Englishmen for that matter, will accuse England of bad faith. No doubt a breach of the Constitution by the Irish Parliament might be remedied by the use of the sovereignty reserved to the British Parliament. But it is difficult even then to see the great advantage of this reservation. In any case in which England would be morally justified in setting aside the terms of the high Parliamentary contract, she would be equally justified in suspending the Constitution by the use of force. The employment of power becomes the more not the less odious because it is allied, or seems to be allied, with fraud. The miserable tale of the transactions which carried the Treaty of Union teaches at least one indisputable lesson—the due observance of legal formalities will not induce a people to pardon what they deem to be acts of tyranny, made all the more hateful by their combination with deceit. For the British Parliament to renounce the exercise whilst retaining the name of sovereignty is the very course by which to run a great risk of damaging the character without any certainty of increasing the power of Parliament.

The plain answer then to the enquiry on which we have been engaged is this :—

Under the Gladstonian Constitution, as foreshadowed in the Government of Ireland Bill, the sovereignty of the

British Parliament is legally rendered doubtful, and is morally reduced to nothing.

2nd Question.—Does the Gladstonian Constitution secure justice ?

The justice which the Constitution ought to secure is twofold—justice to Great Britain, and justice to all classes, including minorities, of Irishmen.

Does Constitution secure justice?

The just claims of Great Britain may roughly be summed up under the one claim, that Ireland should contribute her fair share to Imperial expenditure.

The Gladstonian Constitution, nominally at least, makes fair provision that this claim should be satisfied. But any one who looks into the matter with care will find reason to think that as regards the exaction of payments from Ireland, which are already known by the hateful name of " tribute," Great Britain will find herself involved in this dilemma. She must either surrender the tribute, or else surrender all hope of attaining the main object for the sake of which it is proposed to grant Home Rule to Ireland. If the tribute is exacted, we may be sure that it will have to be exacted in the long run by British officials supported by a British army. Laws, we are told, which are otherwise just are hated in Ireland because they bear a foreign aspect, and come before the Irish people in a foreign garb. If this assertion be false, then the whole case for Home Rule falls to the ground. If this assertion possess even partial truth, then it applies with far greater force to tribute than to law. It is almost an absurdity to suppose that people who hate good laws because they may be termed English will not detest a heavy tax which not only may be called, but in reality is, a tribute to England. It is well to remember that a "publican" was a tax-gatherer, and that Roman publicans were far more hated than Roman judges or Roman law. If England gives Ireland semi-independence, and at the same time makes Ireland pay tribute, all the conciliatory effects of Home Rule will be lost. If Home Rule is to have even a bare chance of producing in Ireland the contentment of Victoria, Ireland, the poorest of all civilized countries, must be freed from Imperial taxation, which would not be tolerated by the richest of our colonies. To this conclusion the advocates and the opponents of Home Rule may, I think, both come without grave dissatisfaction. Of all the sacrifices by which Ireland might be benefited, that sacrifice which England should make with the least regret is sacrifice of revenue. If, however, it be assumed, as the supporters of the Government of Ireland Bill must assume, that justice requires the contribution by Ireland of three or four millions annually to Imperial expenditure, then the Gladstonian Constitution, if it provides for the satisfaction of the claims of Great Britain, does so at the cost of keeping alive Irish discontent. Nor is it at all certain that the payment of the tribute could in effect be easily secured. The practical working of the Constitution might well be that Great Britain were impoverished and Ireland were angered.

Justice to individuals and to unpopular minorities is a matter of far greater importance and far more difficult to secure than the regular payment of Ireland's contribution to Imperial expenditure.

The Gladstonian Constitution ought to provide securities against executive and legislative oppression.

To provide however against the possible oppression of classes or individuals by an Irish Ministry and Irish officials is all but an impossibility, though, as every one knows, the grossest oppression may in any country arise from the wrongful action or inaction of the executive power. The assumption, indeed, is constantly made, though its truth is very hard to prove, that if Ireland were self-governed the law of the land would be enforced. In one sense this assumption may perhaps be well founded. A strong government, or, to put matters plainly, a popular despotism when installed in office at Dublin would, it may be suspected, stringently compel obedience to such laws as the Government approved. The Jacobin Club was no friend to anarchy when anarchy meant defiance of the mandates issued by the Club. But the energy of a strong Government in carrying out laws which it approves is a different matter from the zealous maintenance of even-handed justice. An Irish Executive will immediately on coming into existence be called upon to deal with cases which will severely test its sense of justice. Landlords cannot at once be banished from Ireland; landlords, as long as they exist, must, I presume, have some rights. Is there any security under the Gladstonian Constitution, that these rights—rights, be it remembered, of British subjects, which ought to be neither more nor less sacred than the rights of a British subject in London or Calcutta—will be protected by an Executive of Land Leaguers? There is, I answer, none whatever. To distrust the justice of an Irish Government is not, be it remarked, to show any special distrust of Irish nature. The Irish leaders are of necessity revolutionists, and, it must be added, revolutionists of no high character. Revolutionists on accession to power do not lay aside the revolutionary temperament, and this temperament may have every other virtue, but it knows nothing of the virtue of justice. The Gladstonian Constitution withdraws Ireland from the control of the Government of the United Kingdom, which with all its faults must of necessity possess more impartiality than can a Ministry formed out of the leaders of any Irish faction. The Gladstonian Constitution therefore does leave unpopular classes or individuals exposed to considerable risks of injustice at the hands of the Irish Government.

Though it is from the nature of things almost impossible to take effective steps for ensuring that an Irish Executive shall make a right use of its powers, it is an essential feature of the Gladstonian Constitution that the Irish Parliament shall so far at least use its authority justly as to keep within the limits placed upon its competence. Whether these limitations have been wisely drawn, and whether they may not be in some respects too wide and in others too narrow, are inquiries which, though important in themselves, need hardly detain us. The question in comparison with which all matters of detail sink into insignificance is not what are the limitations which the Constitution imposes on the competence of the Irish

Methods for securing just government. Parliament, but what is the efficacy of the means provided by the Constitution for compelling the Irish Parliament to respect these limitations ? This is the one vital inquiry, for upon the answer to it depends the reality of the constitutional provisions for the maintenance of just legislation. These methods are, as already pointed out, twofold.

The first is the veto of the Lord-Lieutenant. Let us

1. Veto of Lord-Lieu-tenant. assume, though the truth of the assumption is not quite clear, that this veto is combined, as in the case of the colonies, with a further power of disallowance on the part of the Crown, or in effect of the British Ministry. The result is that the British Ministry, or, to put the thing plainly, the British House of Commons, can put a check on such Irish legislation as may be opposed to the letter or to the spirit of the Constitution. The check is in one sense real, but it must, as in the case of the colonies, be but rarely employed. Its constant use, or its use on occasions of great importance, would seem to Irishmen, and with good reason, to nullify

the concession of Home Rule. Suppose the Irish Ministry carry a measure for artificially stimulating Irish commerce, and the Crown disallows it on the ground that it violates the provision of the Constitution forbidding the Irish Parliament to make laws relating to trade. The Irish Cabinet thereupon resigns. No other can be formed. It returns to power and reintroduces the obnoxious Bill. What course can the Lord-Lieutenant take? If he uses the veto, he reintroduces in the most awkward form the interference of the British Parliament with Irish legislation. If he does not use the veto, and the Act is not disallowed, then the right of veto comes to little or nothing. We may be quite sure that in general neither the Lord-Lieutenant nor the Crown will refuse assent to Bills approved of by the Irish Parliament. The veto in its different forms will, in short, be but a very slight check on unconstitutional or unjust legislation.

The second method by which it is endeavoured to check unconstitutional legislation is the use of the authority vested in the English Privy Council. *2. Action of Privy Council.* This method is borrowed from Federalism, as the Lord-Lieutenant's veto is borrowed from the Colonial system. The Privy Council, it should be remembered, may nullify the effect of Irish legislation in two ways:—It may as an administrative body give a decision that a Bill or Act is void. It must, however, be hoped and expected that the Privy Council will rarely adopt this mode of exercising its powers, for such exercise would at once give

S

rise to a direct conflict between the Irish Parliament and
the English Privy Council. That body may, however, act
simply as a Court of final appeal, and as a tribunal decide
whether an enactment of the Irish Parliament is or is not
void. This, we may suppose, is the mode in which the
Privy Council will usually put forth its authority. It is
easy, bearing the experience of America and Canada in
mind, to see how the whole arrangement will, in theory at
least, work. *A.* sues *X.* in an Irish Court, *X.* bases his
defence on some Act passed by the Irish Parliament. The
Privy Council pronounce the Act void, as being opposed
to some provision of the Constitution, and give a judgment
in favour of *A.*, under which he has a right to recover
£10,000 against *X.* Here it will be said the whole
matter is settled. The law was unconstitutional; the law
has been treated as void; *A.* has obtained judgment; *A.'s*
rights are secured. This would be all that was required,
but for one consideration. The object of the plaintiff in
an action is to obtain not judgment, but payment or
execution. What are the means by which judgments of
the Privy Council may be put in force where they happen
not to be supported by Irish opinion, and are opposed, it
may be, to the decisions of the Irish Courts? The answer
is simple: the Constitution provides no means whatever.
The Federal tribunals of America possess in every State
officials of their own, and are supported in the main by
American opinion. The Americans are, moreover, to use
their own expression, "a law-abiding people." Yet for

all this the judgment of the Supreme Court may be worth
little if it runs across State sentiment, and if the President
should happen to sympathise with State rights. A
citizen was unlawfully imprisoned in Georgia; he applied
for a habeas corpus. The application ultimately came
before Chief Justice Marshall, and the writ was granted.
The traditional comment of President Jackson is noteworthy: "John Marshall has given his judgment, let
him enforce it if he can." The Executive would not
assist the Court, and the Supreme Court was powerless.
Switzerland, again, has a Federal tribunal: it is a Court,
as would be the Privy Council, which cannot command
officials of its own to execute its process; it depends
for aid on the Cantonal authorities. This state of things,
I am told on good authority, produces its natural result.
The judgments of the Federal tribunal can be rendered
almost ineffective by the opposition of a Canton.

At this moment the statutes of the Imperial Parliament
bind every man throughout the United Kingdom. The
Courts in Ireland are bound to give effect to every
statute, and the Irish Courts are supported by the Sheriff
and his officers, and in the last resort by the power of the
United Kingdom. Yet the difficulty of the day is enforcement of judgments which run against Irish popular
opinion. Is it common sense to imagine that opposition
which defies, often with success, the authority of the Irish
Queen's Bench Division, or ultimately of the House of
Lords, would not easily nullify the judgments of the Privy

s 2

Council when not only unpopular in Ireland, but in contradiction to a law devised by the Irish Executive, passed by the Irish Parliament, supported by the Irish Judges? The truth must be spoken: the Gladstonian Constitution will, as regards the restrictions placed under it on the powers of the Irish Parliament, inevitably turn out a mere paper Constitution. The methods for compelling the observance of these limitations have neither of them any real efficacy. The veto can with difficulty and but rarely be used; the judgments or opinions of the Privy Council may have a speculative interest, but will possess no coercive power.

If this be so the guarantees afforded by the Constitution for just legislation are nugatory; they are worth neither more nor less than the pompous securities for every kind of inalienable right which have adorned the most splendid and the most transitory among the Constitutions which have during a century been in turn created and destroyed in France—that is, they are worth nothing; nor is it unfair to conjecture that on this point my opinion agrees with the opinion of many English Home Rulers. They think the limitations on the independence of the Irish Parliament useless and destined to disappear; for their avowed belief is that legislation by an Irish Parliament will in the main be just, and that the laws of the Irish Parliament, because they represent the wishes of the Irish people, will obtain easy obedience in Ireland. If this conviction be sound—and it is the almost necessary basis for a policy of Home Rule—let us act upon it, and not impose restrictions which, if needless, must certainly be noxious. Meanwhile in any case let us dismiss the delusion that restrictions which cannot be enforced are any guarantee for justice. The Gladstonian Constitution admits on the face of it that guarantees are wanted. Most Englishmen agree in the opinion implied in this admission. But if I am right in asserting that the guarantees for justice are illusory, then the Gladstonian Constitution does not secure justice, and is therefore not just.

3rd Question.—Does the Gladstonian Constitution hold out fair hopes of finality ?

This is an enquiry which may be answered with some confidence.

Does Constitution possess finality ?

To any one who surveys the Constitution, not as a politician, but as a legist, to any one moderately versed in the study of comparative constitutionalism, few statements which savour of prediction will appear more certain than the assertion that the Gladstonian Constitution cannot be a final or even a lasting settlement of the constitutional relations between England and Ireland.

The grounds of this opinion are, briefly, that the proposed Constitution will, while leaving alive elements of discord, cause disappointment and inconvenience to both countries, and that the mechanism of the Constitution, framed as it is upon a combination of Federalism and of Colonialism, has some of the defects of each system, and promises in its working to produce something like the maximum of irritation and friction.

The two grounds for believing that the Gladstonian Constitution bears no promise of finality run into one another, but they admit of separate examination, and each requires explanation or justification.

The Constitution will cause disappointment and incon-

Constitution will cause disappointment to England.

venience both to England and to Ireland.

Englishmen will on the Gladstonian Constitution coming into operation find to their great disappointment that they have not attained the object which from an English point of view was the principal inducement to grant Home Rule to the Irish people, that is, freedom from the difficulty of governing Ireland. The difficulty no doubt will be diminished, or rather shifted; but the dream is vain that under the new Constitution Englishmen would be able to trouble themselves no more about the concerns of Ireland than they do about the affairs of Canada. Ireland would still be our immediate neighbour. Irishmen would still be divided by differences of class and religion, and England would still, disguise the fact as you may, be ultimately responsible for good government in Ireland. Home Rule is not Separation, and nothing short of Irish independence would greatly lessen English responsibility. This would be true under whatever form Home Rule were established, but it is emphatically true of Home Rule under the particular form contemplated by the Gladstonian Constitution. The army in Ireland—and no one supposes that England can withdraw her soldiers from the country—will be the British Army under the control of the British Government. But the power of the sword is, though we often forget the fact, the sanction by which law is maintained. Hence it follows that the British Ministry remains at bottom responsible for the maintenance of peace and order throughout Ireland. Note the results. If there are riots at Belfast; if unpopular officials are assassinated in Dublin; if evictions give rise to murder in Kerry, the British Army must in the last resort be called in to restore peace or punish crime. If the army are not under the control of the Irish Executive, then the English Cabinet become directly responsible for the government of Ireland. If British soldiers are placed at the disposal of the Irish Ministry, still the English Government must, shift the thing as you will, share the responsibility of the Irish Cabinet. During a riot at Belfast a hundred Protestants or Catholics are shot by British soldiers whilst restoring order. If any one fancies that such slaughter can take place without the English Ministry being called upon in the British Parliament for explanation and defence, he shows utter ignorance of English, or indeed of human, nature. Nor is it for the action only of the troops that the English Executive will incur liability. If British subjects are killed by a mob in Belfast or in Dublin whilst British troops stand quietly by and under the direction of an Irish Home Secretary take no steps to prevent murder, we may rest assured that the Queen's Government in England will be asked whether it is decent that the Queen's forces should be trained to stand as indifferent spectators of outrageous breaches of the Queen's peace.

Take again the question of pardoning crime. Suppose that the first Irish Ministry on their accession to power propose to inaugurate the new era by a free pardon of all the political offenders, dynamiters and others, whose misguided zeal has placed them within the grip of the law, but has also in no small measure contributed to achieve the Parliamentary independence of Ireland. If the request is not granted, then the Irish Administration are refused the means of carrying on the government of the country after their own notions of sound polity. If the request is granted, can the English Government be held entirely irresponsible for the mode in which the Crown exercises its prerogative? Let it be settled that the prerogative of mercy must in Ireland be exercised in accordance with the wishes of the Irish Ministry. Even then the English Government will not really escape responsibility. British soldiers put down a riot at Belfast; they are indicted for the murder of a Catholic rioter, before a Catholic grand jury, convicted by a Catholic jury under the direction of a Catholic judge who has just been appointed by the new Irish Ministry. Popular opinion demands the execution of the convicted murderers, the

Irish Ministry advise that the law should take its course. The general belief in England, shared we will suppose by the English Home Office, is that the convicted soldiers are about to be capitally punished for having simply discharged their duty. Is an English Minister to abstain from advising a pardon? The dilemma is difficult. If he recommends a pardon, the Irish Government are prevented by England from governing Ireland. If the soldiers are hanged, the English Ministry will not keep long in office, and the British Army will hardly maintain its habit of absolute obedience to the civil power.

Englishmen, in the next place, will soon discover that the creation of a statutory constitution for Ireland curiously hampers the working of our own institutions. Questions must arise whether Acts of the British Parliament do or do not trench upon the provisions of the Irish Constitution. Few persons are aware of the number of Imperial Acts which touch the Colonies. To such statutes there is no legal or moral objection, because the principle embodied in the Colonial Laws Act, 1865, that enactments passed by the Parliament of the United Kingdom override any Colonial law with which they conflict, is universally admitted; but, as already pointed out, it is questionable as a matter of law whether the statutes of the British Parliament can repeal Acts duly passed by the Irish Parliament, and it is quite beyond question that for the British Parliament to infringe upon the province of the Irish legislature would involve a breach of good faith.

Changes again in the formation of the British Parliament might under the Gladstonian Constitution become difficult. The abolition of the House of Lords would be hard to reconcile with the right of the Irish Peers to be summoned on occasion to the Imperial Parliament. An increase in the number of British representatives in the House of Commons would be objected to by Irishmen because it diminished the relative importance of the members from Ireland when recalled to take part in the deliberations of the Imperial Parliament. The reduction of the number of members of the House of Commons, though one of the most salutary reforms which could be carried out, would be opposed by every person interested in maintaining the present excessive number of the Lower House, on the ground that to reduce the numbers of the House of Commons, to say 400, would involve an increase in the authority of the Irish members whenever they reappeared on the scene. The moot question whether the British Parliament could on an emergency repeal of its own authority the articles of the Irish Constitution, the extent to which Ireland should be represented on the Judicial Committee of the Privy Council, above all, the vital question whether the reassembled Imperial Parliament were not the true representative of the Parliament of the United Kingdom, and the ultimate sovereign power in the State, would in periods of excitement give rise to disputes hitherto quite alien to English politics, and involving elements of unknown danger.

Ambiguity and obscurity, since they help to pass Bills, are in the judgment of Parliamentary draughtsmen and Parliamentary statesmen characteristics which promote the easy working of Acts. Few delusions are more dangerous. Knives which are made to sell are not knives which are made to cut. The founders of the American Union knew their own minds, and were not well acquainted with the advantages to be derived from the obscurities of modern draughtsmanship. But on two points they tried the experiment of keeping real perils out of sight by omitting to refer to them. "Slave" and "slavery" are words not to be found in the Constitution of the United States. What (if any) was the right of a State to retire from the Union, was a matter purposely left open for the interpretation of future generations. The Abolition movement, the Fugitive Slave Law, the War of Secession tell the result of trying to ignore perils or problems which it is not easy to face or to solve.

The last disappointment of Englishmen would be to find that Home Rule had not satisfied Ireland. For to Irishmen no less than to Englishmen the Constitution must bring disappointment and inconvenience. *And to Ireland.*

That the Gladstonian Constitution cannot satisfy Ireland is all but certain.

To say this is not to imply that its acceptance by Irish Home Rulers is dishonest. In their eyes it is a move in the right direction; they exaggerate, as their English allies underrate, the freedom of action which the Constitution offers to Ireland. It cannot, as already pointed out, by any possibility remove the admitted causes of Irish discontent. It cannot tempt capital towards Ireland, but it may easily drive capital away from her shores; it cannot diminish poverty; it cannot in its direct effect assuage religious bigotry; it cannot of itself remove agrarian discontent. The Land Purchase Bill, even when discarded, remains an involuntary exposure of the futility of the Gladstonian Constitution, and of the unsoundness of the principle on which the demand for Home Rule rests. No friend of Italy ever suggested that Italian independence should be accompanied by a loan from Austria to the Italian Kingdom. For the principle of nationality was the true source of Italian disaffection. If in dealing with Ireland we must calm agrarian misery before satisfying national aspirations, this necessity is all but a confession that Irish unrest is due far more to desire for a change in the land laws than to passionate longing for national independence. I do not doubt that the spirit of nationality has some, though probably a small, part in the production of Irish discontent. But the Gladstonian Constitution is unfortunately so devised as to outrage quite as much as it soothes national sentiment. The tribute will affect every Irishman in his pride no less than in his purse. Can any one suppose that Northerners indignant at recent treachery, and Catholics mindful of ancient oppression, will not join, and justly join, in denouncing as at once ignominious and ruinous the payment of a tribute raised for Imperial purposes at the moment when Ireland ceases to have any voice in the direction of Imperial policy ? Irishmen again will find to their surprise that the Constitution intended to give them independence imposes annoying fetters on their freedom of action. They wish for a protective tariff, and they come across the prohibition to make laws affecting trade ; they desire that the country shall defend herself, and they discover that they cannot raise even a body of volunteers ; they wish to try the plan of concurrent endowment, and they are thwarted by the article of the Constitution prohibiting the endowment of religion. These restrictions are the more annoying because none of them are imposed upon the Colonies. Irishmen will further discover that great achievements of constructive legislation require for their success the command of large pecuniary resources, and that exemption from British control involves the withdrawal of all assistance from the British Treasury.

The Constitution will produce irritation and friction.

Every scheme for uniting into a political whole States which are intended to retain, even when connected together, a certain amount of independence, aims at minimising the opportunities for constitutional collision, or for friction between the different States which are connected together, and also between any State and the Central

Constitution will cause friction.

power. If we compare the mode in which this end is attained, either under the Federal system or under the Colonial system, with the arrangements of the Gladstonian Constitution, we shall easily see how little its authors have attended to the necessity for avoiding occasions of constitutional friction.

Where Federalism, as in America, appears in its best form, the skill with which opportunities for collision or friction have been minimised is almost above praise. The Federal or Central power is so constructed as to represent the whole nation; its authority cannot by any misrepresentation be identified with the power of one State more than another. The Federal Government acts through its own officers, is represented by its own judiciary, and levies its own taxes without recourse to State authorities. Every device which could be thought of has been taken to make it unnecessary for the National Government to come into direct collision with any State. It deals in general with the individual citizens of the United States; it does not deal with the particular States. The result is that on the one hand, whatever may be said against the taxes imposed by Congress, they cannot by any stretch of imagination be looked upon as tribute paid by one State to another, say by Massachusetts to New York, or by New York to Massachusetts. It is again unnecessary for the Federal Government to issue commands to a State. There is, therefore, little opportunity for a contest between a State and the National Executive. Whoever wishes to

understand the elaborate devices necessary to make
Federalism work smoothly should compare the clumsiness
of the arrangements by which the Swiss Confederacy has
at times been compelled to enforce obedience of the
Cantons to the will of the Confederation, with the
ingenuity of the methods by which the Federal authorities
of the United States exert their authority over American
citizens.

The English Colonial system on the other hand, though
far less elaborate than any form of Federalism, does, as a
matter of fact, reduce within very narrow limits the
chances of collision between England and her colonies.
The system, however, succeeds, not because it is a model
of constructive art, but because it attempts very little, and
can, owing to favourable circumstances, leave to nominal
dependencies something little short of complete self-
government. Where collisions do arise they are disposed
of by the habit of the Imperial Government always to give
way.

The Gladstonian Constitution is, as we have already
pointed out, a combination between Federalism and
Colonialism; it may possess some of the merits, but it
much more certainly displays some of the demerits of
each system. From Federalism is borrowed the idea of
leaving the settlement of constitutional questions to a
Court. But the conception is spoilt in the borrowing. All
the difficulties which under a Federal system beset the
enforcement of judgments pronounced by a Federal Court

affect in an aggravated form the attempt to enforce
in Ireland judgments which invalidate Irish Acts, and
are pronounced by a Committee of the English Privy
Council sitting in England. The Privy Council, moreover, while it has every weakness of the Supreme
Court of America, has more than one special weakness
of its own. It lacks moral authority, for it is an English Court sitting in England and representing English
opinion; it lacks jurisdiction, because while it can
pronounce on the validity of Irish, it cannot pronounce on
the validity of British Acts of Parliament; it does not
possess a strictly judicial character, because it is not only
a Court called upon to give judgments, but is also an
administrative body called upon to deliver opinions upon
the validity of Irish Bills and of Irish Acts. Hence its
decrees come into direct collision with the proposals or
enactments of the Irish Parliament, and the Privy Council
is made to appear not as a body of judges deciding cases
between man and man, but as a body of officials whose
duty it is to oppose any unconstitutional action on the
part of the Irish Parliament. From Federalism again is
borrowed the contribution by Ireland towards meeting the
expenses of the Empire. But imposts which under a
Federal system are a tax towards the payment of common
expenditure are under the Gladstonian Constitution a
tribute to a foreign power. From the Federal system
further is taken that restriction of legislative authority
which hardly affects Parliaments such as that of Victoria,

and which under any circumstances is a source of irritation. From the Colonial system, on the other hand, is derived the theoretical supremacy of the British Parliament, the right of veto, and the fatal dependence of the Irish Executive on every vote of the Irish legislature. From the colonies we therefore bring to Ireland sources of dispute, of friction, and of irritation, which are unknown to a true system of Federalism, whilst we do not give Ireland that practical independence, and that immunity from taxation, which prevent our ill-arranged connection with the colonies from causing real dissatisfaction. Federalism has its merits and its defects; English Colonialism works well enough; the sham Federalism and the sham Colonialism of the Gladstonian Constitution must create between Great Britain and Ireland all the causes of discontent which have from time to time tried the strength of the American Union, and all the causes of disturbance which from time to time reveal the weakness of the tie which binds together our Colonial Empire.

Among the hypothetical virtues of the Gladstonian Constitution cannot assuredly be numbered the merit of finality.

The Gladstonian Constitution therefore fails entirely to fulfil for any practical purpose the conditions it is [meant to satisfy. It neither maintains the sovereignty of Parliament, nor makes adequate securities for justice, nor offers a prospect of finality.

A criticism of Home Rule in its four forms gives then this result :—

Home Rule as Federalism means the immediate disloca-
Result of criticism. 1. Home Rule as Federalism. tion and the ultimate rebuilding of the whole English Constitution; it involves the transformation of an old and tried polity which by centuries of experience has been admirably adapted to the wants of the English people, and has fostered the growth of the British Empire, into a form of government in itself not free from defects, and successful, where it has succeeded, only under conditions which the United Kingdom does not present.

Home Rule in the form of Colonial independence in-
2. Home Rule as Colonial independence. volves far less change in the institutions of Great Britain or in the complex arrangements of the British Empire than does Federalism. It appears at first sight to be an application to Ireland of institutions which, as they have been found to answer their purpose in such countries as Canada and Victoria, may also prove successful in Ireland. The appearance is delusive. The true reasons why the Colonial system, self-contradictory as it is in theory and unsatisfactory as it sometimes is in practice, has produced harmony between England and her dependencies, are that the colonies are far distant and are prosperous, that they feel pride in their relation to the mother-country, that whilst contributing not a penny towards meeting Imperial burdens they derive valuable and valued benefits from the connection with the Empire, and lastly that they ·

are not in reality dependencies; the colonies willingly acquiesce in the supremacy of England, because England protects them gratis and does not govern them at all. It is not the Colonial system, but the conditions which make that system succeed, which ought to engross our attention. These conditions will not be found in any arrangement whatever between England and Ireland. It is in the strictest sense impossible that Ireland whilst forming part of the United Kingdom, or even of the British Empire, should enjoy or endure the independence of Victoria. If the Act which gives Victoria her constitution were re-enacted with the necessary verbal changes for Ireland, the constitution which satisfies the Victorians would not satisfy the Irish, and for a good reason : the form would be the same, but the effect would be different. A suffering and discontented people will not accept words for facts.

One condition indeed, which more perhaps than any other ensures the success of our Colonial system, Great Britain has in the case of Ireland the power to reproduce. Immunity from Imperial taxation is one source of Colonial loyalty to the Empire. If Ireland is to accept or to receive the mixed independence and subordination of a colony, she ought to enjoy the substantial advantage of a theoretically inferior position. The Colonial system, as I have already insisted, involves the renunciation of Imperial taxation.

Home Rule as the revival of Grattan's Constitution is

an impossibility. The Constitution of 1782 belongs
3. Home Rule as Constitution of 1782. to a past age, and cannot by any miracle of
political art be at the present day restored to
life.

Home Rule under the Gladstonian Constitution means
4. Home Rule as Gladstonian Constitution. an artificial combination of Federalism and
Colonialism. Its aim is to secure the advan-
tages of two opposite systems; its result is to
combine and intensify the disadvantages of both
systems. It inevitably tends towards the dissolution of
the United Kingdom into a Federation; it immediately
disturbs the bases of the Constitution by creating the
artificial bond of something like a Federal legislature
between England and Ireland; it introduces into the
relations between each of the different divisions of the
United Kingdom elements of conflict which are all but inherent in Federalism; it requires that absolute deference for
the judicial decisions of a Federal Court which, if it exist
anywhere, can exist only among a people like the Americans,
imbued with legal notions, and as it were born with
innate respect for law. That this sentiment cannot exist
in Ireland is certain; whether it exist in the required
intensity even in England is problematical. The Gladstonian Constitution, again, because it contains some
institutions borrowed from the Colonial system without
the conditions requisite for their proper working so to
speak falsifies them. The Imperial supremacy of Great

Britain, the Imperial control over the army, the occasional interference with the Irish executive and the veto of the Crown on Irish legislation, are each and all of them under the Gladstonian Constitution certain to be the source of justifiable dissatisfaction. To the ingenuity of the plan proposed by Mr. Gladstone's Ministry hostile critics have given insufficient praise. But the essential unreality which this ingenuity has concealed has not even yet met with due condemnation. Since the day when the National Assembly of France presented the brand-new French Constitution to the acceptance of Louis XVI. no form of government has ever been seriously proposed for adoption by an intelligent people so radically unworkable as that Gladstonian Constitution which has been instinctively rejected by the good sense of the British Parliament. The Constitution of France lasted out two years; to a jurist it may appear conceivable, though hardly probable, that by the vigorous aid of the British Parliament the new Constitution for the United Kingdom might have lasted for as long a period.

CHAPTER VIII.

CONCLUSION.

LET us here review and summarise our argument.

Survey of argument.　The demand for Home Rule is a demand for a change in the Constitution so fundamental as to amount to a legal and pacific revolution; such a demand requires for its support cogent, we may almost say conclusive, reasons.

The positive arguments in favour of Home Rule are not easy to grasp. Their strength lies in their correspondence with the prevailing opinions of the day. But though public opinion under any form of government, and especially under the system of what is called popular government, deserves great consideration, still the value of a prevailing belief or conviction cannot be determined without examining the elements which have gone to its production. The state of opinion which favours Home Rule is found to result from various and even self-contradictory feelings, some of which belong to the highest and some to the lowest parts of human nature; humanity and a sense of justice are in this instance curiously combined

with indolence and impatience. The arguments again for
Home Rule rest upon one dubious assumption and one
undoubted fact. The dubious assumption is that the root
of Irish discontent is the outraged feeling of nationality.
The undoubted fact is that in Ireland, on all matters either
directly or even remotely connected with the tenure of
land, the law of. the Courts is opposed to the customs, to
the moral sentiment, we may say to the law of the people;
hence the Queen's tribunals are weak because they are
not supported by that popular assent whence judges
derive half their authority; the tribunals of the League
are strong because their decisions commend themselves to the traditional feeling of the people. But the
doubtful hypothesis and the undoubted fact, though one
or other of them lies at the basis of all the strongest
arguments in favour of Home Rule, each invalidate almost
as. much as they support the contention that an Irish
Parliament will prove the specific for the diseases (due
in the first instance to the original vice of the connection
between England and Ireland) under which Irish society
now suffers. If the passion of nationality is the cause of
the malady, then the proposed cure is useless, for Home
Rule will not turn the people of Ireland into a nation. If
a vicious system of land tenure is the cause of lawlessness,
then the restoration or re-creation of an Irish Parliament
is needless, for the Parliament of the United Kingdom
can reform and ought to reform, the land system of
Ireland, and ought to be able to carry through a final

settlement of agrarian- disputes with less injustice to individuals than could any Parliament sitting at Dublin.

Reasoning, however, which fails to establish the expediency of creating an Irish Parliament may prove, and in fact does amply prove, that the task of maintaining peace order and freedom in Ireland is at the present juncture a matter of supreme difficulty. Any possible course, moreover, open to English statesmanship involves gigantic inconvenience, not to say tremendous perils. A man involved in the actual conduct of public affairs may easily bring himself to believe that the policy which he recommends is not only the best possible under the circumstances, but is also open to no serious objection. Outsiders, who in this matter are better because more impartial judges than the ablest of politicians, know that this is a delusion. We have nothing before us but a choice of difficulties or of evils. Every course is open to valid criticism.

The maintenance of the Union must necessarily turn out as severe a task as ever taxed a nation's energies, for to maintain the Treaty of Union with any good effect means that while refusing to accede to the wishes of millions of Irishmen, we must sedulously do justice to every fair demand from Ireland, must strenuously and without either fear or favour assert the equal rights of landlords and tenants, of Protestants and Catholics, and must at the same time put down every outrage and reform every abuse.

To carry out by peaceful means the political separation

of countries which for good and for evil have for centuries
been bound together by position and by history, is an
operation so critical that in the judgment of statesmen
it involves dangers too vast for serious contemplation.

How, lastly, to devise a scheme of Home Rule
which, while giving to Ireland as much of legislative
independence as may satisfy her wants or wishes, shall
leave to England as much supremacy as may be necessary
for the prosperity of the United Kingdom, or for the
continued existence of the British Empire, is a problem
which jurists would find it hard to solve as a matter of
speculative science, and which politicians may (not without
reason) hold to admit of no practical solution.

Yet Maintenance of the Union, Separation, Home Rule,
are names which designate the only paths open to us. To
one of these three courses we are absolutely tied down. Each
path is arduous. To complain about the nature of things is
childish. The course of wisdom is obvious. We must all of
us look facts in the face. " Things and actions are what they
are, and the consequences of them will be what they will be.
Why then should we desire to be deceived?"* We must
calmly compare the advantages of the three steep roads
which lie open to the nation, and then on the strength of
this comparison determine the course which the nation is
bound to follow by motives of expediency and of justice.

Such a comparison we have already instituted:† its

* Butler's Sermons; vii., p. 136, ed. 1726.
† See Chapters V., VI., & VII., *ante.*

results to any reader who assents to my train of reasoning must be obvious.

The maintenance of the Union involves at the outset a strenuous and most deplorable conflict with the will of the majority of the Irish people. It necessitates at once the strict enforcement of law, combined with the resolute effort to strip law of all injustice. It may require large pecuniary sacrifices, and it certainly will require a constancy in just purpose which is supposed, and not without reason, to be specially difficult to a democracy. The difficulties on the other hand which meet us are not unprecedented, though some of them have assumed a new form. We have some advantages unknown to our forefathers : we can, more easily than they could, remodel the practices of the Constitution, modify the rules of party government, or, incredible as it may seem to members of Parliament, touch with profane hands the venerable procedure of the House of Commons. The English democracy, further, just because it is a democracy, may, like the democracy of America, enforce with unflinching firmness laws which, representing the deliberate will of the people, are supported by the vast majority of the citizens of the United Kingdom. The English democracy, because it is a democracy, may also with a good conscience destroy the remnants of feudal institutions, and all systems of land tenure found unsuitable to the wants of the Irish people. Nor, though the crisis be difficult, are there features lacking in the tendencies of the modern world which in the United

Kingdom as in the United States and in the Swiss Confederacy favour every effort to uphold the political unity of the State. Whatever be the difficulties (and they are many) of maintaining the Union, not in form only but in reality, the policy is favoured no less by the current of English history, than by the tendencies of modern civilization. It preserves that unity of the State which is essential to the authority of England and to the maintenance of the Empire. It provides, as matters now stand, the only means of giving legal protection to a large body of loyal British subjects. It is the refusal not only to abdicate legitimate power, but (what is of far more consequence) to renounce the fulfilment of imperative duties. Nor does Union imply uniformity. Unity of Government —equality of rights—diversity of institutions,—these are the watchwords for all Unionists. To attain these objects may be beyond our power, and the limit to power is the limit to responsibility. Still, whatever may be the difficulties, or even the disadvantages, of maintaining the Union, it undoubtedly has in its favour not only all the recommendations which must belong to a policy of rational conservatism, but also these two decisive advantages— that it does sustain the strength of the United Kingdom, and that it does not call for any dereliction of duty.

Separation, or in other words the national independence of Ireland, is an idea which has not entered into the practical consideration of Englishmen. The evils which it threatens are patent: it at the same moment diminishes the means of

Great Britain and increases the calls upon her resources. It lowers the fame of the country, and plants by the side of England a foreign, it may be a hostile, neighbour; it involves the desertion of loyal fellow-citizens who have trusted in the good faith of England. Yet, on the other hand, the material losses and perhaps the dangers involved in the independence of Ireland are liable to exaggeration. Great Britain might find in her complete freedom of action and in restored unity of national sentiment elements of power which might balance the obvious damage resulting from Separation; she might also find it possible to make for the protection of Loyalists terms more efficacious than any guarantees contained in the articles of a statutory constitution. If, further, the spirit of nationality has the vivifying power ascribed to it by its votaries, then Ireland might gain from it blessings which (since no form of Home Rule can transform Ireland into a nation) cannot be conferred by any scheme of merely Parliamentary independence.

For Home Rule it may be pleaded that it offers two obvious advantages: it satisfies the immediate wish of millions of Irishmen, and it facilitates the adaptation of Irish institutions to Irish wants. These advantageous results are the best that can be hoped for from Home Rule. They are real, and to underrate them is folly; the moral gain indeed of meeting the wishes of the body of the Irish people is so incalculable, that did Home Rule involve no intolerable evils a rational man might think it wise to venture on the experiment. Home Rule,

it may be suggested, has the further gain of lessening
English responsibility for the government of Ireland.
What it really might effect is to lighten England's sense of
responsibility for misrule in Ireland. But this, so far from
being a blessing, would in truth be one of the greatest of
evils. The distinguished author of the Gladstonian Constitution denies in his recent pamphlet that the Government of Ireland Bill would, if passed, repeal the Act of
Union. To follow the reasoning by which it is attempted
.to make good this denial is beyond my powers. But there
is one aspect in which the statement, paradoxical though it
be, that the Union is not dissolved by the existence of an
Irish Parliament, has a most serious meaning, which ought
to command hearty and general assent. Under the Gladstonian Constitution, as under any form of Home Rule,
the Government of the United Kingdom must still remain
in the last resort responsible for the administration of
justice throughout the whole realm. Admit for the sake
of argument that the Act of Union, though affected in
every section, is not repealed, then assuredly if men be
wrongfully deprived of their property, if they be denied
their lawful freedom, if they suffer unlawful injury to
life or limb in any part of the United Kingdom, the
responsibility for seeing that right be done falls on the
Executive, and in the last resort on the Parliament, of the
United Kingdom. The delegated authority of a subordinate legislature will not free the principal from the
liability inherent in the delegation of power ; and if Home

Rule in Ireland fosters, as it must foster, the notion that the United Kingdom is not as a whole responsible for misdeeds done in Ireland, this is one of the worst results of the proposed constitutional change.

But putting this matter aside, an examination into the various forms which Home Rule may assume leads to the conclusion that whatever be its hypothetical benefits, it threatens more than countervailing loss to England. There is no need to do more than refer in most general terms to evils which have already been set forth in detail. Home Rule under two of its three possible forms dislocates and weakens the whole English Constitution. Under its least objectionable form—that of Colonial independence— it brings upon England many of the perils which would follow upon the national independence of Ireland; it involves, if the experiment is to have a fair chance of success, large pecuniary sacrifice, and it does not present a reasonable hope of creating real harmony of feeling between Great Britain and Ireland. Home Rule, lastly, under whatever form, whilst not freeing England from moral responsibility for protecting the rights of every British subject, does virtually give up the attempt to ensure to these rights more than a nominal existence, and thus gives up the endeavour to enforce legal and equal justice between man and man. It must also be considered that an examination into the different forms of Home Rule, while it shows that no scheme of legislative independence for Ireland offers any promise of finality, also

suggests that the form of Home Rule least injurious to
England is the form which gives Ireland most independence. The inference from these facts cannot be missed.
Home Rule is the half-way house to Separation. Grant it,
and in a short time Irish independence will become the
wish of England. If any thorough-paced Home Ruler
admit this conclusion, and suggest that Home Rule is a
desirable transition towards Separation, the answer is that
Home Rule is such a transition, but assuredly that such a
transition is not to be desired. If one country is destined
to become independent of another it is better for each not
to experience the disappointment and the heartburning
which accompany a period of unwilling connection.

This is the result of the comparison we have instituted
between the three possible courses open to England. If
the comparison be just the conclusion to which it leads is
obvious. The maintenance of the Union is at this moment
to England a matter of duty even more than of interest.
If the time should come when the effort to maintain the
unity of the State is too great for the power of Great
Britain, or the only means by which it is found maintain-
able are measures clearly repugnant to the humanity or
the justice or the democratic principles of the English
people,—if it should turn out that after every effort to
enforce just laws by just methods our justice itself, from
whatever cause, remains hateful to the mass of the Irish
people,—then it will be clear that the Union must for the
sake of England, no less than of Ireland, come to an end.
The alternative policy will then be not Home Rule but

Separation. We shall save the unity at the expense of lessening the territory of the State; we shall escape self-reproach because having reached the limit of our powers we shall also have filled up the measure of our obligations. But if (as there is every reason to suppose) agrarian misery is the source of Irish discontent, and agrarian misery springs in part from bad administration, and in part from the law governing the tenure of land; if, in general terms, the undoubted ills of Ireland are curable by justice, even though justice proceed from the Parliament of the United Kingdom—an assembly, be it noted, in which the voice of Ireland is freely heard—then there is no need to indulge in speculations, always dangerous, upon a possible remedy which may never be necessary, and which, while the inhabitants of England and Ireland are still fellow-citizens of one State, it is painful even to contemplate. On the whole, then, it appears that whatever changes or calamities the future may have in store, the maintenance of the Union is at this day the one sound policy for England to pursue. It is sound because it is expedient; it is sound because it is just.

This is the case of England against Home Rule; it is a case which, however feebly stated—and I may *Character of Eng-land's case.* well have failed to state it with force—is founded on argument. It is a case which makes and need make no appeal to rhetoric; it is a case which indeed, like all sound views of national policy, is grounded on the interest of the greater number of the

citizens of the State, but it is a case · not grounded
on any mere pride of power, a case not based on any
disregard of justice, a case which above all involves no
unfriendliness to Irishmen, and no assumption, either tacit
or express, that there has fallen to Irishmen a greater
amount of either original or acquired sin than falls to
other human beings, it is a case which does not assume that
real or supposed differences of race are a legitimate ground
for inequality of rights.   Any one, indeed, after having to
the best of his power tried to state what can be said with
fairness on one side of a question such as that now at
issue between the majority and the minority of the
citizens of the United Kingdom, may well call to mind the
conclusion of the noblest statement ever made by genius
of a case involving momentous national interests :—

"It would be presumption in me to do more than to
make a case. Many things occur. But as they, like all
political measures, depend on dispositions, tempers, means,
and external circumstances for all their effect, not being
well assured of these, I do not know how to let loose any
speculations of mine on the subject.   The evil is stated in
my opinion as it exists.   The remedy must be where
power, wisdom, and information, I hope, are more united
with good intentions than they can be with me.   I have
done with this subject, I believe for ever.   It has given me
many anxious moments for the two last years.   If a great
change is to be made in human affairs, the minds of men
will be fitted to it; the general opinions and feelings will

U

draw that way. Every fear, every hope, will forward it; and then they who persist in opposing this mighty current in human affairs will appear rather to resist the decrees of Providence itself, than the mere designs of men. They will not be resolute and firm, but perverse and obstinate."*

The sentiment of these words is one of eternal application. Still at this great crisis in the fortunes of our country, when every course is involved in undeniable perplexity, and surrounded by admitted danger, there are two principles to which we may confidently appeal; for it is by habitual adherence to them that England has grown to greatness. These two principles are the maintenance of the supremacy of the whole State, and the use of that supremacy for the purpose of securing to every citizen, whether rich or poor, the rights of liberty and of property conferred upon him by law. To maintain that any policy, however plausible, by which these principles are violated, must undermine the moral basis of the Constitution, and must therefore lead the nation to calamity and to disgrace, is at any rate to plead a cause which rests upon a firm foundation of plain morality. The case may be ill-stated, the arguments by which it is defended may admit of reply, but it is a case which a just man may put forward without shame, and a humane man may support without compunction.

* See the conclusion of Thoughts on French Affairs, Burke's Works, vol. vii., pp. 84, 85.

APPENDIX.

GOVERNMENT OF IRELAND BILL.*

ARRANGEMENT OF CLAUSES.

* The clauses printed in italics are the clauses of the Bill which are specially referred to in the foregoing pages.

292 *Government of Ireland Bill.*

CLAUSE.
17. Public loans.
18. Additional aid in case of war.
19. Money bills and votes.
20. Exchequer divisions and revenue actions.

Police.

21. Police.

PART II.

SUPPLEMENTAL PROVISIONS.

Powers of Her Majesty.

22. Powers over certain lands reserved to Her Majesty.

Legislative Body.

23. Veto by first order of Legislative Body, how over-ruled.
24. Cesser of power of Ireland to return members to Parliament

Decision of Constitutional Questions.

25. *Constitutional questions to be submitted to Judicial Com mittee.*

Lord-Lieutenant.

26. Office of Lord-Lieutenant.

Judges and Civil Servants.

27. Judges to be removable only on address.
28. Provision as to judges and other persons having salarie charged on the Consolidated Fund.
29. As to persons holding civil service appointments.
30. Provision for existing pensions and superannuation allowance

Transitory Provisions.

31. Transitory provisions in Schedule.

Miscellaneous.

32. Post Office and savings banks.
33. Audit.
34. Application of parliamentary law.
35. Regulations for carrying Act into effect.

A Bill to amend the provision for the future Government of Ireland.

BE it enacted by the Queen's most Excellent Majesty, by and with the advice and consent of the Lords Spiritual and Temporal, and Commons, in this present Parliament assembled, and by the authority of the same, as follows:

A.D. 1886.

PART I.

Legislative Authority.

1. *On and after the appointed day there shall be established in Ireland a Legislature consisting of Her Majesty the Queen and an Irish Legislative Body.* — Establishment of Irish Legislature.

2. *With the exceptions and subject to the restrictions in this Act mentioned, it shall be lawful for Her Majesty the Queen, by and with the advice of the Irish Legislative Body, to make laws for the peace, order, and good government of Ireland, and by any such law to alter and repeal any law in Ireland.* — Powers of Irish Legislature.

3. *The Legislature of Ireland shall not make laws relating to the following matters or any of them:—* — Exceptions from powers of Irish Legislature.

(1.) *The status or dignity of the Crown, or the succession to the Crown, or a Regency;*
(2.) *The making of peace or war;*
(3.) *The army, navy, militia, volunteers, or other military or naval forces, or the defence of the realm;*
(4.) *Treaties and other relations with foreign States, or the relations between the various parts of Her Majesty's dominions;*
(5.) *Dignities or titles of honour;*
(6.) *Prize or booty of war;*
(7.) *Offences against the law of nations; or offences committed in violation of any treaty made, or hereafter to be made, between Her Majesty and any foreign State; or offences committed on the high seas;*
(8.) *Treason, alienage, or naturalization;*
(9.) *Trade, navigation, or quarantine;*
(10.) *The postal and telegraph service, except as hereafter in this*

A.D. 1886.

Act mentioned with respect to the transmission of letters and telegrams in Ireland;

(11.) *Beacons, lighthouses, or sea marks;*

(12.) *The coinage; the value of foreign money; legal tender; or weights and measures; or*

(13.) *Copyright, patent rights, or other exclusive rights to the use or profits of any works or inventions.*

Any law made in contravention of this section shall be void.

Restrictions on powers of Irish Legislature.

4. *The Irish Legislature shall not make any law—*

(1.) *Respecting the establishment or endowment of religion, or prohibiting the free exercise thereof; or*

(2.) *Imposing any disability, or conferring any privilege, on account of religious belief; or*

(3.) *Abrogating or derogating from the right to establish or maintain any place of denominational education or any denominational institution or charity; or*

(4.) *Prejudicially affecting the right of any child to attend a school receiving public money without attending the religious instruction at that school; or*

(5.) *Impairing, without either the leave of Her Majesty in Council first obtained on an address presented by the Legislative Body of Ireland, or the consent of the corporation interested, the rights, property, or privileges of any existing corporation incorporated by royal charter or local and general Act of Parliament; or*

(6.) *Imposing or relating to duties of customs and duties of excise, as defined by this Act, or either of such duties, or affecting any Act relating to such duties or either of them; or*

(7.) *Affecting this Act, except in so far as it is declared to be alterable by the Irish Legislature.*

Prerogatives of Her Majesty as to Irish Legislative Body.

5. *Her Majesty the Queen shall have the same prerogatives with respect to summoning, proroguing, and dissolving the Irish Legislative Body as Her Majesty has with respect to summoning, proroguing, and dissolving the Imperial Parliament.*

Duration of the Irish Legislative Body.

6. *The Irish Legislative Body whenever summoned may have continuance for five years and no longer, to be reckoned from the day on which any such Legislative Body is appointed to meet.*

Executive Authority.

Constitution of the Executive Authority.

7.—(1.) *The Executive Government of Ireland shall continue vested in Her Majesty, and shall be carried on by the Lord-Lieutenant on behalf of Her Majesty with the aid of such officers and such Council as to Her Majesty may from time to time seem fit.*

(2.) *Subject to any instructions which may from time to time be given by Her Majesty, the Lord-Lieutenant shall give or withhold the assent of Her Majesty to Bills passed by the Irish Legislative Body, and shall exercise the prerogatives of Her Majesty in respect*

of the summoning, proroguing, and dissolving of the Irish Legis-
lative Body, and any prerogatives the exercise of which may be
delegated to him by Her Majesty.

8. *Her Majesty may, by Order in Council, from time to time* Use of Crown
place under the control of the Irish Government, for the purposes of lands by Irish
that Government, any such lands and buildings in Ireland as may Government.
he vested in or held in trust for Her Majesty.

Constitution of Legislative Body.

9.—(1.) *The Irish Legislative Body shall consist of a first and* Constitution of
second order. Irish Legisla-

(2.) *The two orders shall deliberate together, and shall vote* tive Body.
together, except that, if any question arises in relation to legislation
or to the Standing Orders or Rules of Procedure or to any other
matter in that behalf in this Act specified, and such question is to
be determined by vote, each order shall, if a majority of the members
present of either order demand a separate vote, give their votes in
like manner as if they were separate Legislative Bodies ; and if
the result of the voting of the two orders does not agree the question
shall be resolved in the negative.

10.—(1.) The first order of the Irish Legislative Body shall First order.
consist of one hundred and three members, of whom seventy-five
shall be elective members and twenty-eight peerage members.

(2.) Each elective member shall at the date of his election and
during his period of membership be bonâ fide possessed of property
which—

> (*a*.) if realty, or partly realty and partly personalty, yields two
>   hundred pounds a year or upwards, free of all charges ; or
> (*b*.) if personalty yields the same income, or is of the capital
>   value of four thousand pounds or upwards, free of all
>   charges.

(2.) For the purpose of electing the elective members of the first
order of the Legislative Body, Ireland shall be divided into the
electoral districts specified in the First Schedule to this Act, and
each such district shall return the number of members in that
behalf specified in that Schedule.

(3.) The elective members shall be elected by the registered
electors of each electoral district, and for that purpose a register of
electors shall be made annually.

(4.) An elector in each electoral district shall be qualified as
follows, that is to say, he shall be of full age, and not subject to
any legal incapacity, and shall have been during the twelve months
next preceding the *twentieth day of July* in any year the owner or
occupier of some land or tenement within the district of a net
annual value of twenty-five pounds or upwards.

(5.) The term of office of an elective member shall be *ten years.*

(6.) In every fifth year thirty-seven or thirty-eight of the elective members, as the case requires, shall retire from office, and their places shall be filled by election; the members to retire shall be those who have been members for the longest time without re-election.

(7.) The offices of the peerage members shall be filled as follows; that is to say,—

    (*a.*) Each of the Irish peers who on the appointed day is one of the twenty-eight Irish representative peers, shall, on giving his written assent to the Lord-Lieutenant, become a peerage member of the first order of the Irish Legislative Body; and if at any time within *thirty years* after the appointed day any such peer vacates his office by death or resignation, the vacancy shall be filled by the election to that office by the Irish peers of one of their number in manner heretofore in use respecting the election of Irish representative peers, subject to adaptation as provided by this Act, and if the vacancy is not so filled within the proper time it shall be filled by the election of an elective member.

    (*b.*) If any of the twenty-eight peers aforesaid does not within *one month* after the appointed day give such assent to be a peerage member of the first order, the vacancy so created shall be filled up as if he had assented and vacated his office by resignation.

(8.) A peerage member shall be entitled to hold office during his life, or until the expiration of *thirty years* from the appointed day, whichever period is the shortest. At the expiration of such *thirty years* the offices of all the peerage members shall be vacated as if they were dead, and their places shall be filled by elective members qualified and elected in manner provided by this Act with respect to elective members of the first order, and such elective members may be distributed by the Irish Legislature among the electoral districts, so, however, that care shall be taken to give additional members to the most populous places.

(9.) The offices of members of the first order shall not be vacated by the dissolution of the Legislative Body.

(10.) The provisions in the Second Schedule to this Act relating to members of the first order of the Legislative Body shall be of the same force as if they were enacted in the body of this Act.

Second order. 11.—(1.) Subject as in this section hereafter mentioned, the second order of the Legislative Body shall consist of two hundred and four members.

(2.) The members of the second order shall be chosen by the existing constituencies of Ireland, two by each constituency, with the exception of the city of Cork, which shall be divided into two divisions in manner set forth in the Third Schedule to this Act, and two members shall be chosen by each of such divisions.

(3.) Any person who, on the appointed day, is a member representing an existing Irish constituency in the House of Commons shall, on giving his written assent to the Lord-Lieutenant, become a member of the second order of the Irish Legislative Body as if he had been elected by the constituency which he was representing in the House of Commons. Each of the members for the city of Cork, on the said day, may elect for which of the divisions of that city he wishes to be deemed to have been elected.

(4.) If any member does not give such written assent within *one month* after the appointed day, his place shall be filled by election in the same manner and at the same time as if he had assented and vacated his office by death.

(5.) If the same person is elected to both orders, he shall, within *seven days* after the meeting of the Legislative Body, or if the Body is sitting at the time of the election, within *seven days* after the election, elect in which order he will serve, and his membership of the other order shall be void and be filled by a fresh election.

(6.) Notwithstanding anything in this Act, it shall be lawful for the Legislature of Ireland at any time to pass an Act enabling the Royal University of Ireland to return not more than two members to the second order of the Irish Legislative Body in addition to the number of members above mentioned.|

(7.) Notwithstanding anything in this Act, it shall be lawful for the Irish Legislature, after the first dissolution of the Legislative Body which occurs, to alter the constitution or election of the second order of that body, due regard being had in the distribution of members to the population of the constituencies; provided that no alteration shall be made in the number of such order.

Finance.

12.—(1.) For the purpose of providing for the public service of Ireland the Irish Legislature may impose taxes, other than duties of customs or excise as defined by this Act, which duties shall continue to be imposed and levied by and under the direction of the Imperial Parliament only.

Taxes and separate Consolidated Fund.

(2.) On and after the appointed day there shall be an Irish Consolidated Fund separate from the Consolidated Fund of the United Kingdom.

(3.) All taxes imposed by the Legislature of Ireland and all other public revenues under the control of the Government of Ireland shall, subject to any provisions touching the disposal thereof contained in any Act passed in the present session respecting the sale and purchase of land in Ireland, be paid into the Irish Consolidated Fund, and be appropriated to the public service of Ireland according to law.

13.—(1.) Subject to the provisions for the reduction or cesser thereof in this section mentioned, there shall be made on the part of Ireland to the Consolidated Fund of the United Kingdom the following annual contributions in every financial year; that is to say,—

Annual contributions from Ireland to Consolidated Fund of United Kingdom.

(*a.*) The sum of *one million four hundred and sixty-six thousand pounds* on account of the interest on and management of the Irish share of the National Debt:

(*b.*) The sum of *one million six hundred and sixty-six thousand pounds* on account of the expenditure on the army and navy of the United Kingdom:

(*c.*) The sum of *one hundred and ten thousand pounds* on account of the Imperial civil expenditure of the United Kingdom:

(*d.*) The sum of *one million pounds* on account of the Royal Irish Constabulary and the Dublin Metropolitan Police.

(2.) During the period of *thirty* years from this section taking effect the said annual contributions shall not be increased, but may be reduced or cease as hereinafter mentioned. After the expiration of the said *thirty years* the said contributions shall, save as otherwise provided by this section, continue until altered in manner provided with respect to the alteration of this Act.

(3.) The Irish share of the National Debt shall be reckoned at *forty-eight million pounds* Bank annuities, and there shall be paid in every financial year on behalf of Ireland to the Commissioners for the Reduction of the National Debt an annual sum of *three hundred and sixty thousand pounds*, and the permanent annual charge for the National Debt on the Consolidated Fund of the United Kingdom shall be reduced by that amount, and the said annual sum shall be applied by the said Commissioners as a sinking fund for the redemption of the National Debt, and the Irish share of the National Debt shall be reduced by the amount of the National Debt so redeemed, and the said annual contribution on account of the interest on and management of the Irish share of the National Debt shall from time to time be reduced by a sum equal to the interest upon the amount of the National Debt from time to time so redeemed, but that last-mentioned sum shall be paid annually to the Commissioners for the Reduction of the National Debt in addition to the above-mentioned annual sinking fund, and shall be so paid and be applied as if it were part of that sinking fund.

(4.) As soon as an amount of the National Debt equal to the said Irish share thereof has been redeemed under the provisions of this section, the said annual contribution on account of the interest on and management of the Irish share of the National Debt, and the said annual sum for a sinking fund shall cease.

(5.) If it appears to Her Majesty that the expenditure in respect of the army and navy of the United Kingdom, or in respect of Imperial civil expenditure of the United Kingdom, for any financial year has been less than *fifteen* times the amount of the contributions above-named on account of the same matter, a sum equal to *one fifteenth* part of the diminution shall be deducted from the current annual contribution for the same matter.

(6.) The sum paid from time to time by the Commissioners of

Her Majesty's Woods, Forests, and Land Revenues to the Con- A.D. 1886.
solidated Fund of the United Kingdom on account of the hereditary
revenues of the Crown in Ireland shall be credited to the Irish
Government, and go in reduction of the said annual contribution
payable on account of the Imperial civil expenditure of the United
Kingdom, but shall not be taken into account in calculating
whether such diminution as above mentioned has or has not taken
place in such expenditure.

(7.) If it appears to Her Majesty that the expenditure in respect
of the Royal Irish Constabulary and the Dublin Metropolitan
Police for any financial year has been less than the contribution
above named on account of such constabulary and police, the
current contribution shall be diminished by the amount of such
difference.

(8.) This section shall take effect from and after the *thirty-first
day of March, one thousand eight hundred and eighty-seven.*

14.—(1.) On and after such day as the Treasury may direct all Collection and
moneys from time to time collected in Ireland on account of the application of
duties of customs or the duties of excise as defined by this Act customs and
shall, under such regulations as the Treasury from time to time excise duties
make, be carried to a separate account (in this Act referred to as in Ireland.
the customs and excise account) and applied in the payment of
the following sums in priority as mentioned in this section; that is
to say,—

First, of such sum as is from time to time directed by the
Treasury in respect of the costs, charges, and expenses of and
incident to the collection and management of the said duties in
Ireland not exceeding four per cent. of the amount collected
there;

Secondly, of the annual contributions required by this Act to be
made to the Consolidated Fund of the United Kingdom;

Thirdly, of the annual sums required by this Act to be paid
to the Commissioners for the Reduction of the National
Debt;

Fourthly, of all sums by this Act declared to be payable out of
the moneys carried to the customs and excise account;

Fifthly, of all sums due to the Consolidated Fund of the United
Kingdom for interest or sinking fund, in respect of any loans
made by the issue of bank annuities or otherwise to the
Government of Ireland under any Act passed in the present
session relating to the purchase and sale of land in Ireland, so
far as such sums are not defrayed out of the moneys received
under such Act;

(2.) So much of the moneys carried to a separate account under
this section as the Treasury consider are not, and are not likely to
be, required to meet the above-mentioned payments, shall from
time to time be paid over and applied as part of the public
revenues under the control of the Irish Government.

A.D. 1886.

Charges on Irish Consolidated Fund.

Irish Church Fund.

15.—(1.) There shall be charged on the Irish Consolidated Fund in priority as mentioned in this section :—

First, such portion of the sums directed by this Act to be paid out of the moneys carried to the customs and excise account in priority to any payment for the public revenues of Ireland, as those moneys are insufficient to pay;

Secondly, all sums due in respect of any debt incurred by the Government of Ireland, whether for interest, management, or sinking fund;

Thirdly, all sums which at the passing of this Act are charged on the Consolidated Fund of the United Kingdom in respect of Irish services other than the salary of the Lord-Lieutenant;

Fourthly, the salaries of all judges of the Supreme Court of Judicature or other superior court in Ireland, or of any county or other like court, who are appointed after the passing of this Act, and the pensions of such judges;

Fifthly, any other sums charged by this Act on the Irish Consolidated Fund.

(2.) It shall be the duty of the Legislature of Ireland to impose all such taxes, duties, or imposts as will raise a sufficient revenue to meet all sums charged for the time being on the Irish Consolidated Fund.

16.—(1.) Until all charges which are payable out of the Church property in Ireland, and are guaranteed by the Treasury, have been fully paid, the Irish Land Commission shall continue as heretofore to exist, with such Commissioners and officers receiving such salaries as the Treasury may from time to time appoint, and to administer the Church property and apply the income and other moneys receivable therefrom; and so much of the salaries of such Commissioners and officers and expenses of the office as is not paid out of the Church property shall be paid out of moneys carried to the customs and excise account under this Act, and if those moneys are insufficient, out of the Consolidated Fund of Ireland, and if not so paid, shall be paid out of moneys provided by Parliament.

Provided as follows :—

(a.) All charges on the Church property for which a guarantee has been given by the Treasury before the passing of this Act shall, so far as they are not paid out of such property, be paid out of the moneys carried to the Customs and Excise account under this Act, and if such moneys are insufficient, the Consolidated Fund of Ireland, without prejudice nevertheless to the guarantee of the Treasury;

(b.) All charges on the Church property, for which no guarantee has been given by the Treasury before the passing of this Act shall be charged on the Consolidated Fund of Ireland, but shall not be guaranteed by the Treasury nor charged on the Consolidated Fund of the United Kingdom.

(2.) Subject to any existing charges on the Church property, such property shall belong to the Irish Government and any portion of the annual revenue thereof which the Treasury, on the application of the Irish Government, certify at the end of any financial year not to be required for meeting charges, shall be paid over and applied as part of the public revenues under the control of the Irish Government.

(3.) As soon as all charges on the Church property guaranteed by the Treasury have been paid, such property may be managed and administered, and subject to existing charges thereon disposed of, and the income or proceeds thereof applied, in such manner as the Irish Legislature may from time to time direct.

(4.) "Church property" in this section means all property accruing under the Irish Church Act, 1869, and transferred to the Irish Land Commission by the Irish Church Act Amendment Act, 1881.

17.—(1.) All sums due for principal or interest to the Public Works Loan Commissioners or to the Commissioners of Public Works in Ireland in respect of existing loans advanced on any security in Ireland shall on and after the appointed day be due to the Government of Ireland instead of the said Commissioners, and such body of persons as the Government of Ireland may appoint for the purpose shall have all the powers of the said Commissioners or their secretary for enforcing payment of such sums, and all securities for such sums given to such Commissioners or their secretary shall have effect as if the said body were therein substituted for those Commissioners or their secretary.

(2.) For the repayment of the said loans to the Consolidated Fund of the United Kingdom, the Irish Government shall pay annually into that fund by half-yearly payments on the *first day of January* and the *first day of July*, or on such other days as may be agreed on, such instalments of the principal of the said loans as will discharge all the loans within *thirty years* from the appointed day, and shall also pay interest half-yearly on so much of the said principal as from time to time remains unpaid at the rate of *three* per cent. per annum, and such instalments of principal and interest shall be paid out of the moneys carried to the customs and excise account under this Act, and if those are insufficient, out of the Consolidated Fund of Ireland.

18. If Her Majesty declares that a state of war exists and is pleased to signify such declaration to the Irish Legislative Body by speech or message, it shall be lawful for the Irish Legislature to appropriate a further sum out of the Consolidated Fund of Ireland in aid of the army or navy, or other measures which Her Majesty may take for the prosecution of the war and defence of the realm, and to provide and raise money for that purpose; and all moneys so provided and raised, whether by loan, taxation, or otherwise, shall be paid into the Consolidated Fund of the United Kingdom.

Marginal notes:

A.D. 1886.

32 & 33 Vict. c. 42.
44 & 45 Vict. c. 71.

Public loans.

Additional aid in case of war.

19.—(1.) It shall not be lawful for the Irish Legislative Body to adopt or pass any vote, resolution, address, or Bill for the raising or appropriation for any purpose of any part of the public revenue of Ireland, or of any tax, duty, or impost, except in pursuance of a recommendation from Her Majesty signified through the Lord-Lieutenant in the session in which such vote, resolution, address, or Bill is proposed.

(2.) Notwithstanding that the Irish Legislature is prohibited by this Act from making laws relating to certain subjects, that Legislature may, with the assent of Her Majesty in Council first obtained, appropriate any part of the Irish public revenue, or any tax, duty, or impost imposed by such Legislature, for the purpose of, or in connection with, such subjects.

20.—(1.) On and after the appointed day, the Exchequer Division of the High Court of Justice shall continue to be a Court of Exchequer for revenue purposes under this Act, and whenever any vacancy occurs in the office of any judge of such Exchequer Division, his successor shall be appointed by Her Majesty on the joint recommendation of the Lord-Lieutenant of Ireland and the Lord High Chancellor of Great Britain.

(2.) The judges of such Exchequer Division appointed after the passing of this Act shall be removable only by Her Majesty on address from the two Houses of the Imperial Parliament, and shall receive the same salaries and pensions as those payable at the passing of this Act to the existing judges of such division, unless with the assent of Her Majesty in Council first obtained, the Irish Legislature alters such salaries or pensions, and such salaries and pensions shall be paid out of the moneys carried to the customs and excise account in pursuance of this Act, and if the same are insufficient shall be paid out of the Irish Consolidated Fund, and if not so paid shall be paid out of the Consolidated Fund of the United Kingdom.

(3.) An alteration of any rules relating to the procedure in such legal proceedings as are mentioned in this section shall not be made except with the approval of the Lord High Chancellor of Great Britain, and the sittings of the Exchequer division and the judges thereof shall be regulated with the like approval.

(4.) All legal proceedings instituted in Ireland by or against the Commissioners or any officers of customs or excise, or the Treasury, shall, if so required by any party to such proceedings, be heard and determined before the judges of such Exchequer division, or some or one of them, and any appeal from the decision in any such legal proceeding, if by a judge, shall lie to the said division, and if by the Exchequer division, shall lie to the House of Lords, and not to any other tribunal; and if it is made to appear to such judges, or any of them, that any decree or judgment in any such proceeding as aforesaid, has not been duly enforced by the sheriff or other officer whose duty it is to enforce the same, such judges or

judge shall appoint some officer to enforce such judgment or decree ; A.D. 1886.
and it shall be the duty of such officer to take proper steps to
enforce the same, and for that purpose such officer and all persons
employed by him shall be entitled to the same immunities, powers,
and privileges as are by law conferred on a sheriff and his officers.

(5.) All sums recovered in respect of duties of Customs and
Excise, or under any Act relating thereto, or by an officer of
Customs or Excise, shall, notwithstanding anything in any other
Act, be paid to the Treasury, and carried to the Customs and
Excise account under this Act.

Police.

21. The following regulations shall be made with respect to Police.
police in Ireland ;

(*a.*) The Dublin Metropolitan Police shall continue and be subject
as heretofore to the control of the Lord-Lieutenant as representing
Her Majesty for a period of *two years* from the passing of this Act,
and thereafter until any alteration is made by Act of the Legislature
of Ireland, but such Act shall provide for the proper saving of all
then existing interests, whether as regards pay, pensions, superannuation allowances, or otherwise.

(*b.*) The Royal Irish Constabulary shall, while that force subsists,
continue and be subject as heretofore to the control of the Lord-
Lieutenant as representing Her Majesty.

(*c.*) The Irish Legislature may provide for the establishment and
maintenance of a police force in counties and boroughs in Ireland
under the control of local authorities, and arrangements may be
made between the Treasury and the Irish Government for the
establishment and maintenance of police reserves.

PART II.

SUPPLEMENTAL PROVISIONS.

Powers of Her Majesty.

22. On and after the appointed day there shall be reserved to Power over
Her Majesty— certain lands

   (1.) The power of erecting forts, magazines, arsenals, dockyards, reserved to
      and other buildings for military or naval purposes ; Her Majesty.

   (2.) The power of taking waste land, and, on making due
      compensation, any other land, for the purpose of erecting
      such forts, magazines, arsenals, dockyards, or other build-
      ings as aforesaid, and for any other military or naval
      purpose, or the defence of the realm.

Legislative Body.

Veto by first order of Legislative Body, how overruled.

23. If a Bill or any provision of a Bill is lost by disagreement between the two orders of the Legislative Body, and after a period ending with a dissolution of the Legislative Body, or the period of *three years,* whichever period is longest, such Bill, or a Bill containing the said provision, is again considered by the Legislative Body, and such Bill or provision is adopted by the second order and negatived by the first order, the same shall be submitted to the whole Legislative Body, both orders of which shall vote together on the Bill or provision, and the same shall be adopted or rejected according to the decision of the majority of the members so voting together.

Cesser of power of Ireland to return members to Parliament.

24. On and after the appointed day Ireland shall cease, except in the event hereafter in this Act mentioned, to return representative peers to the House of Lords or members to the House of Commons, and the persons who on the said day are such representative peers and members shall cease as such to be members of the House of Lords and House of Commons respectively.

Decision of Constitutional Questions.

Constitutional questions to be submitted to Judicial Committee.

25. *Questions arising as to the powers conferred on the Legislature of Ireland under this Act shall be determined as follows :—*

(a.) *If any such question arises on any Bill passed by the Legislative Body, the Lord-Lieutenant may refer such question to Her Majesty in Council ;*

(b.) *If, in the course of any action or other legal proceeding, such question arises on any Act of the Irish Legislature, any party to such action or other legal proceeding may, subject to the rules in this section mentioned, appeal from a decision on such question to Her Majesty in Council ;*

(c.) *If any such question arises otherwise than as aforesaid on any Act of the Irish Legislature, the Lord-Lieutenant or one of Her Majesty's principal Secretaries of State may refer such question to Her Majesty in Council ;*

(d.) *Any question referred or appeal brought under this section to Her Majesty in Council shall be referred for the consideration of the Judicial Committee of the Privy Council ;*

(e.) *The decision of Her Majesty in Council on any question referred or appeal brought under this section shall be final, and a Bill which may be so decided to be, or contain a provision, in excess of the powers of the Irish Legislature shall not be assented to by the Lord-Lieutenant ; and a provision of any Act which is so decided to be in excess of the powers of the Irish Legislature shall be void ;*

(f.) *There shall be added to the Judicial Committee when sitting*

A.D. 1886.

for the purpose of considering questions under this section, such members of Her Majesty's Privy Council, being or having been Irish judges, as to Her Majesty may seem meet.

(g.) *Her Majesty may, by Order in Council from time to time, make rules as to the cases and mode in which and the conditions under which, in pursuance of this section, questions may be referred and appeals brought to Her Majesty in Council, and as to the consideration thereof by the Judicial Committee of the Privy Council, and any rules so made shall be of the same force as if they were enacted in this Act.*

(h.) *An appeal shall not lie to the House of Lords in respect of any question in respect of which an appeal can be had to Her Majesty in Council in pursuance of this section.*

Lord-Lieutenant.

26.—(1.) Notwithstanding anything to the contrary contained in any Act of Parliament, every subject of Her Majesty shall be eligible to hold and enjoy the office of Lord-Lieutenant of Ireland, without reference to his religious belief. *Office of Lord-Lieutenant.*

(2.) The salary of the Lord-Lieutenant shall continue to be charged on the Consolidated Fund of the United Kingdom, and the expenses of his household and establishment shall continue to be defrayed out of moneys to be provided by Parliament.

(3.) All existing powers vested by Act of Parliament or otherwise in the Chief Secretary for Ireland may, if no such officer is appointed, be exercised by the Lord-Lieutenant until other provision is made by Act of the Irish Legislature.

(4.) The Legislature of Ireland shall not pass any Act relating to the office or functions of the Lord-Lieutenant of Ireland.

Judges and Civil Servants.

27. A Judge of the Supreme Court of Judicature or other superior court of Ireland, or of any county court or other court with a like jurisdiction in Ireland, appointed after the passing of this Act, shall not be removed from his office except in pursuance of an address to Her Majesty from both orders of the Legislative Body voting separately, nor shall his salary be diminished or right to pension altered during his continuance in office. *Judges to be removable only on address.*

28.—(1.) All persons who at the passing of this Act are judges of the Supreme Court of Judicature or county court judges, or hold any other judicial position in Ireland, shall, if they are removable at present on address to Her Majesty of both Houses of Parliament, continue to be removable only upon such address from both Houses *Provisions as to judges and other persons having salaries charged on the Consolidated Fund.*

X

A.D. 1886.
———
of the Imperial Parliament, and if removable in any other manner shall continue to be removable in like manner as heretofore ; and such persons, and also all persons at the passing of this Act in the permanent civil service of the Crown in Ireland whose salaries are charged on the Consolidated Fund of the United Kingdom, shall continue to hold office and to be entitled to the same salaries, pensions, and superannuation allowances as heretofore, and to be liable to perform the same or analogous duties as heretofore ; and the salaries of such persons shall be paid out of the moneys carried to the customs and excise account under this Act, or if these moneys are insufficient, out of the Irish Consolidated Fund, and if the same are not so paid, shall continue charged on the Consolidated Fund of the United Kingdom.

(2.) *If any of these said persons retires from office with the appro-bation of Her Majesty before he has completed the period of service entitling him to a pension, it shall be lawful for Her Majesty, if she thinks fit, to grant to that person such pension, not exceeding the pension to which he would have been entitled if he had completed the said period of service, as to Her Majesty seems meet.*

As to persons holding civil service appointments.

29.—(1.) All persons not above provided for and at the passing of this Act serving in Ireland in the permanent civil service of the Crown shall continue to hold their offices and receive the same salaries, and to be entitled to the same gratuities and superannuation allowances as heretofore, and shall be liable to perform the same duties as heretofore or duties of similar rank, but any of such persons shall be entitled at the expiration of *two years* after the passing of this Act to retire from office, and at any time if required by the Irish Government shall retire from office, and on any such retirement shall be entitled to receive such payment as the Treasury may award to him in accordance with the provisions contained in the Fourth Schedule to this Act.

(2.) The amount of such payment shall be paid to him out of the moneys carried to the customs and excise account under this Act, or, if those moneys are insufficient, out of the Irish Consolidated Fund, *and so far as the same are not so paid shall be paid out of moneys provided by Parliament.*

34 & 35 Vict. c. 36.

(3.) The Pensions Commutation Act, 1871, shall apply to all persons who, having retired from office, are entitled to any annual payment under this section in like manner as if they had retired in consequence of the abolition of their offices.

(4.) This section shall not apply to persons who are retained in the service of the Imperial Government.

Provision for existing pensions and superannuation allow-ances.

30. Where before the passing of this Act any pension or super-annuation allowance has been granted to any person on account of service as a judge of the Supreme Court of Judicature of Ireland or of any court consolidated into that court, or as a county court judge, or in any other judicial position, or on account of service in the permanent civil service of the Crown in Ireland otherwise than

A.D. 1886.

in some office, the holder of which is, after the passing of this Act, retained in the service of the Imperial Government, such pension or allowance, whether payable out of the Consolidated Fund or out of moneys provided by Parliament, shall continue to be paid to such person, and shall be so paid out of the moneys carried to the customs and excise account under this Act, or, if such moneys are insufficient, out of the Irish Consolidated Fund, and so far as the same is not so paid, shall be paid as heretofore out of the Consolidated Fund of the United Kingdom or moneys provided by Parliament.

Transitory Provisions.

31. The provisions contained in the Fifth Schedule to this Act relating to the mode in which arrangements are to be made for setting in motion the Irish Legislative Body and Government and for the transfer to the Irish Government of the powers and duties to be transferred to them under this Act, or for otherwise bringing this Act into operation, shall be of the same effect as if they were enacted in the body of this Act.

Transitory provisions in schedule.

Miscellaneous.

32. Whenever an Act of the Legislature of Ireland has provided for carrying on the postal and telegraphic service with respect to the transmission of letters and telegrams in Ireland, and the post office and other savings banks in Ireland, and for protecting the officers then in such service, and the existing depositors in such post office savings banks, the Treasury shall make arrangements for the transfer of the said service and banks, in accordance with the said Act, and shall give public notice of the transfer, and shall pay all depositors in such post office savings bank who request payment within *six months* after the date fixed for such transfer, and after the expiration of such *six months* the said depositors shall cease to have any claim against the Postmaster-General or the Consolidated Fund of the United Kingdom, but shall have the like claim against the Consolidated Fund of Ireland, and the Treasury shall cause to be transferred in accordance with the said Act the securities representing the sums due to the said depositors in post office savings banks and the securities held for other savings banks.

Post Office and savings banks.

33. Save as otherwise provided by the Irish Legislature,—

Audit.

(a.) The existing law relating to the Exchequer and the Consolidated Fund of the United Kingdom shall apply to the Irish Exchequer and Consolidated Fund, and an officer shall from time to time be appointed by the Lord-Lieutenant to fill the office of the Comptroller General of the receipt and issue of Her Majesty's Exchequer and Auditor-General of public accounts so far as respects Ireland; and

A.D. 1886.

29 & 30 Vict. c. 39.

Application of parliamentary law.

(*b*.) The accounts of the Irish Consolidated Fund shall be audited as appropriation accounts in manner provided by the Exchequer and Audit Departments Act, 1866, by or under the direction of the holder of such office.

34.—(1.) The privileges, immunities, and powers to be held, enjoyed, and exercised by the Irish Legislative Body, and the members thereof, shall be such as are from time to time defined by Act of the Irish Legislature, but so that the same shall never exceed those at the passing of this Act held, enjoyed, and exercised by the House of Commons, and by the members thereof.

(2.) Subject as in this Act mentioned, all existing laws and customs relating to the members of the House of Commons and their election, including the enactments respecting the questioning of elections, corrupt and illegal practices, and registration of electors, shall, so far as applicable, extend to elective members of the first order and to members of the second order of the Irish Legislative Body.

Provided that—

    (*a*.) The law relating to the offices of profit enumerated in Schedule H. to the Representation of the People Act, 1867, shall apply to such offices of profit in the government of Ireland not exceeding ten, as the Legislature of Ireland may from time to time direct;

    (*b*.) After the first dissolution of the Legislative Body, the Legislature of Ireland may, subject to the restrictions in this Act mentioned, alter the laws and customs in this section mentioned.

Regulations for carrying Act into effect.

35.—(1.) The Lord-Lieutenant of Ireland may make regulations for the following purposes :—

    (*a*.) The summoning of the Legislative Body and the election of a Speaker, and such adaptation to the proceedings of the Legislative Body of the procedure of the House of Commons as appears to him expedient for facilitating the conduct of business by that body on their first meeting;

    (*b*.) The adaptation of any law relating to the election of representative peers ;

    (*c*.) The adaptation of any laws and customs relating to the House of Commons or the members thereof to the elective members of the first order and to members of the second order of the Legislative Body ; and

    (*d*.) The mode of signifying their assent or election under this Act by representative peers or Irish members of the House of Commons as regards becoming members of the Irish Legislative Body in pursuance of this Act.

(2.) Any regulations so made shall, in so far as they concern the procedure of the Legislative Body, be subject to alteration by Standing Orders of that Body, and so far as they concern other matters, be subject to alteration by the Legislature of Ireland, but shall, until alteration, have the same effect as if they were inserted in this Act.

36. Save as is in this Act provided with respect to matters to be decided by Her Majesty in Council, nothing in this Act shall affect the appellate jurisdiction of the House of Lords in respect of actions and suits in Ireland, or the jurisdiction of the House of Lords to determine the claims to Irish peerages.

37. *Save as herein expressly provided all matters in relation to which it is not competent for the Irish Legislative Body to make or repeal laws shall remain and be within the exclusive authority of the Imperial Parliament, whose power and authority in relation thereto, save as aforesaid, shall in nowise be diminished or restrained by anything herein contained.**

38.—(1.) Except as otherwise provided by this Act, all existing laws in force in Ireland, and all existing courts of civil and criminal jurisdiction, and all existing legal commissions, powers, and authorities, and all existing officers, judicial, administrative, and ministerial and all existing taxes, licence, and other duties, fees, and other receipts in Ireland shall continue as if this Act had not been passed; subject, nevertheless, to be repealed, abolished, or altered in manner and to the extent provided by this Act; provided that, subject to the provisions of this Act, such taxes, duties, fees, and other receipts shall, after the appointed day, form part of the public revenues of Ireland.

(2.) The Commissioners of Inland Revenue and the Commissioners of Customs, and the officers of such Commissioners respectively, shall have the same powers in relation to any articles subject to any duty of excise or customs, manufactured, imported, kept for sale, or sold, and any premises where the same may be, and to any machinery, apparatus, vessels, utensils, or conveyance used in connexion therewith, or the removal thereof, and in relation to the person manufacturing, importing, keeping for sale, selling, or having the custody or possession of the same as they would have had if this Act had not been passed.

39.—(1.) *On and after the appointed day this Act shall not, except such provisions thereof as are declared to be alterable by the Legislature of Ireland, be altered except—*

(a.) *by Act of the Imperial Parliament and with the consent of the Irish Legislative Body testified by an address to Her Majesty, or*

(b.) *by an Act of the Imperial Parliament, for the passing of which there shall be summoned to the House of Lords the peerage members of the first order of the Irish Legislative Body, and if there are no such members then twenty-eight Irish representative peers elected by the Irish peers in manner heretofore in use, subject to adaptation as provided*

* This clause is printed as I am informed that it ought to have been originally printed in the Bill.

A.D. 1886.

Saving of powers of House of Lords.

Saving of rights of Parliament.

Continuance of existing laws, courts, officers, &c.

Mode of alteration of Act.

by this Act; and there shall be summoned to the House of Commons such one of the members of each constituency, or in the case of a constituency returning four members such two of those members, as the Legislative Body of Ireland may select, and such peers and members shall respectively be deemed, for the purpose of passing any such Act, to be members of the said Houses of Parliament respectively.

(2.) *For the purposes of this section it shall be lawful for Her Majesty by Order in Council to make such provisions for summoning the said peers of Ireland to the House of Lords and the said members from Ireland to the House of Commons as to Her Majesty may seem necessary or proper, and any provisions contained in such Order in Council shall have the same effect as if they had been enacted by Parliament.*

Definitions.

40. In this Act—

The expression " the appointed day " shall mean such day after the *thirty-first day of March in the year one thousand eight hundred and eighty-seven* as may be determined by order of Her Majesty in Council.

The expression "Lord-Lieutenant" includes the lords justices or any other chief governor or governors of Ireland for the time being.

The expression "Her Majesty the Queen," or "Her Majesty in Council," or "the Queen," includes the heirs and successors of Her Majesty the Queen.

The expression "Treasury," means the Commissioners of Her Majesty's Treasury.

The expression "Treaty" includes any convention or arrangement.

The expression "existing" means existing at the passing of this Act.

The expression "existing constituency" means any county or borough, or division of a county or borough, or a University returning at the passing of this Act a member or members to serve in Parliament.

The expression "duties of excise" does not include a duty received in respect of any licence whether for the sale of intoxicating liquors or otherwise.

The expression "financial year" means the twelve months ending on the *thirty-first day of March.*

Short title of Act.

41. This Act may be cited for all purposes as the Irish Government Act, 1886.

FIRST SCHEDULE.

A.D. 1886.

FIRST ORDER OF THE IRISH LEGISLATIVE BODY.

Electoral Districts.	Number of Members.	Rotation.

SECOND SCHEDULE.

PROVISIONS RELATING TO THE FIRST ORDER OF THE IRISH LEGISLATIVE BODY.

THIRD SCHEDULE.

BOUNDARIES OF DIVISIONS OF THE CITY OF CORK FOR THE PURPOSE OF RETURNING MEMBERS TO THE SECOND ORDER OF THE LEGISLATIVE BODY.

FOURTH SCHEDULE.

PROVISIONS AS TO SUPERANNUATION ALLOWANCES OF PERSONS IN THE PERMANENT CIVIL SERVICE.

FIFTH SCHEDULE.

TRANSITORY PROVISIONS.

www.ingramcontent.com/pod-product-compliance
Lightning Source LLC
Chambersburg PA
CBHW020240290326
41929CB00045B/1111